# Six-Figure Incomes

## Six-Figure Incomes:

# Profit From America's Best Communicators

### Peter Stankovich

Wall Street Press

Published by Wall Street Press
518 N. 80th Street, Seattle, WA 98103-4302 U.S.A.

Printed in Canada

First Printing: September 2006

10  9  8  7  6  5  4  3  2  1

ISBN: 0-9778127-0-7
ISBN 13: 978-0-9778127-0-7

Library of Congress Control Number:  2006923446

Visit this publication's website at: Six-FigureIncomes.com

*Cover and interior design by Kate Race Graphic Design*

**ATTENTION: SCHOOLS AND CORPORATIONS**
Wall Street Press books are available at quantity discounts with bulk purchase for educational, business, or sales promotional use. For information, please write to:
SPECIAL SALES DEPARTMENT, WALL STREET PRESS, 518 N. 80TH STREET, SEATTLE, WA 98103-4302

## *Dedication*

*To all who strive to better themselves
and the lives of others*

# PREFACE

This research began as a personal quest for self-improvement, not to be shared with others. I had always noticed how easy it was for some people to work with others. They had a special way about them and always left others better off than before they found them. They gave people energy instead of taking it.

As I interviewed more and more top communicators, I began to realize that they were all successful, regardless of occupation, what they sold, or for which company they worked. Each had a unique ability to connect, communicate and work extraordinarily well with others. And equally important, each was genuinely happy in life.

Soon the correlation between their ability to effectively communicate and their extraordinary success in life, both personally and professionally, was obvious. This book is the collection of thoughts, ideas, research, and conversations I've had with these people–the six-figure communicators.

I have learned a great deal from them. They have exponentially helped me in my personal and professional life to become more successful. As I learned their valuable secrets, the world suddenly became simpler to me and made so much more sense. I began to see the world like I had never done before. I then decided to share their secrets with others.

Will this book help turn a light on for people? Absolutely. Will it change their lives? Maybe. But if this book does nothing more than make life just a little easier for others, it will have certainly been worth it.

For most professions, it is extremely difficult to earn a six-figure income consistently, if at all, without having strong communication skills. Though many people enjoy talking to others, six-figure income earners are exceptional at doing the hard things or the things most people are uncomfortable with, like prospecting for new clients, networking, building rapport quickly with key people, getting important introductions to others, and developing people to be centers of influence.

Become good at what few people are good at and you will prosper. Develop yourself first and the money will follow. The money and a higher quality of life are only natural by-products of highly effective communication. Most people continually struggle because they are constantly chasing people and money without first becoming the person they need to be, the six-figure communicator. Develop the right skills now and profit for life!

This book is specifically designed for two types of people: (1) those with average communication skills who want to dramatically improve them, and (2) those who want to significantly improve the quality of their own lives. I focused on communications between individuals and small groups because this is where most of our communication takes place.

In writing this book, I researched human communication extensively, and much of this research is primary, meaning firsthand, not rehashed from others. I drew on 10 years of my journal notes, observations, and key anecdotes, and interviewed scores of six-figure communicators in the real world, not Ph.D. theorists. It is practical information for practical people.

While developing this book, one question intrigued me: Are six-figure communicators using hundreds of little communication tips or are they simply applying two or three fundamentals consistently? Most natural-born communicators would tell me simply to "be yourself," "treat others as you would want to be treated," and "just be natural." For them, understanding, talking to, and working with people is simple. They are intuitive with people and build rapport effortlessly. Self-taught communicators, on the other hand, would tell me they learned to be six-figure communicators little by little over many years of trial and error.

I wrote this book to bridge the mysterious gap between what natural-born six-figure communicators know and do and what self-taught six-figure communicators have discovered. It has been my privilege to cross industry lines and learn from talented professionals in a wide range of fields. Each had a different area of expertise and life experience, and each shared with me his or her communication secrets.

Here are a few reasons you will benefit from developing extraordinary communication skills:

- Communication is a highly rewarded skill—professionally and personally.
- You use it everywhere, not just at work.
- You can use improved skills right now!

- Good communication skills help you become more accomplished.
- Good communicators enjoy respect and admiration from others.
- Your improved communication skills will last a lifetime!

As you read these pages, look for the communications concepts that work for you. Experiment with them and have fun. Let this book expand your horizons and open your mind. You will begin to notice the close relationship between good communication skills and good people skills, and how they overlap. It's exciting to know that just one new concept or idea can dramatically change your communication style, thereby improving your life forever.

I believe all of us have a natural gift or talent inside us that makes us special or unique. I have always admired people who share their talent in a way that improves the lives of others. I believe my own talent has always been having a genuine interest in others and the ability to watch and learn from them. I hope you benefit from what I have learned from the six-figure communicators.

Best of luck in all your endeavors, and happy learning!

**Peter Stankovich**

# ACKNOWLEDGMENTS

CW5 Arnold, U.S. Army; Ash, Ahsanuddin, M.D.; Ted Balfour, J.D., Divisional V.P., AXA Advisors; Scott Blake, AstraZeneca; Kirk Branam, Nissan; Charles Bou Abboud, M.D.; Adam Buksh, Saturn; Dwight Bundy, D.O.; Rich Camacho, Hyundai; Peter Chung, Toyota; Major General Robert Dail, U.S. Army; John Daniel, M.D.; Michael Deerling, Mazda/Hummer; Joyce Dontigny, Larry Pasco Properties; Bruce Dorn, Inflatable Boatworks; Maija Eerkes, Premier Banking Executive, Bank of America; Russ Evans, VP & Chief Financial Officer, Boeing Capital Corporation; Lance Frigard; Cycle Barn; Dolores Gandy, TCI Cable; Ann Gosch, byGosch Editorial Services; Michael Haught, M.D; Major Hermans, U.S. Army; Patty Hickman, Abbott Pharmaceuticals; Gary Hopkins, Isuzu, GMC, Buick; Michael Ivanow, Ferrari and Maserati; Hassan Jaffery, M.D.; David Jones, Regional V.P., Lazyboy Residential, Inc.; Rev. Lee Kapfer, Saint Joseph Church; Connie Knight, Coldwell Banker; Eric Lavale, M.D.; Alex Lopez, Shering Oncology BioTech; Ardith Lupton, V.P., Doulos Service Corp; Charles McClung, D.O.; Gary McGill, Director of Development, Children's Hospital Foundation; Cindy McRoberts, Director of Major Gifts, Northwest Women's Law Center; Richard Meadows, D.O.; Colleen Meriwether, D.O.; David Meriwether, M.D.; Marilyn Milnor, Professional Storyteller; Joseph Minasola; Solocup; Husam Nazer, M.D.; Andrew D. Norman, Divisional V.P., AXA Advisors; Savitha Pathi, Women's Funding Alliance; Bill Patton, Executive Director, Raleigh County Solid Waste Authority; Vijay Paul, Eli Lilly; Barry Perdue, Novartis Pharmaceuticals; Dale Phillips, AstraZeneca; Tonja Phillips, PDI; Kelly Pittembarger, M.D.; John Pluta, Grand Yachts Northwest; Frank Poland, D.O.; Gary Poling, D.O.; William Powers, D.O.; Valerie Quick, R.N.; Frank Quintero, Takeda Pharmaceuticals; Kate Race, Graphic Design; George Ramirez, AstraZeneca; John Ray, D.O.; Brian Richards, M.D.; Carl Roberts, Amsouth Bank; Joanna Roberts, M.D.; Juan Rodriguez, U.S. Army;

## Acknowledgements

Mardi Rogers, John L. Scott; Sister Judy Ryan, Saint James Convent; Debbie Sams, D.O.; Craig Sanderson, Saturn; Joe Schnepf, Philips; Seattle Folklife Festival's "Tall Tales, Fibs and Whoppers" Liars Contest 2004; Seattle Storytellers' Guild; Jennifer Shanholtz, Parker, Smith, Feek; Mr. Snover, U.S. Army; Judy Spencer, PA-C; Brian Stafford, PA-C; Colonel Peter Stankovich Sr., Special Forces (retired); Steven Stankovich, Avalon Communities; Brice Stewart, Novartis; Jon Taschner, Honda; Sarah Taylor, Taylor Presentations; Steve Thoreson, Sea Ray; Toastmasters Chamber Club 540 (Seattle); Toastmasters Division B International Speech Contest (2004); Toastmasters Regional International Humorous and Speech Contests (2004), Seattle; Paul Underwood, KOS Pharmaceuticals; Neal Vonada, MENSA International; Robert Walker, AstraZeneca; Jeff Wing, Saturn; LeeAnn Wykle, Merck; Wayne Yonke, Lexus

# CONTENTS

# FOREWORD

Whether you have a six-figure income or not, communication is critical to your success. In fact, communication is arguably the single most important contributing factor to your proficiency in life. Whether you spend your days as a high-powered executive, a salesperson, a back office employee, or a busy parent, you communicate constantly with others. In the course of any day, you'll find you need to get other people to understand your point of view, convince them to agree to your wishes, take and give accurate directions, explain your position, build rapport with someone new, empathize, sympathize, influence, and empower. Each of these situations involves communication; how successful you are depends on how well you can communicate with others.

If you look in a thesaurus, synonyms for the word *communicate* include: converse, talk, speak, and correspond. It's no surprise, then, that most people think that communication means speaking. Others, who are a bit more astute, understand that communication has much more to do with listening than speaking. Some point out that body language plays an important role as well. But Pete Stankovich is one of the few people I know who really understands that communication is so much more than just speaking, listening, and body language. Pete points out that communication starts long before two people ever come into contact. Communication starts with your state of mind, and with understanding the nature of people.

In this book, Pete not only gives you the information you need to be a top communicator, but he also gives you the tools you need to put that information to use. I have found that if you put his advice into action, you will see a profound change in your life.

I have known Pete for several years now and have always marveled at his ability to not only communicate, but also make an incredible impression on everyone he meets. Now I know his secrets, and you will too once you've read his book. Keep Six-Figure Incomes close at hand. You will refer to it again and again – it is the ultimate user's manual for communication.

**Sarah Taylor, MBA**
President, Taylor Presentations
Author of "Secrets of Successful Pharmaceutical Salespeople"
Gig Harbor, Washington
December, 2005

# INTRODUCTION

**Y**ou can run, but you can't hide. People are everywhere! There is no escape. Interacting with people can be one of the most rewarding, gratifying, and satisfying parts of our lives. It also can be one of the most maddening, saddening, and painful parts. People can make you feel better than you have ever felt—or far more miserable. And the same person can make you feel both. Thus, the better we are at understanding people, talking with them, and working with them, the better our lives become—as well as the lives of everyone with whom we come in contact.

The information in this book can't undo the past, but it can save you from pain and agony today and well into the future. You don't have to reinvent the wheel or change your personality. You just have to learn simple proven skills and have fun using them.

The purpose of this book is to answer just one question: What do six-figure communicators do that average people do not? Poor communicators have not yet learned these secrets and are destined to continue making the same mistakes until they learn these lessons. Six-figure communicators, however, practice these secrets and have gone on to do extraordinary things in their lives. What is that "something special" that some people have? What do they know about positive and effective communication that others don't? Why is it that some people are so easy to talk to, work so well with others, and can get anyone to open up, while others just get more and more frustrated?

If you already have good communication skills, this book will sharpen them—guaranteed! But if you believe (or know) you have poor communication skills, this book will help you improve your communication with others. It will give you a strong foundation to make your dealings with others easier and more enjoyable. You will learn why people do the things they do and what is needed to gently persuade them to your way of thinking.

This book is filled with no-nonsense skills to help you improve your communication, make extraordinary connections, and get results now. Applying these skills in your personal life will help you strengthen your relationships and attract the friends, family, and resources you need to accomplish your goals. Using these skills in your professional life is sure to help you improve your productivity, increase your value to your organization, and even help you earn more.

## How to Use This Book

This book is designed to be an easy-to-follow practical guide. You can start at the beginning and do a chapter a day sequentially, or randomly choose chapters according to your needs and interests. Most skills and techniques are divided into several short sections to give you essential information quickly. The exercises at the end of each chapter will help you turn communication theory into communication reality.

Although most of these skills are simple to learn, some skills take time to develop before they come naturally. It will take time to incorporate some of these skills into your own approach with people as you move from feelings of incompetence to competence and ultimately to second-nature communication ease and success.

This book is not designed to change who you are as a person. It merely contains the techniques that six-figure communicators use to project incredible confidence, likeability and trust. Although many people skills are fundamental, every skill and idea may not apply perfectly to every individual or situation. After all, we have each been raised differently, in different regions, with different life perspectives. Still, remember that just one new idea or skill could make a huge difference in your life.

## How This Book Is Organized

*Six-Figure Incomes* **is divided into four parts, as follows:**

### Part I: Developing the Right Mind-Set

If you are not in the right mind-set, all of the people skills in the world will not do much to fix your situation. The greatest secret to successfully working with people lies within you, not others. This part emphasizes the importance of your state of mind and the power of a strong, positive mind-set. You'll learn how to break unproductive patterns to get into and stay in a more powerful mind-set.

## Part II: Understanding People

The easier it is to understand people, the easier it is to talk and work with them. Part II reveals keys to reading people, finding and avoiding hot buttons, setting people at ease, understanding charisma, learning someone's true colors quickly, and listening and letting others talk during conversations. In this part, you'll learn a simple, universal strategy for understanding people.

## Part III: Talking to People

This part explores interpersonal and conversational dynamics. You'll learn how to apply communication skills from this book while in conversation with others. Topics discussed include the power of words, body language, and conversational dialogue.

## Part IV: Working with People

In this part, you'll polish your communication skills and strategies to better work with others. Topics in this part include recognizing what drives the human heart, dealing with angry people, righting important relationships, bringing out the best in others, leading others using personal power, establishing and using a network, and using simple ways to develop yourself.

# PEOPLE-SKILLS QUIZ

**Answer yes or no to each question below. Rate your communication skill level at the end of the quiz.**

| | Yes | No |
|---|---|---|
| Do you find that understanding, talking with, and working with people is fairly easy to do? | | |
| Are you skilled at working with people you encounter in everyday situations? | | |
| Do you enjoy talking with and working with people? | | |
| Do people energize you? | | |
| Do you deal well with angry people? | | |
| Are you a good judge of character? | | |
| If you were driving around lost, would you feel comfortable pulling over and asking a stranger for directions? | | |
| After a conversation, can you remember three things about the person you were speaking with? | | |
| Are you good at establishing rapport? | | |
| Are you comfortable with most of your conversations? | | |
| Do you have strong personal relationships? | | |
| Do you have strong professional relationships? | | |
| Do you rely on your charisma and communications skills, rather than on your position or title, in leadership situations? | | |
| If you glanced into a mirror at work, while driving or in a shopping mall, would you have a neutral or smiling face rather than a scowl? | | |

|  | Yes | No |
|---|---|---|
| Do people ever call you when they need help or someone to talk to? |  |  |
| Do you bring out the best in others? |  |  |
| Are you good at networking? |  |  |
| Do you have an active network? |  |  |
| If you lost your job today, could you find another job quickly? Are your communication, networking, and people skills up-to-date? |  |  |
| If you were new to your neighborhood and locked out of your house, would you feel comfortable asking neighbors you didn't know for help or to use their phone? |  |  |
| Do you have three or more people you could call at 1 A.M. for help in an emergency? |  |  |
| Do you have three or more people you could call at 1 A.M. for money in an emergency? |  |  |
| TOTALS |  |  |

**How many "no" answers did you have? Use the following scale to rate yourself:**

0–3 "no" answers = Great communicator
4–8 "no" answers = Good communicator
9–13 "no" answers = Fair communicator
14–22 "no" answers = Poor communicator

# Part I

Perhaps the greatest of all people skills is the ability to get into and stay in a strong, positive mind-set. In this state of mind, magic happens. People are mysteriously drawn to positive people and want to associate with them. In this mind-set, people are funnier, happier, and more pleasant to be around. It is easy to talk with others when you are in this state, and it is easy to talk to others who are in this state.

When you are not in a strong, positive mind-set, talking to and working with people is tough, regardless of how many people skills, tricks, tips, and techniques you know. People quickly see through someone faking a positive mind-set.

Part I of this book addresses the importance of this distinctive mental state called the "personal power mind-set."

# The Personal Power Mind-Set

## In This Chapter:

- Discover the unlimited power of mind-set
- Assess your Personal Power IQ
- Set the law of attraction in motion
- Use the Golden Minute every day, everywhere
- Learn how to develop and keep the personal power mind-set

Have you ever been introduced to a stranger and gotten a feeling of whether you liked the person—before he even opened his mouth? Whether we realize it or not, we are constantly sending out an enormous amount of information about ourselves and receiving information from others. We cannot not communicate. Before we open our mouths we get a sense of others and they get a sense of us. People get a feel for our mood and what kind of conversation is going to occur during the first few seconds. They get a sense for us and make up their minds about us extremely quickly.

## The Golden Minute

A fascinating report on National Public Radio on November 5, 2001, told about counselors using dogs to help grief-stricken victims open up and cope after the terrorist attacks on the World Trade Center in New York. One counselor mentioned that if there was a group of three people, and two people didn't like dogs, the dog naturally gravitated to the person who liked dogs. The dog somehow could sense this, even though no one went up to the dog to pet it!

In his classic job-search book, *What Color Is Your Parachute,* Richard Bolles says that when interviews are lost, they are most often lost within the first 30 seconds to two minutes. And this applies to when interviewers have taken extra time to screen candidates who could be with the company for years. The rest of the interview merely justifies the interviewer's initial impression. All things being equal, job interviewers are primarily trying to "sniff out" if they like you, as do dogs and most people.

In fact, the first minute is the most critical time when talking with people. It is during the first 60 seconds of a conversation or exposure to others that people decide whether they want to talk to us, hire us, do business with us, or ignore us. This is when they access our mind-set, determine who they think we are, and make their decision. I call this critical time the golden minute. For it is during this golden minute that the majority of interactions with others are won or lost.

Salespeople making numerous sales calls per day are especially alert to this phenomenon. Almost without exception, within the first 60 seconds of walking into an office or making an approach, the direction and tone of the conversation are determined. When salespeople are in a bad mood, they will have to wait a long time to see the customer or they will have to come back another day—gatekeepers somehow can sense this. When salespeople are in a great mood, then gatekeepers seem to get them in to see the client as quickly as possible. People can spot a "mood faker" right way.

## The Right State of Mind

Reading all the books in the world on persuasion, selling, parenting, and communication will do you little good if you are not in the right mental state to transmit this information. By the same token, you could be in a room full of people who love you, but if you are not in a receiving state, you will not reap any of the benefits. What then is the missing key?

The missing key for so many people is state of mind, or mind-set. The fact is you can transmit and receive certain traits only in certain states. Certain qualities and traits are unattainable in certain states. You cannot transmit love, caring, patience, understanding, empathy, charisma, charm, class, or confidence when you are outraged. It is impossible. People will see right through you if you try to fake it. You will come across as insincere and fake. We are but mirror reflections of our present state.

The following chart lists traits people possess while in various states. The more distinctive the state, the more definitive its traits. Notice that you cannot transmit these traits or receive them unless you are in that particular state (or similar state). Also notice that certain traits are unique to certain states. By learning to get into more powerful mind-sets, you will be able to better transmit and receive more dynamic traits. Though you have control only over yourself in this process, you will learn how to subtly lead others into powerful states too.

## Achievable Traits per State

| ← Negative | | | State | Positive | | → |
|---|---|---|---|---|---|---|
| Hatred | Sadness | Frustration | Apathy | Appreciation | Happiness | Love |
| Send/Receive | Send/Receive | Send/Receive | Send/Receive | Send/Receive | Send/Receive | Send/Receive |
| disgust | disappointment | anger | indifference | recognition | joy | warmth |
| anger | grief | aggravation | hesitation | gratitude | lightheartedness | affection |
| rage | worry | irritation | low esteem | trust | contentment | passion |
| fear | hopelessness | agitation | doubt | praise | enjoyment | concern |
| alienation | hurt | uncertainty | disengaged | admiration | pleasure | admiration |
| worry | discouragement | impatience | carelessness | understanding | satisfaction | kindness |
| mistrust | defeat | helplessness | detachment | awareness | bliss | generosity |
| dislike | sorrow | oppression | | confidence | hope | compassion |
| scorn | misery | confusion | | motivation | energy | understanding |
| loathing | dejection | desperation | | support | goodwill | thoughtfulness |
| hostility | unhappiness | | | | | patience |
| malice | gloom | | | | | humility |
| antagonism | | | | | | empathy |
| animosity | | | | | | trust |
| | | | | | | respect |
| | | | | | | strength |

Which column best describes your daily mental state? Do you intentionally get in this state or is it habitual, or even accidental? How many hours a day do you spend in this state? How does this state affect your life or the lives of others? Can you become the person you need or want to be if you continue to stay in this state? If you don't learn to get into a more powerful state, what would it cost you now and in the future?

*"Men do not attract that which they want, but that which they are."*
— **James Allen, As a Man Thinketh**

# The Power of a Positive Mind-Set

Ever have a day when everything goes great? You wake up feeling good and your day just keeps getting better and better. You get the last great parking space, the elevator just happens to open when you walk up to it, a stranger wishes you a good morning, and you get great news as soon as you get to the office.

When you are in this mind-set, life is good, and you know it. People naturally gravitate to you, start up conversations with you, and you feel unstoppable. You glow! You are in a state of exuberance and you think more creatively, more clearly, more positively. You get better ideas and have an unusual sense of well-being. You soon begin to expect and attract more good things into your life as your luck continually multiplies. Projects and tasks that were once difficult are now easy to do, and you complete them quickly. You are in a strong productive mind-set that allows you to accomplish more and communicate better with others.

This mind-set unleashes the all-powerful law of attraction. This law states that we attract like things around us. Like attracts like. The better it gets, the better it gets. The worse it gets, the worse it gets.[1] It has also been described as being "in the zone" or as the snowball theory. Things start off good or bad and just seem to snowball in that direction, getting bigger and bigger.

Maybe you've had a day that snowballed in the wrong direction. You woke up late, spilled your coffee, got cut off in traffic, got a flat tire, forgot you had an early-morning meeting—and the whole day just seemed to get worse before it really even began. Everything you said came out wrong and everything you did just seemed to make everything else worse. Your day continually spiraled downward.

You were clearly out of the zone and in a negative state. It's dangerous to talk to and work with people in this state because you can do more harm in it than good. Similarly, it is dangerous to do major thinking in this state because outcomes may not be rational or factual, but based solely on negative thoughts and emotions. Suicides, fights, arguments, and accidents are the result of making bad decisions in negative states.

Mind-set is simply about getting into a good mood and staying positive. Nothing is more important. Good things always happen when you are feeling good! You make the best decisions and do your best work. Nothing good comes from being down—nothing!

---

Cheerful people, by age 34, make $14, 000 a year more than less happy people, adjusting for family background.[2]

---

# Escaping from a Negative Mind-Set

Bad things are going to happen in life. That is just part of life. You do not always have power over them. People are going to have accidents, get injured, and even die. Companies will close, relocate, lay off, fire, downsize, and restructure. You will work with difficult, angry, frustrated, irrational, and unfair customers. People will lie, cheat, and steal. You will have many reasons to get into a bad mood daily and throughout your life. But how you get into this negative mood isn't what's important—it happens. What is important is how to get out of this negative state.

Mind-set is about control. Control is being aware of your mood and knowing what you need to do to get out of a bad mood and into a better one. That is the first priority. A positive mind-set is simply replacing negative thoughts with positive thoughts. It is about releasing unpleasant thoughts and choosing more desirable ones. This takes practice.

Six-figure communicators know that a powerful mind-set protects them and infects others. It is simple physics, the principle of diffusion. Energy particles always move from the higher concentration to the lower concentration—never the other way around. People with a higher energy level always alter people with a lower energy level, regardless whether that energy is positive or negative. Whoever has the strongest mind-set wins.

For example, if you feel tired and rundown, and you run into an angry person, that anger will rub off on you. That person's mind-set and energy level are stronger than yours and after that interaction, you will become angry too. You were in a decent mood but now you, too, are mad at the world.

But when you are in a strong mind-set, others will not zap your energy and leave you angry, frustrated, broken, and bent. Negative people will not rub off on you. Instead, you will rub off on them! You will "infect" them with your abundance of positive energy, for your energy level is stronger. You will win the energy/state battle.

> *"I believe we are masters of our lives—*
> *we hold all the cards and it is up to us to use them right."*
> **—Flight attendant Vesna Vulovic, who in 1972 survived an airplane crash from 33,330 ft. She was found unconscious with her legs sticking out of the fuselage. She is listed in the *Guinness Book of World Records* for the highest fall survived without a parachute.**

# Personal Power vs. Position Power

The power you possess within yourself to influence others can come from one of two sources: personal power or position power. The power of position is influencing people, or getting people to do things for you, based solely on your position, status, or title. People who use their people skills to influence others are exercising their personal power.

Parents, teachers, doctors, police officers, and judges are among those who have position power. No doubt you have heard a parent say to a child (or have said this yourself), "I am the parent and you are the child, and you are going to do what I say." Or an Army officer says, "Move out, Sergeant, and make it happen." These are examples of the power of position in action. There are times, such as in the presence of danger, when the power of position must be used. But its overuse shows poor leadership and leads to hurt feelings, resentment, and lowered respect.

People who can talk and work with anyone, regardless of position or status, are using their personal power. Six-figure communicators have developed their people skills to the point that—even if they have the power of position—they know they can accomplish just as much or more using their personal power. Using personal power, you might say, "Come on, guys, let's get this done so we can go home early." People with these skills have what might be called a "sixth sense" when talking and working with others.

Using personal power instead of position power is a well-kept secret of six-figure communicators. Six-figure communicators know they always have this power and can use it anywhere, anytime, on anyone, even on vacation. It allows them to earn the respect and admiration of others in a way that the power of position never can.

When we combine personal power with a powerful mind-set, we are unstoppable. Personal power begins to magically increase as the law of attraction is activated. We automatically say and do the right things. Good things flow into our lives as our interactions with others become more meaningful and enjoyable. And when we use this powerful combination, communication and influence thrive.

## The Value of People Skills

Without strong people skills, we are scared to change jobs, go back to school, move to our dream city, or try something we have always wanted to do. We don't take chances with our shadow security. It is "shadow security" because if we lost our jobs, we would not have the people skills to network, interview, and get a job with similar income or benefits. Without strong people skills, we do not have the confidence to try something new. Instead, we stress about keeping our existing job.

## Choosing Personal Power over Position Power

I had the privilege to hear a former Chicago police officer, Donald Woelfle, speak about the influence of personal power in a speech titled "He's a Good Boy." He related a story of being called in to control a hostile situation in which an irate man threw a steel radiator through a wall and was yelling, screaming, and out of control. It was Woelfle's job to take this man into custody and escort him to a mental institution. But this enormous man didn't want to go. Three other police officers couldn't get close enough to the man to handcuff him.

Officer Woelfle learned that the man's grandmother lived in the building and asked her to talk to him. She told the man to "be a good boy and do what the police officer said." With pressure from his grandmother, the man reluctantly agreed to cooperate. Woelfle moved in to handcuff the man quickly and soon realized that the man's wrists were so massive that the handcuffs wouldn't fit. This angry giant would be free to mash the officer like an Idaho spud.

Officer Woelfle quickly remembered hearing that this man was a former Marine. He told the man that he had always heard that Marines were men of honor and that they always kept their word. He asked the man if that was true, and he agreed. With little choice, Woelfle told the man that he wouldn't handcuff him if he promised, as a Marine, not to try to get away or hurt anyone. The man earnestly agreed and cooperated with the police. Both men were able to walk out of the building with a little dignity.

Later Officer Woelfle learned that this was a recurrent problem and that this was the first time the man had ever been brought to a mental institution under his own accord. Experience had taught the institution guards that 12 of them should greet the giant at the door. But the man quietly walked into the mental institution without incident. The guards were utterly amazed at how the police officer had persuaded the man to get into his patrol car willingly and walk into the institution quietly and confidently.

Police officers have enormous power and resources to protect and serve the public. They can fight criminals all out if they have to. But most of them prefer to use tact and diplomacy instead of force. It makes their jobs easier and safer and reduces incidents. Though Officer Woelfle had the power of position, his quick thinking and personal power may have saved not only his life, but the lives of three other police officers.

# What's Your Personal Power IQ?

Your Personal Power IQ is a measure not of how much personal power you possess at any given time, but of your ability to get into and stay in a powerful mind-set all day. It measures your capacity to get into and remain in a productive mind-set for long periods. You can rate your Personal Power IQ by answering the following questions:

1. What is your dominant mood? Give yourself 10 points if it is almost always positive, five points if it tends to be positive, and no points if it is usually "blah," or negative.

2. Are you active? Do you have a core group of friends that you socialize with, are you a member of a club, or do you get out of the house and do things frequently? If you do, give yourself five points, and if you do not, do not give yourself any.

3. What percentage of your conversations with others is positive? Give yourself 10 points if more than 90 percent are, five points if at least 75 percent are, and no points if less than 75 percent are.

4. Do you get upset easily? Estimate how often you get upset. If you get upset three times or fewer weekly, give yourself 10 points. If you get upset three to six times weekly, give yourself five points. If you get upset more than six times weekly (daily), do not give yourself any points.

5. Can one person ruin your morning? Give yourself 10 points for "almost never," five points for "at times," and no points for "frequently."

6. Is your mental state more positive or less positive by lunchtime? Give yourself 10 points for being "more positive," five points for "the same," and no points for "less positive."

7. Do you take the time to enjoy the present? Do you savor your conversations with others, time spent with them, and the time taken to enjoy the good things in life? If you do "usually," give yourself 10 points. If you do "sometimes" or "rarely," do not give yourself any points.

8.  Can you pull yourself out of a bad mood? If you can more than 90 percent of the time, give yourself 10 points. If you can do so 89–75 percent of the time, give yourself five points. If you can do so less than 75 percent of the time, do not give yourself any points.

9.  Do the people you typically surround yourself with inspire you, uplift you, and bring out the best in you? If they do, give yourself five points. If they do not, or you are indifferent, do not give yourself any points.

10. Does your environment uplift you, inspire you, and bring out the best in you? If it does, give yourself five points. If it does not, or you are indifferent, do not give yourself any points.

Total Score _____

Add up your points to find your total score and rate it on the chart below.

Personal Power IQ:

<55    Nonexistent or Minimal Personal Power
55–65   Limited Personal Power
>65    Above Average, Highly Productive Personal Power

Your score is indicative of your ability to attract the good things into your life—for when the mind is ready, the body and success will follow. If your mind-set is off, all of the tricks and tips in the world will not help you. People will see right through you.

## The Relationship Between Mood and Personal Power

The illustration on the following page shows that the more positive your mood, the easier it is to get into the personal power mind-set. Getting into this mind-set is easier with just a little bit of love in your heart than with a whole lot of appreciation. But love and appreciation both work. Also notice that the weaker your mood, the more emotional intensity you need to be able to get into the personal power mind-set. The more grateful you are, the easier it is to get into the personal power mind-set. But notice, too, that a negative mood, at any intensity, will never increase your personal power.

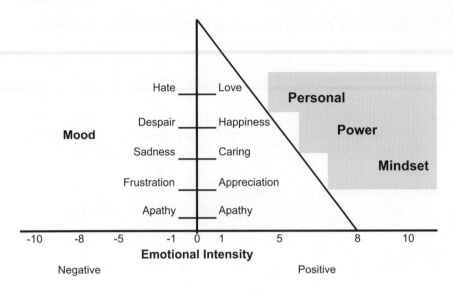

By understanding these relationships, you will better understand how to improve your own mind-set. Sometimes it is easier simply to increase the intensity of a positive emotion and other times it is easier to improve your mood. Creating the personal power mind-set is crucial to talking to and working with people, especially difficult people. And if you are not at a level nine or 10 (some say level 12), you will have trouble dealing with them.

## Three Steps to the Personal Power Mind-Set

Do you think six-figure communicators accidentally get into a powerful mind-set? Or does it happen by chance? Does "the world" decide their mood or what kind of day they are going to have? Or do the communicators themselves have a hand in it?

People who use a high degree of personal power have the unique ability to get in and stay in an exceptionally strong mind-set, regardless of people or circumstances. This enabling mind-set allows them to do great things. It is that something special that allows them to handle difficult people with confidence and class. It gives them their charm, personality, and charisma when talking and working with others. People using the personal power mind-set have their share of obstacles like everyone else, but they have the unique ability to turn negative situations to their advantage.

Most people have trouble getting into this powerful mind-set. They frequently get stuck in a negative state and do not know how to get out of it. They get stuck in this negative state for days, weeks, and even years. When this happens, their personal power drops to almost zero and they have little choice but to rely on their power of position. Their low energy is habitual.

Getting into the personal power mind-set involves three fundamental steps. Six-figure communicators consciously or unconsciously go through these steps daily to get into this advanced state. Think carefully about each step to see where your strengths and weaknesses lie. Use these steps to pinpoint and improve areas that restrict energy so that you can get the most out of each and maximize the personal power mind-set.

## Step 1: Choose Your Focus

It is not the positive thinking that is important, it is the focus. Positive thinking is the by-product and the end result of focus. It is extremely difficult to think positively when you focus on doom and gloom, even the most positive people can't do this–it is too hard for anyone!

Every situation has two sides, just like a coin, but it is the side of the coin we choose to focus on that determines all subsequent thoughts, and thus our reality. If the positive side of the coin is "heads" and the negative side is "tails," you might hear people yelling and complaining because there is a "tails" on one side of the coin. Who put a tails on this coin?! I wish there wasn't a tails on this coin. Everything would be great if there wasn't a tails on this coin. Instead, six-figure communicators look for and focus on the "heads" in life.

Six-figure communicators habitually have a different focus than poor communicators! They are "others focused" and not "self-focused," says Emmy Hagar, a successful businesswoman and a district governor for Toastmasters International, an organization that helps people improve their communication skills. When you focus on others, it not only helps them, it helps you. When your focus is on others, you don't waste time worrying about your own problems and concerns, attracting more negative thoughts. Your own problems and concerns seem to vanish. This small distinction changes everything! Your focus changes the source of all thoughts.

Focusing on others instantly changes your mind-set and makes talking to and working with others easier and more enjoyable. People quickly learn where your heart is and where your intentions lie, and they treat you accordingly. This mind-set enables positive thoughts to flow effortlessly and helps you forget about your own problems and misfortunes and instead focus on finding solutions for others. Focusing on others changes where your attention lies and thus changes your thoughts.

Learning to choose your focus takes work. Losers always find the negative side because a negative focus is easier to find. But six-figure communicators find and focus on the positive. They know that the "heads" side of the coin is always there; it just takes a little more work to turn the coin over.

Our focus changes the way the human body functions. The brain's cerebral cortex creates thoughts and interprets external stimuli. When feelings of rage, anger, excitement, and pleasure are generated, the cerebral cortex sends this information, via neurons, to the hypothalamus, which is the brain's mediator for converting emotion into physical response. The limbic system, the brain's emotional headquarters, also sends signals to the hypothalamus. The hypothalamus processes this information and affects your state by sending signals to the autonomic nervous system to increase heart rate, constrict blood vessels, and increase blood pressure by sending signals to the brain's pituitary gland (connected by the pituitary stalk) to change state through chemical factors.

## Step 2: Combine Focus with Action

Although choosing our focus is a good first step in getting into a strong mind-set, it must be combined with action. Why? Because sitting on the couch watching television or lying in bed thinking positively usually does not create emotions or thoughts strong enough to release brain chemicals. People are usually no different after watching four hours of television. But physical action, such as running, walking, eating certain foods, and talking to happy people can release brain chemicals to physically change your state.

Be aware of how you operate. Figure out what makes you happy and the ingredients you need to get into a positive mind-set. Knowing what uplifts you is a good start. One way to do this is to make a list. The more uplifting things you are aware of, and the more of them you do, the easier it is to replace negative thoughts with positive actions.

### Sample List:
- Do a favor for someone
- Pay someone a compliment
- Exercise (lift weights, hike, golf)
- Whistle, sing, hum
- Take a hot shower or bath
- Breathe deeply
- Call or visit an upbeat friend or acquaintance

- Watch your favorite television show (Bonanza?)
- Read a favorite book

*"Even if you're on the right track, you'll get run over if you just sit there."*
— **Will Rogers (1879-1935)**

## How Action Changes Body Chemistry to Influence Mood and Mind-Set

Nerve cells within the brain (neurons) generate small electrical impulses (action potential) and pass on electrical impulses from other neurons. But there is a space between these neurons that the electrical signal (traveling at up to 250 mph) cannot jump, no matter how strong the signal. When this signal comes to the end of the neuron, neurotransmitters—chemicals manufactured and stored in the neuron—are released. They bridge this gap (synapse) so that the electrical impulse can continue.

The brain doesn't work like cable television, simply sending electricity through a cable wire. Instead, each electrical signal continually alternates from being electrical to chemical and then back to electrical as it surges from one neuron to the next, coursing through the brain. Amazing!

More than 18 major neurotransmitters are in the brain. Each specializes in passing on a different signal, triggering different states and behavior within the brain. Serotonin sends signals of well-being and relaxation; affects perceptions, focus, and concentration; and helps you sleep better at night. Thoughts release dopamine from the pituitary that affects desire, pleasure, and assertiveness. Dopamine has been linked to memory, problem solving, and attention. Norepinephrine, a precursor chemical of adrenaline, is associated with the fight or flight response, heightening alertness and increasing heart rate, dilating airways and constricting blood vessels.

Endorphins are the body's natural pain killers released during pain, stress, and pleasure. When the body is in pain, endorphins block pain signals to the nervous system. And during times of pleasure, they create a sense of euphoria.

Endorphins, not adrenalin, are responsible for the "runner's high" and similar pleasures. They give bungee jumpers and sky divers their energy rush after landing safely on the ground. Endorphins also give us a sense of well-being.

Action stimulates the release of endorphins and other neurotransmitters. Exercise, chocolate, chili peppers, and sexual activity have been shown to specifically increase endorphin levels. Hugs, laughter, acupuncture, massage, sugar, music, and even ultraviolet light may also increase endorphin levels. These increased levels may lower blood pressure and stimulate the immune system (immune system cells have endorphin receptors).

In a recent study published in a veterinary journal, researchers took blood samples from dogs and their owners. Then they had the owners and their dogs spend time together relaxing for up to 30 minutes, and then they took another blood sample. Endorphin, dopamine, oxytocin, and prolactin levels doubled in the bloodstream of not only the owners, but also the dogs! And blood pressure fell.[3]

Researchers already knew that beta-endorphin was released during exercise, but they wanted to determine exactly how much exercise and time it took to increase beta-endorphin levels in the blood. To test, they put eight healthy males on stationary bikes and then inserted a venous catheter in each one to make it easy to take blood samples at regular intervals. They had the men exercise for 25 minutes at 60, 70, and 80 percent of peak output volume, as measured my oxygen levels. They took blood samples at five-minute intervals during exercise.

Exercising at 60 and 70 percent peak output did not increase beta-endorphin levels. But cycling at 80 percent output for 15 minutes did! In fact, beta-endorphin levels increased continuously up to the 25-minute endpoint.[4]

So what does all of this mean? It means that action changes the chemistry of the body and helps influence not only our moods, but our mind-set. It means that such diversions as being active with family and friends, exercising, eating certain foods, and spending time with a significant other can play a major role in our mental and physical health, initiating electrical and biochemical activity to improve mind-set.

## Step 3: Savor the Present

This is the missing step for most of us. While we are doing the action, most of us are already thinking about what we are going to do next, what else we have planned that day, how much time we have to do the next task on our list, and what we want to cover at the meeting next week.

Instead, we must learn to savor the now. Savor the present. Enjoy action. Really savor how good action feels. Make it a point to consciously savor your time with friends and family, the weather, and having fun. Don't wait till Thanksgiving or Christmas to appreciate all of the blessings in your life and revel in how good the activity feels.

Live in the moment! Too many of us are living in the past or the future. Savor the present. That is all we have. Too many people don't realize—until the days are gone—that these are the "good old days" right now. The "golden years" are now!

## Putting It All Together

Choose your focus, take action, and then savor the action. This builds the personal power mind-set and starts a continual cycle of improving thoughts. This gets the law of attraction moving in the right directing. Taking action and then savoring that action improves the next thought. Then taking action on that thought and savoring it improves the next thought, continually building a powerful mind-set.

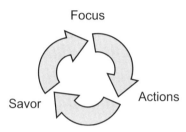

**Here are some examples of applying the three steps toward achieving the personal power mind-set:**
1.  **Situation #1**
    Focus and subsequent thought: I want to get in shape.
    Action: Go running.
    Savor the sun's warmth and how good it feels to exercise and do something good. Enjoy seeing other runners, admire the sunset, and relish in the fact that you are getting healthier.

    New thought: I feel great; I might as well do a few pushups, too, to strengthen my arms.
    New action: Do some pushups.
    Savor: That felt good. I should work out more often. I forgot how good it makes me feel!

2.  **Situation #2**
    Focus and subsequent thought: I want to improve my relationship with God.
    Action: Go to church.

Savor the organ music, church choir, and the uplifting feeling of being in a holy place.

New thought: Maybe I should join the choir.
New action: Get information on the choir, when and where it meets.
Savor: I forgot how much I love to sing. This is so much fun!

3. **Situation #3**
Focus and subsequent thought: I am down and need to break this negative state.
Action: Go dancing and invite friends along.
Savor: I love dancing and socializing with happy people.

New thought: What are you guys doing next weekend? Do you want to go kayaking?
New action: Go kayaking.
Savor: I love this group! This is so much fun!

Research shows that people who do what they love have a far easier time getting into and staying in the personal power mind-set compared with people who work only for a paycheck. This subtle difference allows those of us who like what we're doing to accomplish far more than people who don't. We are likeable people who are habitually in a good mood. Others can sense this immediately.

# Keeping the Mind-Set

Once you are in a powerfully productive mind-set, the next trick is to stay in it long enough to use it, to profit from it, to put it to work, and to get the most mileage out of it. You are ready to accomplish all you set out to do—if you can keep the mind-set!

But as soon as you walk out of the house in the morning, you get challenged from all sides. People may cut you off in traffic, complain, defy you, or be intentionally rude. Your personal power is constantly being tested. Who could blame you for getting angry? After all, rude people should get what they deserve. But getting angry drains our batteries and robs us of the critical energy needed to effectively work with others. Sagging energy cripples communication and disables the personal power mind-set.

This section offers strategies for helping to preserve your personal power mind-set. Some strategies work on preserving this mind-set through thoughts and others through actions. Choose strategies that work best for you.

# Cognitive Behavioral Strategies (Thoughts)

Sigmund Freud described the id and the ego in his psychoanalytical approach to therapy. The id works on the pleasure principle, attempting to maximize personal gratification by satisfying raw impulses. It does not care about morals, society, or other people. It is rooted into the limbic system, the primitive brain. It is our "spontaneous dangerous side" that seeks pleasure.[5] It is animalistic, tactless, undiplomatic, and hot-headed. It seeks immediate gratification. Make the id angry, and it will react harshly, often too harshly. Like an arrow shot from a bow, words once released can never really be taken back. The damage has already been done.

The ego, on the other hand, is the logical and rational part of the brain, the neocortex. The ego will delay satisfying the id's desires until it can be done safely and successfully. It uses socially accepted methods for dealing with people and understands the consequences of its behavior. It looks at the larger picture, the circumstances, and the environment before reacting. The ego helps us better work with others.

Cognitive behavioral strategies use the ego to reduce conflict and, more important, reduce energy drain. This ensures that the personal power mind-set has the energy it needs to successfully work with others. In this section we will see how *predetermined beliefs*, *battle drills*, *reducers*, *immediate statements*, and *perspective* all help to preserve the personal power mind-set and help us come across with more charm, personality, and grace under pressure.

## Predetermined Beliefs

We do more to pull ourselves "out of state" than anyone else. Here is an example:

On one of my office calls as a pharmaceutical sales representative, the receptionist greeted me with a smile as soon as I walked through the door. She asked for my business card and said it would be a few minutes. I waited about 10 minutes and then she called me back to wait for the physician. I was in a good mood. I waited for five, 10, and then 25 minutes. Soon I had been back there for an hour, and I had six more sales calls to make that day in another town. By now I was hopping mad and told the receptionist that I was late for another appointment and had to leave. She smiled and said she would see me next time.

The receptionist was pleasant, but I was upset. My personal power instantly stopped, and I started to get upset. I really wasn't in the mood to be charming or understanding at that point. Why? I did nothing wrong, the receptionist was pleasant, and the physician probably just got hung up with a patient through no fault of his own. What happened?!

The same thing happens daily to all of us. Before anyone says or does anything to us, we have consciously or unconsciously predetermined how we will interpret and perceive future comments and events. After all, comments and events have no meaning except for the meaning we give them. And this meaning is established long before the actual event.

This may be a good or a bad thing, depending on the response. In my case it was a bad thing. I pulled myself out of a perfectly fine mood by my predetermined belief, in this example, to get mad if I waited more than an hour to see a customer. That's how predetermined beliefs work—they determine future actions and reactions.

The trick is to predetermine your beliefs and attitudes now, before you need them. They are modifiable. When faced with challenging situations, your actions will be more productive and less stressful if you think about them in advance.

Why is this so important? It is important to stop negative feelings before they snowball. Negative feelings rob you of vast amounts of energy and leave you exhausted. Moreover, large amounts of energy (which you've already lost) are required to get back into the personal power mind set. The personal power mind-set is sacred and you shouldn't allow anything to pull you out of it. Remember, you do more to pull yourself out of this mind-set than anyone else.

So what is meant by changing predetermined beliefs? How do you modify them? Will this change who you are? Let's take a look at a few common predetermined beliefs and modify them.

**Predetermined Belief:**
If someone says something to me that I don't like, I will get angry.
*Modified Belief:*
Losers complain and yell; I'm glad I am not one of them. What an unhappy life they must live. They probably get taken advantage of a lot.

**Predetermined Belief:**
I will be nice to people until they hurt me or make me angry.
*Modified Belief:*
I will give 100 percent to everyone and care for them 100 percent. I will expect nothing in return.

(Incidentally, this is why children are often happy. They give unconditionally to people and don't get hung up if someone doesn't care or ignores them—they just go on with their lives. Perhaps this is due to their short attention spans. Adults, however, stew about and hold grudges from comments or actions that others make.)

**Predetermined Belief:**
People make me so mad sometimes.
*Modified Belief:*
To really be happy, I need people. The "good" feelings and emotions, such as love, affection, companionship, humor, pride, charisma, admiration, caring, and friendship require someone else. I can be sad, grumpy, angry, outraged, hateful, and frustrated all by myself.

Predetermined beliefs are like solving for X in an algebraic equation. Events plugged into the equation determine your reaction. Events determine whether you are having a good day or a bad day. And these minor events add up all day and snowball negatively. Six-figure communicators have already "rigged" their equations so that regardless of the event or situation, their value for X will be a positive value, not a negative one. Rigged positive beliefs and attitudes help us keep the personal power mind-set.

## Battle Drills

America's elite 82nd Airborne Division continually practices battle drills. They practice seizing an enemy airfield, reacting to a sniper, reacting to an ambush, and reacting to indirect or direct fire. They practice these drills over and over in peacetime so when their lives depend upon them, they respond effectively and efficiently. By having and rehearsing battle drills, they don't get flustered or stressed in difficult situations. Their minds don't shut down, and they immediately respond in a predetermined fashion. They know that most people don't feel stress from the situation itself, but from its initial shock, deciding how to handle it, and second-guessing their decisions and actions.

But you don't have to be a paratrooper to have battle drills. By knowing how to respond ahead of time to everyday situations, you will reduce stress, come across more professionally, and have more fun. Listed below are a few examples of battle drills for non-paratroopers, used in tandem with pre-determined beliefs. (Specific battle drills for dealing with angry people are discussed later in this book.)

- **Situation:** Someone blows up at me for no apparent reason.
  **Predetermined Belief:** People get upset sometimes and just need to vent. I will not take it personally.
  **Battle Drill:**
  1. Comment: "It sounds like you are having a tough day. I'm sorry. I hope your day gets better."
  2. Action: I leave.
  3. Think: Poor guy, it sure sounds like he is having a bad day. I hope his day gets better.

- **Situation:** One of my pieces of luggage misses its connection at the airport and will arrive late.
  **Predetermined Belief:** I will not get upset with things that are out of my control.
  **Battle Drill:**
  1. Comment: "I understand that these things happen sometimes. What do you need from me so that I can get my bag back?"
  2. Action: Leave hotel information.
  3. Think: At least now I don't have to lug my bag around. Instead, they will transport it to the hotel for me.

We cannot think out all actions in advance, but by taking a minute to think about how we will react to general events, before they happen, we will act smoothly and in control when similar events happen. This reduces stress, anger, and second-guessing.

By doing this, you will come across as calm, cool, and collected, and as a person with class and finesse. Come up with a few of your own battle drills or polish old ones. Battle drills help you preserve energy and keep your personal power mind-set.

**Reactionary Mind-set** ⟶ Belief ⟶ Trigger Id ⟶ Poor Response (panic/anger)

**Personal Power Mind-set** ⟶ Predetermined Belief ⟶ Trigger Ego ⟶ Great Response (battle drills)

## Reducers

Reducers are another way to instantly reduce a bad or unpleasant circumstance before you even have time to get upset or angry. This short-circuits negative energy and prevents negative emotion from quickly building and starting a negative chain reaction or snowball. Reducers are essentially rationale you can use when you hear negative comments from others or people who treat you poorly. And you will probably be right nine times out of 10. Let's look at a few examples.

- **Situation #1**: A child is upset and yelling about something.
  **Reducer:**
  Instead of getting upset, you instantly reduce the intensity of the situation and think: This is a child, and he is probably scared or hungry and just wants his mother. Or if the child is an adolescent, realize that she has no real-world experience and is only talking theory or repeating what one of her friends have said.

- **Situation #2:** Someone is upset.
  **Reducer:**
  Think: Perhaps this person has been up all night and is exhausted, or this person may be under a lot of stress.

- **Situation #3:** Someone speeds by you in traffic and cuts you off.
  **Reducer:**
  Boy, that guy is really moving. Whatever he is late for must really be important to him. I hope it is not an emergency.

Thinking the way of the reducer, you will be right most of the time. From time to time, everyone is under stress or has a bad day. There is no reason to take what people say or do literally or personally. This quick thinking will help keep you from getting upset or will mitigate your anger if you do, thereby preventing a negative chain reaction.

Use reducers to comfort others. If a friend of yours said she had a fight with someone or that someone said harsh words to her, you could use a reducer and say, "Don't take it too personally; John is going through a hard time in his life now. He is edgy about the layoffs, hasn't been sleeping at night, and his little girl is in the hospital." Again, when you really think about it, you can usually figure out the real motivation without getting too upset.

Reducers help to minimize negative situations, thereby helping you keep the personal power mind-set.

## Immediate Statements

One of the easiest ways to change your focus is to say immediately "this is good," "great," "very good," or "all right!" as soon as it happens, regardless of what just happened. As soon as these words escape your mouth, it forces you to come up with reasons that you are right, before your brain comes up with reasons for how bad something is. It forces you to justify your position and look for and see the positive side. If others are around, this strategy will be amplified—you will have to think even harder to come up with why a situation is positive because your reputation is on the line.

But do you know the best part of this strategy? You will be right! One morning, for example, I got a call asking me to give a speech less than 48 hours out. Speeches take a lot of work to prepare and I had a tight schedule that week. I called apologetically to ask to help another day in another way, but the woman who asked me to speak was in a real jam. I hesitated to accept the speaking engagement, but reluctantly agreed.

As soon as I hung up the phone, I said to myself, "Yea! All right! I get to speak in front of a live audience Thursday! I can't believe my luck. This is going to make me a better speaker and give me more experience. And it will help me get certified as a speaker more quickly. I will probably meet a lot of interesting people too!"

As soon as I said "Yea! All right!" I stopped any negative thoughts from attracting other negative thoughts and snowballing into a horrible mood. I caught myself and got my snowball moving in a positive direction, making me feel better instead of worse. Again, I felt better after that conversation and not worse. Most people would have felt worse. This is taking control of your mind-set.

---

Accomplished public speakers speak extemporaneously from general outlines rather than reading or memorizing a speech verbatim, so the same speech can go 16 different ways depending on the speaker's mood at the time. Different moods summon different words, and change the speech tone, emphasis, details, pitch, and speech direction. This is why it is so important to be in the personal power mind-set before speaking.

## Perspective

Perspective changes thoughts. Perspective consists of time, experience, and the distance from a situation. The more time that goes by, the more places you visit, the more people you meet, the more experience you gain, and the further you distance yourself from situations, the better decisions you will make.

Things that have bothered us in the past don't necessarily bother us today. We learn from the past and gain greater perspective as we gain more experience. A *USA Today* poll asked Americans about their top regrets in life. The No. 1 answer was worrying too much. Things that we thought were such a big deal 10 years ago turned out not to be. And things that we think are a big deal now won't be in 10 years. That is just how time works.

No doubt you have noticed the special relationship between a child and a grandparent. There are many reasons for this, and here is one: Grandparents have a greater perspective on life, for they have more experience. It is this broader perspective of life that makes them generally more likeable and pleasant to be around. They are slower to anger and have more patience.

One day I was sitting in a doctor's office and a proud grandmother started to tell me about her new grandson. I asked her about this special relationship that grandparents have with their grandchildren and why it was. She looked at me with the warmest smile, paused, and then said, "God gives us a second chance."

She went on to say that if a child spilled milk on the carpet, as a parent she would get angry. But as a grandparent she knew that kids are just being kids and there isn't much she could do about it; those things just happen. She said that she just laughs now when her grandchildren fumble with their little hands.

> *"The reason grandparents and grandchildren get along so well is that they have a common enemy."*
> — **Sam Levenson (1911–1980)**

Over time all of us develop a greater prospective. We don't get upset as easily. It just takes a little time, experience, and distance from a situation. We tend to mellow with age. We realize that, most of the time, people are really doing the best they can. We realize that we are too quick to judge if something is bad. Looking back, we realize that something might have been the best thing ever to have happened to us. Perspective helps us get our priorities straight and keep the personal power mind-set.

# Positive Action to Keep the Mind-Set

Thoughts change actions and actions change thoughts. Both are intimately intertwined. This is important to remember. Sometimes, no matter how hard you try, you cannot think more positively. You may be tired, wet, cold, and miserable. You may be at wit's end. You are tired of people telling you to think more positively. You are angry and frustrated. You are not in the mood to think more positively.

Taking positive action will prevent you from getting to this stage. And if you are already there, then positive action will get you out of it. If thinking positive thoughts is impossible, then change your actions. Changing your actions naturally, effortlessly, and cleverly changes your thoughts and jerks you out of a negative state. This puts you in control of your mind-set, instead of being held hostage by it. The following are suggested actions you can take to help you quickly change your mental state, thus your thinking.

**Fifteen Actions to Transform a Mental State:**
- Change your physical surroundings (buildings, view, desk, room, inside/outside, etc.)
- Change your physical activity level (walk, run, lift weights, etc.)
- Change your environment (go to the park, restaurant, shopping mall)
- Change your city, state, or country
- Change your activity (take a shower, do something fun, go on vacation)
- Change the variety of people around
- Take a nap or rest
- Call a happy or pleasant person
- Change your focus (other-focused vs. self-focused)
- Change clothes (dress up or down)
- Listen to different types of music
- Laugh
- Help people
- Do something nice for someone (send flowers, write a note, etc.)
- Go shopping (you don't necessarily have to buy something)

One of the most common reasons people are not happy is that they are not surrounding themselves with the right people. We cannot change people, but they can change us. The people we surround ourselves with can definitely change our moods. They can either push us down or bring out the best in us. They can make us feel stagnant and unproductive, as if we are not growing as a person.

I believe there are few bad people, just people who do not match. Dating is a great example of this. Two wonderful people could love each other very much, but be so different that they bring out the worst in each other. They become miserable trying to change each other.

When your heart is in the right place, you may want to help people. But slowly you can get sucked into others' problems. Their snowball is rolling downhill out of control and you walk up and get flattened, no matter how much you wanted to help. There was nothing you could have done.

So stay away from or limit your exposure to problem people and situations. If you get caught up in one, you must fight your way out. Protect yourself by keeping your eye on the solution, not the problem—or avoid sticky situations altogether. Don't try to change people—just surround yourself with the right people for you.

If you change your environment, you change your mood. It is impossible to think habitual thoughts when you are not in your habitual environment. Stray thoughts in your new environment will soon creep in and lead to new thoughts that will lead to still more. One thought attracts another thought that soon attracts another. Thoughts begin to snowball. And when your state positively changes, you talk and work with people more easily.

If you go on a trip to another part of the country, for example, you can't help but think different thoughts. You are tasting different foods, sleeping in a different bed, looking at different buildings and people, hearing different sounds (and perhaps even different languages), feeling a different climate, and smelling different smells. You will meet people who grew up differently from you and may be in different walks of life. Your conversations will be different from the usual, giving you new ideas and a new perspective on life. Simply going someplace else can instantly change your mind-set.

## Considering the State of Others

Not only is your own state of mind important in determining the outcome of your communication with others, but so is their state. Just because you are in a great mood and have the time to chat doesn't mean this is true for

others. Your results can vary dramatically depending on your timing, location, others' moods, and what is happening at the time. All golden minutes are
not created equally. Some minutes are just more valuable than others.

During the workday, people tend to be rushed and stressed with ringing
phones, traffic jams, and hundreds of people moving in and out of offices.
This tends to be the worst time to get any quality conversation with people,
especially if you need something from them. During the workday people,
have their guard up and are short on time. The quality of these interactions
will be mediocre at best. Be aware of this and if possible, choose the time
and place of your golden minute.

Finding the right environment will not only change your state, but it will
change the state of others and improve the quality of the golden minute. So
many times as a salesman I tried to talk to clients in their offices and they
were short, busy, and occasionally rude. But when I got them out on a golf
course or talked to them over a cup of coffee, they could be the nicest
people in the world. The only thing that changed was their state, not mine.

So don't take offense if the conversation is not going the way you would
like. Just realize that the other person's state has a lot to do with it and know
that the suggestions in the list of 15 ways to transform a mental state can
work not only on your mind-set, but also on others'.

# Chapter Summary

- **The Golden Minute:** The most critical time during a conversation, or exposure to others, in which people decide whether they want to talk to you, hire you, do business with you or ignore you.

- **The Right State of Mind:** You can transmit and receive certain traits only in certain states. Certain qualities and traits are unattainable in certain states.

- **Positive Mind-Set:** Getting into a good mood and staying positive. This enacts the law of attraction to bring you more good things in life. Bad things happen to everyone. But mind-set is about control, the awareness of mood, and knowing what you must do to get out of a bad mood and into a better one.

- **Personal Power:** The ability to talk to, work with, and influence others using your people skills and not your authority, rank, position, or status.

- **Three Steps to the Personal Power Mind-Set:**
  1. Choose your focus. There are always two ways to interpret a situation—be careful of which one you choose. Your focus determines all subsequent thoughts. Six-figure communicators are others-focused and look for and choose the positive.

  2. Combine focus with action. Action physically changes our mental state and stimulates the release of neurotransmitters, thus altering our body chemistry. This gives us a sense of well-being, pleasure, and excitement.

  3. Savor the present. Enjoy the now. Make it a point to consciously savor your time with friends and family, the weather, and fun activities.

- **Keeping the Mind-Set:** The trick is to keep the personal power mind-set regardless of people and circumstances. Getting angry drains our batteries and robs us of the critical energy needed to effectively work with others and do great things.

- **Cognitive Behavioral Strategies (Thoughts)**
    (1) Predetermined beliefs: Before anyone says or does anything to you, you have consciously or subconsciously predetermined how you will interpret and perceive future comments and events. The trick is to predetermine your beliefs and attitudes before you need them so that you will not expend energy getting angry or upset when negative situations arise.

    (2) Battle drills: By thinking about how you will react to events in general, before they happen, you will act smoothly and in control when similar events happen.

    (3) Reducers: Do not take people's comments too literally or personally but quickly "reduce" the significance of what they say by telling yourself that the other person is upset from being under stress on the job, problems at home, having a bad day, and the like.

    (4) Immediate statements: Change how you interpret a situation by saying to yourself immediately, "this is good," "great," or "all right!"— regardless of what just happened. This forces you to come up with reasons why you are right, before your mind has time to see the negative. It forces you to justify your position and look for and see the positive side.

    (5) Perspective: Time, experience, and distance from a situation change your thoughts on it. The more time that goes by, the more places you visit, the more people you meet, the more experience you gain, and the further you distance yourself from situations, the better decisions you will make.

- **Positive Action to Keep the Mind-Set**
    Thoughts change actions and actions change thoughts. If you are at wit's end and cannot think positively, change your actions. This will help you naturally to change your thoughts and either keep you from getting into a negative state or pull you out of one. Do one of the 15 actions to transform your mental state.

- **Consider the State of Others:** The same conversational topic can go two different ways, depending on your state, the other person's state, your timing, and the environment.

## Daily Challenge

Today's challenge is to deliberately get into the personal power mind-set. Use the three-step formula. Become cognizant of what gets you in a good mood and lifts your spirits, and then write it down. This will be helpful on tough days. If your mood begins to shift, change your focus or your actions. Activate the law of attraction and get it working for you, giving you the energy to effectively communicate with others.

## Executive Challenge

Today, work on keeping the personal power mind-set. Examine one disempowering predetermined belief and modify it. Create a battle drill for a situation you commonly find yourself in, to help you react smoothly and effortlessly in future situations. Try out a reducer to see how it changes your thinking or the thinking of others. Play around with different catchphrases to immediately change your focus and start thinking positively.

# Part II

Although none of us is exactly alike, we all share basic human truths. And the better we are at understanding these truths, the easier it is to talk and work with others. The result is that we improve not only our own lives, but the lives of everyone we come in contact with.

Many psychology books divide people into categories and subcategories. It can be difficult not only to remember all the categories, but also to keep track of who is in which. People may be divided into thinkers or visionaries or judgers, owls or wolves or bears, into color groups such as orange, blue, and green, and into various other categories. But most people don't neatly fit into any one category. And people's moods, stress levels, and lives constantly change.

"Typing" people is difficult and inconsistent. After all, just because someone seems or acts interested in something today doesn't mean the person really is or that the person will be interested in it tomorrow. It is far more valuable to learn to read people and understand human nature. Part II of this book provides a simple, universal strategy for doing this.

This part shares the secrets of working with and understanding people you encounter in your everyday life. It teaches how to develop both the two- and three-track minds to better read people and situations. You'll learn the theory of "buttonomics" to help you better understand how to mentally "click" with others during conversations. "People spooking" will be explored, and you'll learn some practical "anti-spooking" techniques to help you build rapport. Part II also will present the eight qualities of charisma, though the specifics on developing charisma will be presented in Part III. Lastly, this part covers how to quickly learn people's true colors and why it is so important to let other people talk.

# Eight Secrets to Dealing with Everyday People

## In This Chapter:

- Make dealing with everyday people easier and more enjoyable
- Discover the hidden benefits to building rapport
- Learn why unpleasant people are the way they are
- Better understand how people respond, and use it to your advantage
- Harness the power of empathy
- Learn to give people a pat on the back

Everywhere we go, in everything we do, we are dealing with people. People can drive us mad and make our lives miserable. But if you know how to work with the people you encounter in your everyday dealings, you will have an easier time of it. It becomes a mutually beneficial relationship.

If you "take care" of the people you encounter in public, then they will take care of you, a sort of symbiotic relationship. You will notice you'll start to get the good deals and the lucky breaks. You'll get the last flight, the last seat, the last room, and the last ticket. And as if by a stroke of luck, you may even get other perks along the way.

Oh sure, you'll run into difficult people like everyone else, but you'll have a special way of handling them. You'll understand human nature and always seem to come out ahead. So what is it that you're about to learn that others don't know? What will you do differently? Read on for the eight "secrets"!

# 1. Build Rapport with Everyone

People who can quickly build rapport create friends, contacts, and a virtual support group wherever they go. When this happens, great things happen. People who were once strangers are now more willing to help, if needed. This help is honest help—different from the help people give when they don't care. Showing a genuine interest in others will lead you to establish rapport.

When you do not establish rapport, people don't particularly care about you. And it shows. They do the minimum required and make only halfhearted attempts. They never go out of their way to help. Often they simply tell you that they can't help and then tell you to go somewhere else.

## Improved Service at the Tire Center

One day I noticed that my car had a bad tire, and another was borderline. I went to a local tire service center to see about getting them replaced. I consciously and deliberately built rapport with Karen, the woman behind the counter (I later learned she was the store owner) and then explained what I wanted. She asked one of the mechanics to walk out and make sure they had the right tire for my car and that it was what I needed. I built rapport with the mechanic as we walked to the car to inspect the tires.

The mechanic noticed that I had two different-sized tires on the vehicle. Then he had me turn the steering wheel so he could better inspect the tires. He noticed that the inside of one tire was particularly worn. I told him that I might be selling the car soon, and he told me that new tires would make anyone in the car safer and would make the vehicle ride better. He said that if I did sell the car, new tires would increase its resale value. He gave me reasonable and logical advice without trying to "up-sell" me (persuade me to buy more than I'd intended).

In the end, the mechanic took extra time to genuinely study my situation. This prevented future problems and increased my safety. Karen worked in a $40 discount and charged me $100 less than the mechanic estimated the tires would cost. She gave me a free gift for "special customers" (a baseball with a lottery-type card enclosed). And the service center threw in a free inspection and got me out quickly.

Six-figure communicators consciously and deliberately build rapport with others. They do it genuinely and sincerely. In the process, they are continually building goodwill all day, every day. This makes life better for them and better for others.

You must give to receive. And when you do this, other people, too, are more genuinely and sincerely willing to help.

# 2. Rapport May Get You Favors

It's an old adage that "flattery will get you nowhere," but the truth is that rapport can get you far more than you may have thought! People will rarely volunteer the fact that they can do more for you than they let on—unless you have established rapport and they like you. Often they can bail you out of all sorts of situations whether it is your fault or not. It's interesting how flexible—or stringent—rules can be, depending on whether people like you.

## Little Things Add Up

My trip to Tampa is an example. My plan was to drive the short distance from my home to Richmond, Virginia, meet a friend for dinner, spend the night, and then fly to Tampa early the next morning. On the way to Richmond I was pulled over by a state trooper for speeding. After I talked with the trooper for a brief period, he came back and said he had to give me the ticket but he reduced the reported speed. He also made a notation to the court clerk so the ticket would not affect my insurance.

Later I pulled into a gas station, filled my tank, and went in to buy a soda to stay awake. I talked briefly with the clerk, and she told me that I could get a larger soda for the same price. I got it.

I got to Richmond and went to a hotel. The desk clerk was having a hard time because she was the only one at the front desk that night and the phones were ringing off the hook. I smiled and told her to take her time. She eventually got back to me, we talked briefly, and I gave her my credit card to book the room. She then asked me, "Do you want the corporate or the AAA discount?" I smiled and said that I really didn't have either. She told me that I didn't understand her, and she repeated the question. I asked her which one was better and she gave me the corporate rate.

Later that night I went to dinner with my friend Joe Minasola. It was an incredible Cuban restaurant called Havana 59. We split the dinner bill and then the server brought the drink bill. My friend said that he'd get the bill and quickly paid it. What class!

The next day at the airport I went to check in and the airline clerk told me that my flight was cancelled! She said that I'd have to wait two and a half hours. She said there was nothing she could do. But after I chatted with her for a few minutes, she said: "Wait, let me try something." She somehow got me on a flight to arrive three minutes earlier than my original one!

That trip certainly taught me that people can help us far more than we realize! And those were examples from only one trip. Just think of the weekly or monthly impact. Most people try to help people they like, and they'll go out of their way for people they really like.

# 3. Be Nice and You Will Be Rewarded

People who work with the public get yelled at, treated rudely, and taken advantage of. It's a hard and stressful job working with the public. Remember that.

My brother Joe, for example, is a police officer in a major U.S. city. He gets lied to and abused every day by people who are trying to get out of speeding tickets, have gotten into an auto accident, or are going to jail. He says, "All perps have excuses and lie." He deals with all types of nasty people, whether criminals or law-abiding citizens.

No wonder that state trooper who pulled me over for speeding near Richmond reduced the reported speed on my ticket. He was probably just grateful to encounter someone nice. People have a greater propensity to reward those who are warm and charming—for it is these people who make their jobs tolerable and even rewarding.

One day I was talking with a McDonald's employee in a local doctor's office waiting room. She was one of the nicest people I have ever met, with a smile that would melt your heart. I commented that in working in that restaurant over the last 12 years, she probably had dealt with just about every type of person. I asked her which type was the hardest to handle. She replied, "The ones that throw the food at you if the order was not quite right."

I saw such a person in action one day at a fast-food restaurant in Summersville, West Virginia. I heard a man screaming at a high school girl behind the counter. She couldn't have been more than 17. It had something to do with pickles. I don't know if he wanted pickles on his burger and there weren't any; or he didn't want pickles on his burger and they were there. It was obvious that the girl was doing the best she could. She finally said, "Fine, I will go fix your burger." She walked back into the kitchen and stayed there, out of sight for a little while.

She then reappeared with a devilish grin on her face. She looked the man dead in the eye and slowly handed him a neatly wrapped burger and said, "Here, I made this burger especially for you!" Everyone in the restaurant held their breath as she spoke these words. Everyone wondered if she had done anything to that burger. It wasn't even my burger and I was scared to eat it! The man probably ordered the burger with pickles and was right, but he lost when he started to yell at the minimum-wage restaurant employee who had little to lose.

Often you may feel that you are at the mercy of others any time you leave the house, and to a certain degree you are. But remember that you will always get further when you are pleasant—always! Knowing this, don't ever get upset and yell at anyone. You will lose big! And yelling at others will cause you to enact the all-powerful law of attraction: Negative begets negative (or positive begets positive). Your day will start snowballing downhill, making all new interactions with people worse and worse.

So the third secret is to make people feel good and you may get rewarded for it. Your reward may be better service, more or exclusive information, or whatever the person can do to make your encounter more enjoyable. Do it genuinely and sincerely to brighten their day or make the job just a little better for them, and the aftereffect may be a room overlooking the water.

# 4. Limit Your Dealings with Hostile People

Unpleasant people have every reason to be rude and short with others because they themselves get abused every day. It is a vicious circle that is difficult to escape from. They get treated poorly simply because they are unpleasant. No wonder unpleasant people feel it's okay to be ugly with others!

Their guiding principle is that it is fine to be nice, but if things even start to get ugly, they would rather "win" the situation than get further abused. But their attempts to "win" too often result in their being taken advantage of. They don't get the "good deals" or the "lucky breaks" in life. They never get the "last room," and they never get great service.

Then, when they get back into a situation where they have any position power, such as "gatekeepers" of any kind, it's payback time. They prefer using the power in their position over trying to establish rapport or negotiate with others because it is easier. They are not in the mood to chat with others.

So avoid wasting your time and energy dealing with people of this type. Just move on. Don't take their abuse personally. As soon as they're done with you, they will just move on to the next person, and then the next—continuing the cycle of abuse.

## 5. Offset People's Frustration or Anger with Civility

If you are polite to people who treat you poorly, they usually will feel bad about their behavior. About one-third of them (a higher percentage if you know them) will come back later and apologize for their behavior in their own way, feeling bad for how they treated you.

This doesn't necessarily mean a formal apology, but they will realize the need to somehow make it up to you or make things right. They may do you a favor, do something nice for you, or even verbalize an apology. This happens only if you are extremely nice from the start and remain consistently pleasant.

Another one-third of frustrated or angry people to whom you were polite will not say a word. But they will still feel bad about their behavior.

Always remain pleasant and treat people well, even though they might not deserve it. You just might get better service or an apology—or at least make the person rethink their bad behavior.

## 6. Empathize with People

Up to 90 percent of the reason people complain or get upset is that they want empathy or sympathy. They don't necessarily want a fix to the problem. Usually people understand that circumstances are beyond your control; they just want to feel better about it with a little empathy. Give it to them.

Let's say you have dinner plans with someone, and something at work comes up that forces you to cancel your plans. Most people will understand that these things happen. But when you say this to the person with whom you've just cancelled your plans, that person gets angry or upset. Then you say there was nothing you could have done, and you get defensive because you can't believe the other person won't cut you some slack. After all, it wasn't even your fault.

The problem is not that people don't understand this; usually they do. But they are disappointed or hurt. Instead, realize this immediately and express empathy. Say something like: "I feel terrible about this; I have been looking forward to this all week," or "If anyone deserves a wonderful evening, it is certainly you. Let me make it up to you." This takes some of the sting out of it.

Phrase it yourself, but empathize and tell the person how bad you feel or how much you were looking forward to the activity. Remember to acknowledge others' feelings. (Chapter 18 will go into specifics on dealing with angry people.) This is far more important than explanations.

# 7. Express Appreciation or Encouragement

When people feel overwhelmed or frustrated or are just having a bad day, a little expression of appreciation or encouragement can go a long way. Give people a verbal pat on the back for helping you or just hanging in there. An ideal time for this is when you see clerks, receptionists, or others fumbling at the computer, juggling multiple tasks, or barely composing themselves because they are overrun with customers. Just a short line or two from you acknowledging their efforts or showing appreciation for their help can serve as a quick picker-upper.

Not too long ago a group of colleagues and I were flying home from a company meeting in Detroit. After waiting a long while in line at the airport ticket counter, we finally reached a ticket agent. Little did we know that though our tickets listed the airline counter we had been waiting at, our flight was subcontracted to a smaller airline at a different location. With the flight leaving shortly, time was a critical factor.

Unfortunately the customer in front of me started to yell and scream at the ticket agent for the misunderstanding. She yelled out of fear of missing her flight because she was being directed somewhere far away with her luggage.

Then it was my turn. As I looked up, the ticket agent looked at me with cold eyes and sweat beading on her forehead. I was a little nervous knowing that she had the power to send me wherever and whenever she desired at that point, for we were flying back to a very small airport. And I knew it was probably our own fault for not reading our tickets more closely.

This was a great time to use the seventh secret when dealing with people. "You sure did a great job handling that lady. You must be a very patient woman," I said. "I was patient—(pause)—once." Then I smiled and waited for a reaction.

The agent just stared at me for a second and then burst out laughing. "Thank goodness," I thought, "now she can deal with my situation in a better mood." She ended up checking in my bag and me at her counter (saving me a trip across the airport) and getting me on my scheduled flight.

You don't give people a pat on the back just to help your own situation; you do it genuinely and sincerely because people sometimes need it. And it makes all of our lives easier when we pick people up who need it. The result of a simple smile or a few sincere words will do more for them than we can imagine.

I almost feel guilty about "picking up" people who are having a hard time and then "magically" getting the window table, the room that wasn't yet ready, or special passes to local events. One woman working at an airport information booth even offered me an apple and her sandwich after hearing that I had traveled all day without getting a chance to eat. All I had done was tell her how much I appreciated her helping me.

# 8. Use Extraordinary Manners

The final secret to dealing with people is a powerful one. This one secret will prevent and stop people problems before they start or progress. It works on people from every culture and background and will clearly separate you from 90 percent of the public. Using this secret, you will make more friends, soften harsh situations, influence more people, come across with class, and most important, make life easier. The eighth secret is to use extraordinary manners.

Minimum manners don't cut it. Most people think that simply saying "please" and "thank you" is using good manners. This is only the bare minimum. If you want to have extraordinary luck working with people, you must have extraordinary manners. Let's take a look at just six ways six-figure communicators mind their manners:

- Hold the door open an extra moment if someone is walking in behind you. And gentlemen, open doors for women.
- Address people as sir or ma'am or by their title or their name (shows respect).
- When you bump into someone, say "pardon me" or "excuse me."
- Don't talk on a cell phone around other people. If your cell phone rings around others, and you must take the call, pardon yourself or say "Excuse me, I must take this call" and then move away from people. It is rude to drop a conversation with someone you're speaking with in person to start talking to someone on the phone.
- Thank people after they have done something for you. It doesn't matter if a server refills your drink or someone brings you a report you asked for—thank the person. Thank people for their time, thoughts, ideas, and help. In fact, most conversations or actions "require" a thank-you. This simple phrase is underused and always appreciated.

- Say "I'm sorry" to show that you care about something that has gone wrong. This phrase doesn't admit responsibility, but lets the other person know that you care—"I am sorry that happened to you." Often when people think that you don't care, they keep getting angry, trying to get you to care. By using this phrase early in the conversation, empathizing with them, people will get over their frustration more quickly.

I once saw a man spill coffee all over someone's notebook at a coffee shop and then walk off. I was amazed this man didn't say something like "pardon me," "let me help you with that," "I'm sorry," or anything else. The man with the wet notebook didn't ask him to clean it up or pay for the notebook. He didn't even care whose fault it was. He only wanted a word of understanding and empathy. Outside in the parking lot I overheard the men's confrontation. The man with the notebook kept saying that he didn't care about the notebook; he just wanted a simple, courteous "I'm sorry," or an "excuse me." The man who spilled the coffee kept shouting that he didn't think it was his fault—"the girl set my coffee on your notebook."

Always treat people extraordinarily well. Minimum manners don't cut it! The better we treat people, the better they will treat us on the whole. This last secret is guaranteed to work wonders daily and make your dealings with people easier.

# Chapter Summary

- **Secret #1:** Consciously and deliberately build rapport with people.

- **Secret #2:** Rapport may get you favors. People are often able to do more for you than they let on.

- **Secret #3:** Be nice and you will be rewarded. People who work with the public are often abused by the public, so they are grateful to encounter a warm and charming person. You will always get further with people being nice and pleasant—always.

- **Secret #4:** Limit your dealings with hostile people. Unpleasant people get caught in a vicious circle: They are unpleasant to people, so people are unpleasant to them. So then if things even start to get ugly, they would rather "win" the situation, especially if they have position power. Don't waste your time and energy on these people; just move on.

- **Secret #5:** Offset people's frustration or anger with civility—and then they will feel bad that they treated you poorly. If you are polite to frustrated people, about one-third of them will later come back and apologize for their behavior in their own way, making it up to you somehow.

- **Secret #6:** Empathize with people. Up to 90 percent of the reason people complain or get upset is that they want empathy or sympathy, not necessarily for you to fix the problem. Most of the time people realize that circumstances are beyond your control, but will feel much better if you give them a little empathy.

- **Secret #7:** Express appreciation or encouragement when people seem to be feeling overwhelmed or frustrated or just having a bad day. Just a short line or two will serve as a quick picker-upper.

- **Secret #8:** Use extraordinary manners. The better you treat people, the better you will be treated on the whole. Problems will be prevented, your life will get easier, and you will come across with more class, regardless of the situation.

CHAPTER 3:

# The Multi-Track Mind

## In This Chapter:

• Learn what is really happening during a conversation.
• Evaluate whether what people say and do are congruent.
• Begin learning how to read people.
• Learn the power of focus during conversations.

One of the most important communication skills you can develop to better understand people is using the two-track and three-track minds. Too many people are oblivious to what actually happens during a conversation and are unaware of how much information people continually send. This goes way beyond body language. Using the two- and three-track mind to develop conversational and situational awareness opens you up to a world you never knew. This chapter explains all three tracks.

## The Two-Track Mind

The two-track mind consists of one track focusing on the conversational dialogue and the other track carefully watching the other person during a conversation. Doing this enables you to see better whether what someone says matches what they do.

Mothers are good at this. They may be talking to their child about school and immediately notice that the boy is walking with a limp, has a tear in his pants, or has a scrape on his leg. Or the child may say that he was upstairs doing his homework while his mother was gone, but she notices paint on his hands.

Someone may ask you, "How are you doing?" but do so without facing you, but instead facing a door to leave. Someone may tell you how good it is to see you while her eyes keep glancing at her watch. Maybe a neighbor carrying a heavy bag of groceries up the stairs happens to see you and, to be polite, asks you how you are doing. If you were using the two-track mind, you would notice the neighbor shifting his body weight trying to hold onto the bag and you would limit your answer to a few words. Someone not using the two-track mind would go ahead and answer the question in detail, oblivious to the neighbor's struggling with the heavy bag.

Wherever someone's eyes point is where their attention is. If their eyes look over your shoulder or another direction, that person is distracted and not listening to you, feigning interest or attention.

As you converse with others, notice their mood, their eyes, how they are dressed, and what they may be holding. To see how genuine people are, watch their face to see if it changes—it should be animated. People who are genuine and sincere move their face more than uninterested or insincere people. Watch people's eyes to see how frequently they bounce around, if they widen or squint, or if the pupils dilate or constrict. Their eyebrows, as well as the corners of their mouth, will also move.

---

When I was master of ceremonies at a Toastmasters event, my seat was up front so I had an up-close and personal view of the speakers. After the meeting, one of the speakers asked me what I thought of her presentation. I asked her if she started out nervous for the first three minutes or so, got over it for about a minute, and then got nervous for the last two minutes. She smiled and said, "Yes! How did you know?"

Using the two-track mind, I had noticed that she developed red splotches on her neck that lasted for about three minutes. Then they began to fade away. But when she started to lose her train of thought and summarize her points, the splotches came back. Other speakers might develop beads of sweat on their foreheads, sweaty palms, or a dry and scratchy voice.

---

We all get nervous; it is normal. But people who use the two-track mind are astutely aware of what is really happening. They are better judges of character. They read people better. They note what others are going through and when to step in and help. They use this information to reassure people and make better decisions.

The secret of the two-track mind is carefully listening to what people are saying and watching what their body is doing to see if the two are congruent. This gives you important information about what is really happening with someone. It is a fundamental skill in learning to read people. It takes a little practice to listen and watch someone or talk and watch someone. But you will be amazed that what people are saying and what they are doing are often contradictory—or what their body says that their mouth doesn't.

# The Three-Track Mind

With the three-track mind, one track is paying attention to the conversation, one track is watching the other person, and the third track is astutely aware of the surroundings. You can pick up on a lot of information before a conversation even begins or while it is going on. Notice freshly delivered flowers (possible birthday or anniversary), pins or other jewelry people are wearing, pictures on the desk, diplomas on the wall, unusual behavior, interesting objects, what is sitting on the counters, and so on.

It is just as important to be aware of other people in the room. People often act differently when others are around. Other people intensify someone's emotions. People are more sensitive when others are around. If they are proud, they are twice as proud when other people see them. If they are embarrassed, they get more embarrassed when other people are watching. Be more careful of the words used when others are around—for the walls have ears!

---

A pharmaceutical sales manager once told me that when he walks into a crowded waiting room at a hospital or clinic, he is particularly sensitive to the patients. He knows they often have been waiting a long time to see the doctor. But his job is to meet with doctors, letting them know about any new drugs, clinical information, formulary changes, and so on. Because there are so many offices to serve, he often ends up seeing the doctor before some patients.

Astutely aware that patients are not only in the room, but could be listening as he checks in at the front desk, he might say something along these lines to the receptionist:

- "I have brought free samples to help your patients. I will be more than happy to give them to you, but I will need to go back and get a quick signature from the doctor."

---

> • "Wow, you are really packed today. You must be either out of samples or in desperate need of some. Would you mind if I go back to check on them?"
>
> This way the patients hear that he is there to help so they are more likely to understand why he may get in to see the doctor before they do.

In my own experience using the three-track mind, I have intentionally complimented people with their boss, manager, or spouse within earshot. I might thank them for their great service or their professionalism, or tell them how much I appreciate a friendly staff. The person I compliment often smiles or even winks back at me as if to say "thank you for saying that in front of" the boss or manager. It makes the person look good and it makes me feel good, and I always seem to get exceptional service afterward.

Regrettably, people who are oblivious to the three-track mind aren't aware of who may be listening to a conversation. They are focused solely on the conversational dialogue. They may say things they shouldn't around others standing nearby, ignore people, catch people at awkward times, ignore spouses, and have no idea what is happening in their general vicinity. It is common for people with this kind of tunnel vision to be doing most of the talking.

## The One-Track Mind

The one-track mind is very different from the two- and three-track minds. The latter two are astutely aware of the other person's state and the surroundings. But the one-track mind is not interested in reading body language, determining congruency, or noticing what is happening in the surroundings. The one-track mind is about absolute focus. You can use it in one of two ways.

Have you had a conversation with someone and felt so unbelievably connected that you lost track of the time, temporarily forgot where you were, forgot about the world, and forgot about yourself? You were totally engrossed in the conversation. You weren't sure whether you were in a quasi-hypnotic state or one of absolute focus. But what you were sure of was that you felt extraordinarily connected to this person in some way. The world seemed to stand still during that conversation. This may not happen often, but when it does, it is powerful.

This is what happens when you're using the one-track mind. You completely focus on the conversation and forget about the surroundings. You give your full and undivided attention, so much so that others can feel it in their soul. This is one secret to an extraordinary ability to connect with people: giving others 100 percent of your focus, energy, and attention.

The second way to use the one-track mind is to focus totally on what you yourself are saying while you speak, so much so that other people can see it in your eyes. Then other people know not to interrupt this powerful flow of information; they simply remain quiet and listen. Again, others can feel your high level of concentration in their soul.

When this happens, people act differently and go into a one-track state themselves. A strong connection with other people begins. Common characteristics of people using the one-track mind to listen or to speak are the following:

- In a room full of people, they never look over someone else's shoulder or at another person. They break eye contact occasionally, but never to look at other people. People can sense even a temporary lapse in attention and will be hesitant to fully connect with distracted people. Six-figure communicators can go 60 to 90 minutes and never look at anyone but the person they are talking to.
- They keep all of their attention in a small, confined area. They look at people and objects only within this area, such as on a table—a pen, chart, or notepad. Their attention might alternate between looking at the other person and writing notes on a notepad.
- They have great eye contact with the other person. When connected, their eyes naturally dart back and forth during the conversation, in very small movements. This is a sure sign someone is using the one-track mind.
- As the communicator focuses totally on the conversation, people in the background begin to fade out.
- One-track communicators can't hear anyone else. All background noise is indistinguishable or totally shut out.

People immediately sense whether they have someone's attention. Without this attention, people are hesitant to talk to others, give additional information, or provide additional help. Conversations are shallower and less meaningful. People are less effective when talking to and working with others when they aren't focused. But six-figure communicators can turn on the one-track mind when they need to, like a light switch. Their extreme focus while talking or speaking changes everything.

# Progressing Through a Conversation

Each track will help you better understand what is happening while talking with others. You will read people and situations more efficiently and improve conversational outcomes. You don't necessarily have to use the tracks in a particular order. But a typical progression of conversation is as follows:

1. Use the two-track mind as you greet and meet others. Look at the other person to judge his mood, how busy he is, and so on.
2. While he is talking, become aware of other people in the room and your surroundings (three-track mind).
3. Then give the other person your undivided attention, and he will sense this. Using this one-track mind, you will slowly make a strong connection.

## Chapter Summary

- The two-track mind consists of one track focusing on the conversational dialogue and the other track watching the other person carefully during the conversation. By doing this in concert, you will be better able to see if there is congruency between what people are saying and what they are doing. You will also have greater conversational and situational awareness.

- The three-track mind consists of one track paying attention to the conversation, one track watching the other person, and the third track astutely aware of the surroundings.

- The one-track mind is about total focus during conversations, whether listening or talking to others. Six-figure communicators give others 100 percent focus, energy, and attention. Others immediately sense this and act differently, going into a one-track mind themselves. This strengthens connections. People open up more, provide more information, and are more willing to help.

## Daily Challenge

As you talk with people today, practice using both the two-track and three track-mind. Keep one track on the conversation and the other track watching for such things as how people are facing, what they are doing with their hands, what their eyes are doing, and the spatial distance between you and the other person. Also observe what is happening in the room and who is present. Try this with at least three people you talk with today.

## Executive Challenge

While using the two- and three-track minds today, find at least three incongruities between what people are telling you and what their body is telling you. Use the one-track mind at least once today to go into a state of absolute focus. Shut out background noise, people, and distractions. Notice how this special state feels different. Also notice how other people act differently when you are in this state.

# Engaging People Using Buttonomics

## In This Chapter:

- Learn to energize people positively
- Learn to "click with people"
- Reduce small talk and make conversations more substantial
- Make conversations real and seem less awkward
- Improve the quality of your interactions with others.

This chapter is about learning what makes people tick, finding out what really "juices" them, and getting their energy flowing in a positive direction with an extraordinary technique call "buttonomics." The more skilled you become at using buttonomics, the smoother and more enjoyable your conversations will become. Conversations will be less superficial and more meaningful, and people will genuinely enjoy talking with you. Enjoy this section and have fun playing with this unique technique.

## Simplified Buttonomics

What in the world is "buttonomics"? It is connecting with people on a mental level. It is the art of finding and pushing people's positive hot buttons and staying away from their negative ones. Hot buttons are topics that emotionally charge people.

As you learn to do this, you will notice that conversations will become more substantial with less small talk. Conversations become authentic. People awaken and get truly excited about the conversation. And the more they talk, the more they like you. People begin to think that you are an excellent conversationalist without realizing you've hardly spoken a word.

Take someone you know well, for example. You know that she may love talking about sports, travel, or her ambitions. The more she talks about these subjects, the more excited she gets. It is as if she almost takes over the conversation and just needs a little prompting, a question or comment now and then, to keep her energy going.

Ironically, simplified buttonomics takes a lot of pressure off you during the conversation. You don't have to try to be the funny one; you become that way by pushing the "fun" buttons in other people. That is how some people always seem to end up in the "fun group"; they make any group they are in fun by pushing the "fun" buttons of the other group members. Yes, you can make other people fun, energetic, and interesting. And through association and the law of attraction, you take on the characteristics of the group.

## Recognizing People's Hot Buttons

You can detect when you've hit people's hot buttons by using the two-track mind. Pay attention to the conversation and carefully watch people to see how they react to what is being said. They might talk faster, use more gestures, talk more loudly, or simply laugh or smile more often.

While you are talking to people, look into their eyes. If you hit a button, you will see an energy, as if a light was switched on in their head. If it is a positive button, their eyes will widen and their pupils will dilate. When you see this happen, stay with the topic and expand upon it, for they are genuinely interested and excited about the topic. Pupil dilation or constriction is an involuntary response that cannot be faked.

If you see the pupils suddenly constrict, you have struck a nerve.[1] Be careful! Get away from that negative topic as quickly as possible by changing the subject or apologizing.

Also use the three-track mind to notice the distance between you and the other person. Striking a positive hot button may draw the person closer to you, while a negative hot button may "repel" the person to back off.

One day I was on a sales call with a busy customer in her office. I planted myself leaning against a wall in a busy area while I talked with her. This showed her that I was not going anywhere; I was not going to chase her down or follow her if she wanted to leave. But here is the interesting thing in relation to buttonomics and the two-track mind: When I hit a positive hot button, she would walk closer to me, so I knew she was interested in what I had to say. When I hit a negative button or touchy subject, she would slowly back off and move down the hallway. I could see her move in and out as I talked about the various features and benefits of my product.

How did I use this? When she moved closer I knew to expand upon the point or ask her questions about that specific area. If she moved back, I knew she was not interested in that aspect of the product. She would move forward or backward depending on her interest in the subject matter. My goal was to keep her voluntarily moving closer asking questions. Result: She started to use more of my product—a breakthrough sales call!

## Letting Others Talk

When I started in sales, I thought I would be great because I loved to talk. But I sold very little at first; I really struggled. It was tough getting past the gatekeeper to start a conversation with potential clients. They were all too busy to talk. They all claimed that they couldn't afford any time to talk with a salesperson; they had far too many important things to do. The most time I seemed to get with a prospect was 30 seconds. This was no fun at all! I would just get beaten on all day long—I felt like a piñata.

Then one day it happened. It was a Friday afternoon and my prospect's office was packed with people, as usual. I had been in that office at least a dozen times, but this time something was different. I don't know if it was the alignment of the planets or the cosmic energies of the universe. But to my amazement, I actually got past the gatekeeper and was allowed to go back and see the prospect. I never expected to get as far as I did with this office and was now at a loss for words about what to say. I thought, "I'd better be good, for I may never get a second chance." What charming and intelligent words could I utter?

The client suddenly walked in and, surprisingly, spoke the first words. And then something slipped from his lips. He said he was going to go after work to look at a new boat. He was giving me a button!

I told him that I was always interested in boats but didn't know a whole lot about them. I asked him what type of boat he was going to look at and what kind of boating he did.

He looked at his watch and told me to go into his office, that there was something he wanted to show me. He put his papers down and came into the office and showed me a picture of him and his motorboat. Then he pulled out a picture of the boat he wanted. It was a huge sailboat. He was fascinated with sailboats! The more he talked, the more excited he got. The more he talked, the faster he talked. His hands were moving, his arms were moving, and his head kept bobbing around. He ended up talking for about 30 minutes about the boat he had his eye on. I hardly said a word, just an occasional question here and there. It was a joy to listen to someone so passionate about something. I learned a great deal about him, about boats, and about his love for boats. He seemed like a little kid, giggling as he showed me boat pictures.

That's when I learned an important series of lessons. The more the other person talks, the more he likes you. This sounds strange but it's true. If you let people talk until they run out of steam, then an interesting realization takes place. They realize they have been doing all the talking and then they start to feel guilty. (This is true for angry people as well.) It is funny when this happens because at this point, the person usually hesitates and then has a goofy look on his face as he realizes what has happened. He now feels an obligation to at least ask you how you are doing, if anything is going on with you, or how he can help you. This is hitting the person's *inflection point.*[2] This is the point when the person suddenly realizes that he has been doing all the talking and feels he should give you time to speak.

So what do you do when this point comes? Limit how much you speak. When people hit their inflection point, they want to give you time. But speaking for as long as they did will undo their "good" feeling, the button created. You should always speak for much less time than they did, from just a few sentences to a couple minutes. Let the conversation end with their having spoken 80 to 90 percent of the time.

How did my sales call end? At the inflection point, I quickly mentioned my product and the prospect said he would give it a shot. The relationship flourished for years. I have spent not only a weekend boating with him on the Chesapeake Bay, but also an enjoyable evening with his family. What follows are the lessons learned from this.

# Buttonomics Basics

- When people say they're too busy to talk to you, what they really mean is "I'm too busy to talk to you if you don't find my hot button. If you find one, I will give you as much time as I can."

- Find and pick up on people's positive hot buttons, and stay away from their negative ones.

- Keep hitting multiple positive hot buttons within a topic or on various topics; don't just stop with one.

- The more you let others talk, the more they like you.

- The more that others talk, the more you learn.

- The more you let others talk, the more interesting you become to them.

- Let people talk until they run out of steam.

- Notice and use the inflection point.

- When you find a positive hot button, don't let it go. Make the most of it. Expand the button by asking follow-up questions.

The last buttonomics basic is an important one. Asking follow-up questions shows others that you have genuine interest in them. If you are talking with someone who says she has just written a book, that is probably her hot button and she would love to talk about it. (Use the two-track mind to confirm this. Sometimes work is the last thing people want to talk about.) Ask questions about how long the book took to write, her favorite chapter, the toughest part about writing the book, why she wanted to write a book, and so on. Don't let the positive hot button go. Poor communicators might only say, "How nice, you are writing a book" or ask, "What is it called?" and then drop the button. True positive hot buttons are dying to be pushed, and it is a pleasure to talk with people who have a real passion for something.

Top salespeople use buttonomics to build rapport quickly. They are skilled at quickly finding positive hot buttons to get others talking about themselves and to find out what they have in common. Both will quickly build rapport.

They do this by asking questions and then expanding on them. Other techniques for finding positive hot buttons will be discussed in later chapters.

## Core vs. Superficial Hot Buttons

Although people's core buttons remain constant, their superficial buttons change daily and even hourly. People who love politics, for example, tend to love politics deep down; their core "politics" button is always with them. People who love cooking will probably always have a passion for cooking, and that core button, too, will remain constant. But superficial buttons change often, and they often require a little probing to find.

Usually a superficial button is something that happened to someone that day or within the last week or so. It is whatever is currently on the person's mind. Maybe he just got married, had his house broken into, just started a new job, got a new dog, or just bought a new house. It might be as simple as getting cut off by another car on the way to work or a sore neck from restoring a classic car. Whatever it is, this is a button that is itching to be pushed.

So learn to find and push people's positive core and superficial hot buttons. Just remember that good and bad buttons set off a chain reaction (law of attraction). Negative buttons start off as a "bitch session" and often escalate until there is so much negative feeling that the mood begins to change for the worse.

Instead, use the law of attraction to your advantage and use the principle of buttonomics to control the direction of the conversation and ensure that it picks up speed in a positive direction. Do this by finding people's positive hot buttons and asking questions to keep them focused on a positive topic.

## Avoiding Negative Buttons

People who don't get along push each other's negative buttons. We all have negative buttons, but our friends usually push our positive buttons. Think about it. The people who make us feel good and the ones we like to be around bring out our better qualities. If we like to have fun, we tend to be around fun people. If we like to laugh, we tend to surround ourselves with people who make us laugh. If we are having fun and laughing, we aren't pushing someone's negative buttons.

Unfortunately, we know our spouse's, friend's, and family's negative buttons all too well. We know where they are vulnerable, where their Achilles' heel is. I'm sure if you look back you can think of times when you pushed these negative buttons. "How do you expect to get [fill in the blank] when all you do is [blank]?" or "No wonder you got fired; you have always had a problem with [fill in the blank]!"

In their book *A New Beginning II: A Personal Handbook to Enhance Your Life, Liberty and Pursuit of Happiness*, Jerry and Esther Hicks write that as long as we are focused on the solution, and not the problem, we stay in "positive energy." It is when we focus on the problem (negative buttons) that we attract negative thoughts that snowball and makes things worse.

# Expanding Your Knowledge Base

Six-figure communicators are knowledgeable about many subjects. They can talk to people about anything. And what they don't know, they compensate for with their curiosity and by asking good questions. Vast subject knowledge allows them to find people's hot buttons quickly and spend less time fishing for them.

In her book *How to Talk to Anybody About Anything: Breaking the Ice with Everyone from Accountants to Zen Buddhists*, Leil Lowndes teaches readers about different hobbies, skills, and professions, and how to talk to people in each one. And she teaches the lingo specific to each. This is an excellent way to find people's positive hot buttons quickly.

In *How to Win Friends and Influence People*, Dale Carnegie wrote that Theodore Roosevelt had a great interest in people. The night before a dignitary or other guest arrived at the White House, he would stay up and read about topics his guests were interested in. If the guest was an avid collector of rare tropical butterflies, for example, Roosevelt would read up on the subject the night before. By showing a genuine interest in others and having the ability to talk intelligently about their interests, Roosevelt certainly won a lot of friends and influenced people.

A book that is easy to read and pull a variety of information from is the *Running Press Cyclopedia*, by Diagram Visual Information. It gives a quick overview of geography, religion, science, art, history, weather, and more. You need not be an expert on any of it, but you at least need to be somewhat familiar with various topics or have a resource to go to for more information.

Reading interesting news stories can be a great source of positive hot buttons to help you start conversations and also make you more knowledge-able when others are speaking on the same topics. I like to go online to read from a variety of newspapers.

One quick word on research: You just need to familiarize yourself quickly with a few points from each chapter or article. Although it is great to read almanacs and other fact books cover to cover, with buttonomics, it is more important to have a basic knowledge on a diverse number of subjects. Don't make a career out of reading one book; instead simply study its main points and then move on to the next one. If you want to learn more, ask other people your questions.

Some of the best selling I did took place during mealtimes. Before each lunch or dinner meeting, I would take out a sheet of paper and write a short list of current news, interesting stories, and information on known hobbies or interests of the client. I would have a clean joke ready and of course have key points that I wanted to stress or discuss. Then I was prepared to do business and came across as a natural, well-informed conversationalist. I just call it planning ahead.

## Chapter Summary

- Buttonomics is connecting with people on a mental level. It is the art of finding people's positive hot buttons and staying away from their nega-tive ones. These buttons are topics that emotionally charge people.

- Hot buttons are found using the three-track mind. Pay attention to the conversation, watch the individuals to see how they react to what is being said, and pay attention to the surroundings (such as a sailing maga-zine on the table). When you have hit a hot button, you will see an energy, as if a light was switched on in the person's head.

- Once you hit upon a positive hot button, let the other person talk until they reach their inflection point. This is when people realize they have been doing all of the talking and feel they should give the other person time to speak. This point is often characterized by a slight hesitation, sometimes accompanied by a goofy look.

- **Buttonomics Basics:**
  - When people say they're too busy to talk to you, what they really mean is "I'm too busy to talk to you if you don't find my hot button. If you find one, I will give you as much time as I can."
  - Find and pick up on people's positive hot buttons, and stay away from their negative ones.
  - Keep hitting multiple positive hot buttons within a topic or on various topics; don't just stop with one.
  - The more you let others talk, the more they like you.
  - The more that others talk, the more you learn.
  - The more you let others talk, the more interesting you become to them.
  - Let people talk until they run out of steam.
  - Notice and use the inflection point.
  - When you find a positive hot button, don't let it go. Make the most of it. Expand the button by asking follow-up questions.

- Core buttons remain constant and rarely change. Superficial buttons constantly change. They are topics that are on a person's mind at the moment.

- People who don't get along push each other's negative hot buttons.

- The greater your knowledge about a great number of subjects, the easier it will be to find people's positive hot buttons. Curiosity and asking good questions are the keys to simplified buttonomics. Familiarize yourself with the basics of a variety of subjects by reading from a variety of resources.

- Before an important meeting, write a short list or make a mental note of current news, interesting stories, and the individual's known hobbies or interests. Have a clean joke and your key messages ready. Then you will be prepared for the meeting and come across as a natural, educated, and interesting person.

## Daily Challenge

Talk to at least three people today and find one of their positive hot buttons. Once you find it, expand the button and see how long you can get them talking about it. Notice when they hit their inflection point.

# Executive Challenge

Same as the daily challenge, but when they hit their inflection point, find a different positive hot button and get them talking about that one too. Don't let the focus of the conversation switch to you; keep them talking about their second or even third hot button.

# Setting People at Ease

## In This Chapter:

- Understand how people get spooked
- Use the Magic Formula to get people to open up and feel at ease around you
- Learn simple tips to start a conversation with anyone
- Discover how to tell if people are genuine and sincere or just acting
- Practice the surprising power of "shooting the breeze"

Have you known people who could walk up to anyone and start a conversation? And before you knew it, they are talking about where they went to high school. When we are having a rough day or dealing with issues, with whom do we speak? We seek people with whom we feel comfortable, people we can open up to. Thus, it follows that when you put people at ease, people will open up to you more, befriend you, and trust you more.

As strange as it may sound, we sometimes get "spooked" by others. That is why we naturally put up our guard for our safety and protection when we're out in public. This fight or flight response has been a natural human instinct for thousands of years and has ensured our very survival. This instinct has also been developed throughout our lives from working with and meeting people. It is our gut feeling about people that quickly tells us how we should respond to them.

This instinct is evident when we walk up to a stranger or a stranger walks up to us. We may feel uncomfortable or awkward if a stranger knocks on our door, stops us to ask for directions, or simply stands too close. We may feel uncomfortable approaching someone, or someone else may feel uncomfortable approaching us. Do you "spook" others? The greatest communicators have the ability to set people at ease both in the way they approach individuals and the way they approach a topic.

## Avoiding "Spooking" People

"Spooking" people is the antithesis of setting people at ease. A classic example of people spooking would be sitting among others in silence in a doctor's office waiting room for 20 to 30 minutes—and then turning to the next person and starting up a conversation: "How about those Seahawks?" It would seem unnatural and out of the ordinary; people would wonder where that came from. People would be slightly "spooked."

I remember my first formal interview while researching this book. I was at a car dealership interviewing one of the top salespeople. My first question was, "Do you mind if I record this interview, and if appropriate, use the information in my book?" Immediately the salesman got nervous, his face bunched up, and he seemed uneasy (using the two-track mind). So I offered not to record the conversation.

After that first interview, I realized that I had spooked the salesman right from the start with the idea of a complete stranger recording his remarks. I quit using the tape recorder. I should have known better. From that point on, my interviews were more personable, genuine, and down-to-earth. People were more comfortable opening up to me and speaking frankly, giving me better information. The interviews became "chats" or "conversations" instead. In fact, the more conversational the interview, the more at ease people felt. Then they would give me more of their time and better information.

My tone of voice also mattered when I had to cold-call prospects by phone to get an interview in the first place. If I came across as too energetic, people thought I was trying to sell them something and were resistant to meeting me. One man asked twice for reassurance that I was not going to try to sell him something. I found more success with a confident, soft, and hypnotic tone of voice. The words I used on the phone also mattered. Many people were nervous about a complete stranger "interviewing" them—or one of their staff. I found more success asking to "chat" or "pick their brain."

One day my girlfriend Jennifer (now my wife) and I were driving across a Navajo Indian reservation, on vacation in Arizona. Just ahead we noticed a sign reading "Dinosaur Tracks, one mile ahead." We had the time and thought they would be fun to see. As we approached the designated area, a weathered-looking man, about 40 years old with tattoos on his arm, flagged us down and motioned me to roll down the window. As he approached the car, he didn't identify himself, but asked if we wanted to see the dinosaur tracks.

After we nodded yes, he said he would show us the prints, but he asked if we would take him and his "two brothers" off in the distance into Tuba City. We were hesitant to give these men a ride, but cautiously agreed to his tour. He showed us a few dinosaur footprints by the car and then walked us farther and farther away from it.

Who was this stranger and why was he asking us to take the three of them up the road? Was he legit? Would he hurt us? We were spooked.

**Factors that spook people include:**

- Strangers
- Unknown intentions
- Unknown information
- Attire (significantly out of the ordinary for the situation)
- Position or profession
- Opposite sex
- Shyness
- Not in the mood to talk
- Topic
- Significant time lapse

# The Magic Formula for Building Rapport

Some people are more easily spooked than others, and some subjects spook people more than others. Some people are just a bit touchy and some subjects are just tough to talk about. Have you ever wanted to have a serious talk with someone but it just seemed uncomfortable? You didn't quite know how to start and you felt you might chicken out? You may have tried to ask someone out on a date or to tell a child about the "birds and the bees." The last thing you want to do is spook this person.

What follows is a "magic formula" that smooth communicators consistently use to talk to tough people or to talk about tough subjects.

**The formula involves these five steps:**
1. Approach people smoothly
2. Use a disarming statement or object
3. Smile
4. Shoot the breeze
5. Ask for what you need

Maybe you have tried to ask someone for a favor but they wouldn't hear you out. Follow the five steps explained in this section and try this magic formula for yourself.

# 1. The Approach

An important part of building rapport is helping others feel comfortable with you. How you enter a room or walk up to someone has an effect on how others perceive you. Psychologists have shown that we make an impression on people in as little as three seconds. This is not just for strangers, but people we know. When someone we know walks up to us, for example, we quickly assess what kind of mood he is in, how he is dressed, if we really want to talk to him, and so on. The same is true when we walk up to other people. They quickly make these assessments about us. Conversational outcomes are almost always determined before people even open their mouths.

Remember the different ways to change people's state of mind? People are more or less receptive in different environments and doing different activities. People may be more approachable on a golf course, over dinner, and around certain people. Not only will people think and act differently, but they will also "lighten up."

An Army officer, Major Herman, taught me this approach. When a subordinate unit was having serious logistical problems, Major Herman asked me to go down to the unit and "have a cup of coffee with them." He knew that the unit had a lot of pride in its work and might not be receptive to outside help. But when I met the other officers over coffee, their guard went down and they were more receptive. The meeting seemed more like a chat than an inquisition.

In her book, *Talking the Winner's Way*, Leil Lowndes describes a technique for approaching people that she calls "Hello, Old Friend." And it works incredibly well. She advises to walk into a room and act as if it were a family reunion or you were greeting an old friend. "Heyyyyy, how's it going, Johnny?" Spread your arms and smile as you greet someone you know.

Remarkably, I've actually had strangers or people I did not know particularly well walk up to me and give me a brief hug when I did this! You walk in almost as if you are family and people tend to react as if you are. Try it.

After approaching someone, a lean can help the person feel a little more comfortable. I've seen salespeople casually lean on a wall, counter, door, or doorway while talking with a prospect or customer. Again, this can help some people feel at ease. Just experiment a little to see how it can work for you.

Bill Patton, a successful, retired real estate broker, and I were talking one day about people spooking. He told me that before he ever showed someone a house, he tried learning as much as possible about the person to ensure he "clicked" with that person from the start. He said he tried to "match" the person to create a sense of similarity. If he was showing property to an executive or a lawyer, he would wear a suit and drive his luxury car to show a house that day. If the person was a blue-collar worker, he would leave the suit at home.

He noticed that he did not make sales to people who belonged to local unions if he drove a foreign car. Because jobs were going overseas, these people felt it was important to buy American. So many of the blue-collar workers were turned off by a foreign car before even getting into it, let alone going to see the property. So if Bill knew he was going to be showing a union member a particular property, he would be sure to drive an American car that day.

One day, I arrived early for a meeting I had in a small, rural West Virginia town. It was a little after noon and I decided to go to the public library to do some paperwork. Careful not to spook people, I left my suit jacket in the car and carried in my work. The librarian quickly asked me who I was, where I was from, and what my name was. The whole time I was working, I could see her and her assistant subtly watching me to see what I was doing. She must have thought I was from the government making some sort of secret inspection. Even with my suit jacket off, I spooked her. The point is only that people can be spooked easily.

Remember that as a general rule, if you want to talk with a stranger on a bus or train or to anyone sitting or standing next to you, you have less than a minute and ideally fewer than 30 seconds to start up a conversation (golden minute). If you wait more than that, the conversation tends to feel awkward and people close up. This is also true if you move into a new apartment or house. Meet your neighbors within the first couple of days. The longer you wait, the more awkward it is. It is hard to introduce yourself six months later.

## Have Someone Else with You

It is easy to spook people, but having a second person along will help others feel more at ease. This is because many people act differently when others are present. I don't know if it is due to peer pressure to behave a particular way when peers or others are around or if the other people subconsciously send signals that "I have checked out this person and it is okay to talk with him." (Guys know that it is easier to attract other women at a bar if they are with a female than if they are by themselves or with several guys). Simply having a brother, friend, or spouse along will cause others to relax and open up more. People are less hostile and standoffish.

A third person will also help take the awkwardness out of conversations. It takes the pressure off of you and the other person. You don't always have to be the one that is talking or clicking with the other person. You can take a little break while the other person does some of the talking. This keeps conversational energy levels high. Many late-night talk-show hosts have a sidekick to help keep conversations moving and interesting.

There are many everyday examples of this. Salespeople will tell you that customers act differently when they take their managers with them on sales calls. Strangers in public places are less spooked and more open when a child or a spouse is present. Single people know that they are more approachable at the park with a dog or a friend than by themselves. Having another person (or animal!) along with you changes the way many people act, removing awkwardness and making people more approachable.

## Conversational Approach

Six-figure communicators have also learned the power of a conversational approach when talking to and working with others. They see everything as a conversation: conducting interviews, networking, selling, looking for a job, presenting, and speaking. They harness the power of conversational tone. They know that this approach sets more people at ease, makes them more enjoyable to listen to, helps them come across as more genuine, and builds rapport much more quickly.

Without this approach, it's too easy for interactions with others to come across as cold and canned. This is one of the most common mistakes new salespeople make. They are so worried about selling their product that they forget to be a human being first and simply have a conversation with people. The smoothest sales presentations are conversational.

> The magic word is not "please," but "hi" or "hello." The best communicators use these words before they say anything else, setting people at ease. It is a simple and effective way to start a conversation, particularly if accompanied with a smile. Never be lost for words again.

When listening to the best speakers, you feel that it is a private conversation between you and them. You feel that they are talking to you and not at you. One Harley-Davidson salesman I interviewed said that he enjoys talking about the Harley rallies, rides, and camaraderie with other Harley owners. Only later do customers ask him how to "get" one.

## Shock and Awe Approach

When people are startled, they act differently. Hare Krishnas used this technique to their advantage. They were known to startle people at airports by coming up to them suddenly or from behind a column or corner. The startled individuals were shocked out of whatever state they were in and were momentarily confused. Their habitual defenses went down and their thoughts were scattered. Then the Hare Krishna offered a "gift" (acting out the law of reciprocity). It might have been a book or a flower; it did not matter. The Hare Krishna would not take back the "gift," but asked for a donation to their organization. The startled individuals, without thinking, often made donations without confrontation.

People larger than life also use this technique. They walk into a room as if their hair were on fire. "Heyyy, what is going on?!" They startle the people in the room, who are then momentarily disarmed and confused. The ones who do the startling disable the others' resistance and then quickly fill the void and build rapport.

## 2. The Disarming Statement or Object

The disarming statement is your "opening comment" to someone. It is a general statement that other people can agree with that has nothing to do with what you want. The use of a little humor or careful sarcasm can make the statement even better. A co-worker of mine, Bob Walker, does this well. He may walk up to someone and say with a big grin, "It looks like you are so happy that you can't stand it." After the disarming statement, he might follow up with another disarming statement such as, "You look organized. I was organized—once," and then smile.

This kind of approach breaks the ice and helps you decide if the other person is approachable, if the person is in the mood to talk, or whether you should talk with the person. If the person doesn't want to talk or is in a bad mood, leave her alone. If the person feels like talking, then shoot the breeze with her.

I like to use disarming questions or neutral statements. I might sit down next to someone on a train or in a waiting room and say something like, "Boy, it sure is hot out there!" If the other person feels like talking, he will usually answer with a little more than "yep." Asking someone a general question such as "Is it supposed to cool off any this week?" can also get the ball rolling if the person wants to talk. "You look deep in thought" is a good way to get people talking if they want to. But whatever you say, just remember that you have a golden minute or less to give this statement, to try out a conversation.

The disarming object is simply something you're holding that "disarms" people. It may be a baby, puppy, or unusual electronic gadget. It acts as an icebreaker for others. Top salespeople might wear an unusual pin or carry something around to prompt inquiry from others. In general, I have found that holding something in my hand, even a cup of coffee or a pen, helps to set people at ease. Someone holding a cup of coffee just doesn't seem as threatening.

You can see master salespeople using the disarming object at conventions. They want to entice passersby to come into their booths and look at their products. If three or four salespeople are standing together or huddled up, people tend not to walk up to them; they keep walking. The best salespeople stand by themselves and hold something in their hands, to avoid spooking anyone and to appear more open to approach. The object might be a brochure, a pen, or a giveaway. Whatever it is, it makes the passersby more likely to approach the booth.

When I was vacationing in Mexico, I saw countless waiters standing outside of their restaurants trying to entice passersby to dine at their restaurants. They were very aggressive. I watched one waiter, in particular, from a distance. Soon I saw a small, white kitten crawl out from under the restaurant's deck. The waiter reached down to pick it up (some temporary company) and soon a group of three women walked up to the waiter and started to pet the kitten. He smiled and chatted with the women for a few minutes. The women then walked off, and the waiter dropped the cat and went back to hustling people. Those three women were the only people who stopped to talk with the waiter. The waiter didn't realize he was holding a disarming object.

# 3. The Smile

A smile is that something extra to help people feel comfortable with you. Once you utter your disarming statement or question, always smile. This will subconsciously persuade others to move in your conversational direction and talk with you. People will begin talking with you without even realizing it. Most people are too stingy with their smiles.

Smiling before your disarming statement also will help ensure that the statement will be taken well. When babies or children smile at us, few of us can resist them. We always smile back. They disarm us momentarily and the tension leaves our bodies. It makes us feel good to return a warm genuine smile—and it works on more than kids!

## How Powerful Is a Smile?

Let's look at a real-life military example told by Mark Strassmann, an embedded CBS News reporter with the 101st Airborne Division during the war in Iraq, April 3, 2003.[1] As Strassmann told it, U.S. troops moved into the city of Najaf, Iraq, and were arranging a meeting with the mosque's cleric who issued a decree urging Muslims to remain calm and not hinder U.S. forces. The cleric asked for protection, and troops moved toward his home. Unfortunately, the crowd mistook this action as troops wanting to storm the mosque. A volatile standoff ensued.

"The biggest resentment for this crowd was the thought of U.S. soldiers carrying guns into the mosque," said Strassmann. "That's exactly what the Fedayeen had been doing for years." U.S. forces faced a nervous and hostile crowd, shouting at them in a foreign language and waving crude weapons. The 101st Airborne Division had automatic machine guns, grenade launchers, and close air support available to them. But with all of that firepower, how could they disarm the crowd and reduce tensions?

Commander Chris Hughes had to decide how his soldiers were going to handle the situation. One gunshot could start a riot leaving many injured and others dead. "Everybody smile. Don't point your weapons at them," he told his soldiers. U.S. troops withdrew. "Turn back slowly and smile," Hughes told his soldiers. "These people don't understand that he asked us to come in."

Talk about a disarming smile, literally. Soldiers withdrew, the incident was defused, and no one got hurt. The potential for injuries and loss of life existed, but was narrowly avoided in large part because of the quick-thinking commander. Certainly smiling can show others that your meaning is earnest and well intentioned.

## Put on a Happy Face

A smile naturally puts people at ease and is so easy to do. People tend to gravitate toward happy people. I learned this lesson the hard way. As a young Army lieutenant, I walked around with a scowl on my face, trying to look tough. I wanted to look strong and mean so people would fear and respect me. The problem was that no one wanted to be around me—I was no fun. Worse than that, soldiers felt more apprehensive about confiding in me for fear I would pounce on them.

Then I left the Army and went into sales. There, the tough approach did not work well at all. I was forced to smile. I remember during the first two weeks of selling that my cheeks were so sore from smiling all day. I was using muscles I didn't know I had, for I was not used to using them. I would lie in bed at night and massage my cheeks, "Ooohhh, my cheeks are sooo sore!"

Whom would you rather talk with—a happy person or a mean and bitter person? Winners make a conscious effort to surround themselves with the right kind of people. No one likes to be around a grouch, especially if they have a choice. The late Fred Herman, a professional speaker, meeting planner, and renowned salesman, once said, "A forced smile is better than a sincere grouch." He has a point. He said the Chinese have an age-old expression: "He who cannot smile shouldn't open shop."

Most people don't realize they rarely smile. Most people think they are smiling. Pictures and videos, however, reveal the truth. Quickly look into a mirror sometime to see what "look" is habitually on your face. You might be surprised.

Try something new. When you smile at the next person, give her an all-out smile; unleash the smile from within! Don't hold it back. Halfhearted smiles get halfhearted results. Or worse, they show sarcasm, fear, or insincerity. Unleash your smile and let there be no doubt it is genuine and meant exclusively for the other person. Don't chicken out halfway through it; be brave. That's what makes the smile so wonderful; it is your gift to the person of your choosing. Your smile is something special you share with others.

A smile can also be used as an approach, in place of a disarming statement. For example, if you are walking through a parking lot with a smile on your face, people will be inclined to smile back at you if you make eye contact with them. Everyone wants to be around happy people and in on the good feeling. They are put at ease by you and may ask you about the weather. "It's a beautiful day, isn't it?"

But if people make eye contact with you and you give a grimace or a smirk, they will look away from you and keep walking, pretending to ignore you or pretending not to have noticed you. Halfhearted smiles get halfhearted results. Give the gift of a confident smile.

## Real or Fake?

Can you tell a fake smile from an authentic one? Can others? The answer is yes. Put a piece of paper over your mouth and look into the mirror. Smile. Did the smile reach your eyes? If you can't see your eyes "smiling," keep smiling bigger and bigger until they do. Genuine smiles are with the eyes, cheeks, and the corners of the mouth. That is why the entire face seems to illuminate with a great smile. Play around with it by squinting your eyes slightly, showing your teeth, raising your cheeks, and crinkling your nose and eyes. This looks and feels very different from smiling with only your lips.

Another way to tell a genuine smile is that the person's entire face seems to relax and the pupils slightly dilate. This facial relaxation is noticeable even looking through a beard. You can tell fake expressions because the face does not relax and remains rigid.

Now that you know what an authentic smile looks and feels like, work on projecting it at will without the paper. And work on detecting fake smiles in others. If people smile only with their lips, you will know it is a fake smile and that they are not genuinely happy or amused.

# 4. Shoot the Breeze

Unless it is an emergency, never walk up to people and immediately start interrogating them about projects, tasks, or other information. Instead, shoot the breeze with them for at least 20 seconds and then ease your way into whatever you want to ask them. Skipping this step is like waking someone out of bed and immediately yelling about doing the day's chores. Building rapport is about giving people time to adjust to you.

A large part of establishing rapport is being like the others you are talking to. If they talk fast, you talk fast. If they talk slowly, you talk slowly. If they like information, facts, and figures, you give them information, facts, and figures. If they are warm and fuzzy, you should be warm and fuzzy. If they are visual, show them what you are talking about. If they are busy and need information quickly, give them the information quickly. The best salespeople are chameleons. That is, they adjust and adapt their speaking style to that of the person they are talking to and that person's situation.

Before you open your mouth, however, use the two- and three-track minds to absorb all of the information you can from someone. This is one reason to let the other person talk first. Notice the other person's energy level, the energy level in the room, how busy someone is, other people who might be standing around or waiting, whether someone is a Type A personality (fast-paced) or more easygoing, and so on. The more information you can absorb quickly, the easier it is to be like the other person.

After absorbing as much information as possible, you have a good shot at establishing rapport. You have a good feel for the other person, her mood and stress level, and how to talk to her. We have only one chance to make a first impression, so six-figure communicators get their act together to make sure that when they open their mouths, "gold" comes out.

Now "shoot the breeze" to build rapport. This step can be as short as 10 seconds or as long as a couple of hours. It depends primarily on the other person, but also on your available time. Adjust yourself and your message accordingly.

Do this before you ask anyone for anything, accuse anyone of anything, or even "chew anyone out." Always shoot the breeze first! Six-figure communicators use their time to consciously and deliberately build rapport, trust, and credibility before doing anything else.

Many professional speakers try to meet as many audience members as they can before they speak. They introduce themselves before speeches and shake a lot of hands. One professional speaker said he tries to make as many friends as he can before speaking. He says it is easier to speak to friends than strangers. He starts building rapport with the audience before even getting on stage.

Six-figure communicators sell themselves first! They are not wasting time, but taking the time to show people they care. Only after rapport is built and they have sold themselves do they ask for something or ease their way into business.

## Cheese-and-Cracker Talk

Twelve hours into a major training exercise, when the sun came up, my commander told me to push back the defensive perimeter 50 meters! We had been digging in the fighting positions all night long and had put major work into developing the perimeter. My soldiers were physically exhausted. He told me to get with the first sergeant and move the perimeter back.

I found the first sergeant sitting next to a tree, opening a package of cheese and crackers. He offered me a few crackers and we sat next to the tree eating cheese and crackers and talking for a few minutes. This was the first time we had sat down in perhaps 12 hours and it felt good.

After chatting for about five minutes, I eased my way into telling him what needed to be done. He didn't like it, but our small talk first certainly took some of the edge off. If I had walked right up to him (after he just sat down to eat for the first time in 12 hours), told him to move the perimeter back, and then left the scene, I might have been shot in the back!

Never forget the power of cheese-and-cracker talk first. It takes a lot of the edge off and puts people in a more receptive state, allowing you to ease your way into whatever you need to tell or ask someone. This establishes rapport that is critical to talking and working with others.

Whether you call it cheese-and-cracker talk, shooting the breeze, or simply chitchatting, it is your chance to build rapport, trust, and credibility around others. This is the most important secret six-figure communicators know. People who cannot do this are rarely successful. Six-figure communicators intentionally and deliberately build rapport, trust, and credibility first.

## The Pitfalls of Rushing into Business

The biggest mistake most people make when they deal with people is that they jump right into business without first establishing rapport. Often the people we dislike are those who haven't established rapport. Ever notice that? Too many people try to sell us or ask us for something without even taking a minute to get to know us. We immediately sense this and back away. That is one reason that we dislike telemarketers. They try to sell us without first establishing rapport.

One day I went fly-fishing in the Yakima River. I noticed a boat tied to a tree with a man sitting in it waiting for someone. I asked him if he had any luck fishing, and he said he caught several fish but threw them back. Then he gave me his business card stating that he was a "guide," and he attempted to sell me his services. He immediately talked about his fee and all of the skills he would teach. I didn't particularly care for this man because he didn't make himself "human" first. He merely assumed I wasn't catching anything, had no idea of my skill level, and tried to sell me before even exchanging pleasantries. There wasn't even a "Good afternoon. Pretty day, isn't it?" or "Any luck?" In essence, he did not yet earn the right to ask for my business. He did not take the time to shoot the breeze.

One time I was dining at a fine restaurant where the waiter, upon approaching our table for the first time, passed out menus and started to push appetizers. Then he came back trying to sell us on the most expensive drinks on the menu. He came back again and pushed expensive dinner specials. Right from the start, we disliked this waiter. He didn't introduce himself, welcome us to the restaurant, ask us if we had been there before, offer a little time to look over the menu, or ask if we had any questions. By trying to up-sell us (to increase our overall bill, thereby increasing his tip), we lost our appetites.

My brother and I had a similar experience when he went with me to look at cars from a couple of local dealerships. The salesman at one dealership didn't ask who the car was for, if it would be used for commuting, if trunk space was important, or if I was from the area. He didn't ask a single question about me or what I would use the car for. He only talked product.

Top salespeople, on the other hand, always shoot the breeze with customers before ever mentioning product. They get to know the other person first, then gradually move into what customers need and what they are looking for. One top car salesman called this the customer interview. He said his secret was to take the time to get to know customers and what they want, and then go get it for them. "It's that simple," he said.

Too many salespeople do not earn the right to close a prospect because they don't take the time to get to know the customer and simply shoot the breeze first. Only after they know a little about someone will they start to talk product. A Harley motorcycle salesman put it best when he told me that he never sells a motorcycle to a "stranger."

## Rapport Eases Negotiation and Cooperation

When rapport is established, both the salesman and the customer are more willing to give in. Both are more willing to compromise. The salesperson is more willing to come down on price or add extra options he would not ordinarily add, and the customer is more willing to pay a higher price when likeability and rapport are established first. Buying and selling are both easier when rapport is established.

John Taschner, the top car salesman at a local auto dealership (who, coincidentally, sold me a car after I interviewed him for this book), told me that he is much more willing to give a break in price to customers he likes. Likewise, customers who like the salesperson are less likely to haggle or quibble over price. A natural give and take happens when people take a few minutes initially to get to know each other and shoot the breeze. Then both people walk away happy and feeling good, instead of feeling emotionally drained.

Moreover, the more time that people have invested in a conversation, the easier it is to work with them. It is especially important to shoot the breeze with someone if you need help, if you have a last-minute request, or if you're asking for a special favor. Once rapport is established, then you can ask anyone for anything.

One day during an emergency deployment-readiness exercise at Fort Bragg, I was working at a restricted parachute-rigging facility. Being a qualified parachute rigger, I was checking heavy equipment, which was to be dropped at night over an objective. A new lieutenant walked up to me, and I asked her how she was doing. She ignored me and went on with her business. Two minutes later she walked up to me blasting me about a missing vehicle, asking where she could find this vehicle and why no one would help her. I should have helped her, but as a young lieutenant myself, I just shrugged and she moved on to someone else.

Now let's suppose that, instead, the new lieutenant had first walked up to me and said, "Boy it's hot out here. What a day I am having. I haven't met you; my name is Carrie. Say, I am having a terrible time trying to find a vehicle. Could you help me?" The odds are she would have gotten my help. Without shooting the breeze and establishing rapport, a person has nothing to work with. You should sincerely enjoy talking with people to begin with, but if you find yourself needing a little help later, you will be in a better position to ask and get real help instead of a brush-off.

While shooting the breeze, you establish trust, credibility, and rapport. This is key. Without it, your technical expertise and experience hardly matter! Shooting the breeze is far more important than most people realize.

A side benefit to establishing rapport is purely social. Top salespeople often find customers inviting them to social occasions. "Most people become your friends," said one salesman. Customers frequently ask him and his wife out to dinner. I, too, have been invited to dinner in my customers' homes, gone on vacation with them, attended family weddings, and asked to go boating, hunting, running, weight lifting, drinking, golfing, rafting, and to parties and church. In addition, top salespeople are constantly being offered jobs by clients or competitors. Why? Because they sell themselves first, and talk product later.

## 5. Ask for What You Need-or-Build Subject Rapport

Only after they have established rapport with people will six-figure communicators ask for what they need. They might preface the asking with one of the following phrases:

- "Say, let me ask you a question …"
- "I'm having trouble with …; can you help me?"
- "By the way, I am from out of town and am looking for …; would you point me in the right direction?
- "Before I forget, I need help with …"

Asking for help in a "by the way" or a "before I forget" tone suggests you are now friends and you're merely asking "Would you mind … ?" Establishing rapport gives you the "right" to ask and expect reasonable help.

### Building Subject Rapport

Once they have established rapport with people, six-figure communicators go to work building rapport for their subject. If you do not do this, people will mentally switch off and not care what you have to say. You must warm people up to a particular subject before blowing full steam into it!

You can get people thinking or talking about a subject by asking questions, chatting, and gathering facts. This is how you learn the needs or desires of others. When you learn this, you are better able to tailor your information to others to come across more effectively. Only after you've established rapport for a particular subject should you begin discussing it.

You might build rapport for a topic by creating common feelings for a subject: "Don't you hate it when …?" Or you might build sympathy or empathy into the subject: "You can't imagine what it is like to ...?" or "Has this ever happened to you ...?" Such queries enable you to gently start talking about a topic, and then you can lead into what you want to discuss. If you warm people up a little first, they can better relate to a subject because they have "been there" too. Build common feelings into a subject first and then you can proceed to discuss it.

Why is this so important? Because it is useless to talk about a particular subject unless people care about it, are ready for it, or want the information. People must be in the receive mode first. If people don't get into this mode, they will feel they are being preached at and lectured to. Six-figure communicators instinctively know that they are just squandering the rapport they worked so hard to build if others are not ready for the information they want to convey.

At a local town meeting, a speaker walked up to the microphone and started lecturing the audience about a particular country. The speaker never introduced himself, never said who he was or why he had an interest in that country. He just started lecturing the audience. This speaker did not build rapport with the audience or build rapport for his topic. The audience couldn't have cared less for this man or his topic. His message was rendered ineffective in less than 30 seconds.

Contrast this with a teenager at a local speaking competition. He wore camouflage pants and had a black bandana tied around his head. When he walked up to the microphone and began speaking, the audience immediately noticed his lisp. But the first words were: "This is my first time ever speaking in front of anyone. I don't know if I am more scared of you or you are more scared of me." Then he started to tell a story about a popular local baseball player whom everyone knew.

Everyone in the audience was pulling for this kid from the start. We liked him before he even began his story, so we wanted him to do well. His story was one everyone could quickly relate to and identify with, so building rapport for the topic was easy. He won third place. The audience loved him.

# Sell Yourself First

Too many salespeople (and others) tend to forget the importance of selling yourself first before asking for anything else. They try to sell without first establishing rapport. If people do not like or trust you, you will not make the sale, no matter how much people want your product. If people trust you, you will sell yourself and your product. If they don't trust you, they may pick your brain for information and then go elsewhere to buy. They will think they can do better somewhere else. They will be more willing to shop around for a better deal. They will look for a salesperson with whom they feel more comfortable or one who is less "pushy." They will use you for what you are worth and take up your time.

In this age of the Internet, there is less and less need for salespeople to establish subject rapport. Top auto sales personnel, for example, know that people probably don't wander into a dealership unless they are at least interested in the cars for sale there. And the odds are that "window shoppers" have already done research online before they walk in. Often they already know the technical information of the cars they are looking at. But technical information is not necessarily what people see a salesperson for anyway. Indeed, the top Mercedes salesman in the country a few years ago scored only 35 percent on his technical assessment test. He claimed he didn't know cars, but he knew people!

Potential customers can find all of the stats, facts, and safety information online for products as diverse as pills and planes. People can also find pricing information. And this is why people skills are more important than ever. Fail to win over a customer and the customer will go somewhere else to buy. If salespeople have weak people skills, potential customers will merely pick their brain and then go elsewhere to buy. Making sales depends on people skills.

Whether selling cars or selling yourself, life is a people business. And people don't change. Learn people and you will succeed. Basic people skills—making time to get to know people, selling yourself first, being conversational, building trust and rapport, reading people, and working with others—will ensure success.

### Epilogue on the Navajo Reservation

The stranger on the Navajo Reservation turned out to be a legitimate guide. The sun was close to setting, and he simply wanted to get himself and his two brothers home before dark, particularly if he was going to take 20 or 30 minutes to give us a tour. We were spooked because he did not use the magic formula. He should have used the time during his tour to sell himself and build trust and credibility. He should have built rapport with us first! Then, following the magic formula, he should have said something along the lines of "By the way, it is almost dark; could I trouble you two to give us a ride home? My brothers and I were just about to walk home when you drove up."

## Chapter Summary

- The greatest communicators have the ability to set others at ease both in the way they approach people and the way they approach a topic. Communicators who do this find that people open up to them more, befriend them, and trust them.
  - **Factors That Spook People:**
    Strangers
    Unknown intentions
    Unknown information
    Attire (significantly out of the ordinary for the situation)
    Position or profession
    Opposite sex
    Shyness
    Not in the mood to talk
    Topic
    Significant time lapse

  - **Use the Magic Formula to Build Rapport:**
    1. Approach people smoothly
    2. Use a disarming statement or object
    3. Smile
    4. Shoot the breeze
    5. Ask for something or build subject rapport

- A disarming statement is an opening comment to someone. It is a general statement or question that the person can agree with that has nothing to do with what you want. It simply breaks the ice and helps you decide whether someone is approachable, whether she is in the mood to talk, or whether you should talk with this person. If the person doesn't want to talk, or is in a bad mood, leave her alone. If the person feels like talking, then shoot the breeze with her. A disarming object is something that sets someone at ease or makes breaking the ice easier. Examples include an unusual pin, a baby, a puppy, a kitten, or a cup of coffee.

- Don't be bashful with your smile—smile all out. Halfhearted smiles get halfhearted results, or worse, show sarcasm, fear, or insincerity. The smile is your gift to the person of your choosing.

- Always "shoot the breeze" with people, and then ease your way into whatever you want to ask someone. This is an important step in building rapport. It is how you establish trust, credibility, and likeability. The biggest mistake most people make when dealing with others is that they jump right into business without first establishing rapport.

- Only after establishing rapport with others should you launch into asking for something you need. Establishing rapport gives you the "right" to ask and expect reasonable help.

- Once you've established rapport with others, you can build rapport for your subject. Get people thinking or talking about a subject by asking questions, chatting, gathering facts, and sensing people's feelings. Only after you establish rapport for a particular subject should you begin discussing it. If you don't, people will mentally switch off and not care what you have to say.

## Daily Challenge

Approach five people today and start up a conversation with each of them using the Magic Formula.

## Executive Challenge

Study other people today to see which elements of the magic formula they use and which ones they do not use. What could they have done differently to improve outcomes?

# Unlocking the
# Secrets of Charisma

## In This Chapter:

*   Learn six secrets of charismatic people
*   Find out what charismatic people do that makes them special

**M**ost people can't tell you what charisma is, but they know it when they see it. It seems magical and mysterious. People who have it have a special style and class about them. It is a miraculous elixir that enables its host to achieve more, earn more, and move on to higher levels of performance. It has been described as charm, personality, grace, and finesse. But what exactly is it, where does it come from, and how do people get it?

Are people born with charisma? Whoever heard of a charismatic baby? While some charismatic traits come naturally to a select few, much of it is learned and developed. The more charismatic qualities you learn and develop, the more charismatic you will become. Learn only one new skill and become just a little more charismatic. Learn two or three new skills and become even more charismatic.

True charisma comes from using your personal power and not your power of position. People who can talk and work well with anyone, anywhere, are charismatic, regardless of position. A charismatic person can be just as effective talking and working with tourists in Hawaii as being president of a major bank on the mainland.

Charles Lindholm, a Harvard anthropologist, says that charisma "can be revealed only in interaction with others."[1] It is a collection of specialized people skills. Charisma is the ability to draw people to you using only your personal power, relentless belief, and uplifting rapport.

Uplifting rapport is not about likening or adapting yourself to others, like traditional rapport, but positively differentiating yourself, giving people so many positive feelings that they are attracted to you and want to be around you. There is something about you that others like and they want more of it. Uplifting rapport includes positive energy, passive likeability, the ability to help others feel better, class, and humor.

If charismatic behavior is learned, so is non-charismatic behavior. But to become charismatic, you need not undo non-charismatic qualities. You simply need to put into practice charismatic ones. Developing the six skills that follow will give you charisma to apply in any situation such as parenting, managing co-workers, leading people, teaching, coaching, or selling.

# 1. Belief

People want to believe in you, trust you, do business with you, and follow you. But the minute you doubt yourself, hem and haw, show awkwardness, or stumble with your words, people begin to doubt you, and charisma begins to fade. You go downhill fast and soon all charisma is lost. Your opportunity is over, and the person leaves.

You cannot attract anyone without relentless belief. Charisma does not work without it. This belief has to be extremely strong and consistent the entire time you talk with someone. You must almost overpower people with your certainty. Developing belief in yourself, your role, or your purpose is the first and most important step to becoming charismatic.

The secret to charisma is to believe in something so strongly that you are unshakeable. You are relentless; you are in the personal power mind-set with a solid purpose. It is about focusing on your strengths and not on your weaknesses. Belief must come from deep within you. Many people can quickly create belief in what they are doing by linking something they believe strongly in or what they are very good at to their cause, role, to others, or to their speech.

Let's take the sales profession, for example. I know a woman who spent years as a nurse, who changed careers and went into selling capital equipment, mainly office equipment. She struggled and struggled getting started, calling list after list of random companies, trying to set up appointments. She set up very few. She felt awkward on the phone and felt uncomfortable cold-calling businesses.

One day she realized that she was a nurse and should be calling on hospitals. She knew and understood hospitals better than any of her counterparts or competitors. She understood who the decision makers were in the hospital, which departments needed which pieces of equipment, and the general layout of hospitals. She instantly excelled in that market and became a top producer for her company.

She linked what she had experience in, and what she understood, to selling capital equipment. But what really changed was that she was no longer awkward, uncertain, or uncomfortable in sales. She was a nurse again who happened to help various departments with their office needs. She knew their problems and frustrations and the appropriate office solutions. Though her market changed, what really changed was her belief and confidence in herself.

People can see it in your eyes when you firmly believe in something and when you don't. Take U.S. Senator Zell Miller, a Democrat from Georgia, who spoke at the 2004 Republican National Convention about why he thought President George W. Bush, the Republican, would make a better president than John Kerry, the Democrat. He was so focused that he didn't even wait for the audience to applaud during his speech. And when they did, he rarely paused. He was not in it for the applause; he was in it to deliver what he strongly believed in. His face had a "don't stop me" look throughout the speech and you could see it in his eyes. He believed in his message so much that he crossed party lines to do it. The result was that he inspired a crowd and, some say, swayed the election in Bush's favor.

An extreme example of speaking with unrelenting belief in a message happened in 1912 when President Theodore Roosevelt was about to give a speech in Milwaukee, Wisconsin. At that point a would-be assassin aimed a pistol at him and pulled the trigger. Roosevelt was shot in the chest. Dripping in blood, he pulled himself to the podium and said, "I am going to ask you to be very quiet and please excuse me for making a long speech. I'll do the best I can, but there is a bullet in my body. I have a message to deliver and I will deliver it as long as there is life in my body." He spoke for 90 minutes and then collapsed.

He ad-libbed the speech because his written speech, which was in his breast pocket, was shot through. (His 50-page speech, folded in half, and his eyeglass case helped to absorb the bullet's force.) Teddy Roosevelt certainly believed in the message enough to deliver it dripping in blood. And because it was so important to him, he ad-libbed it for 90 minutes. You better believe that people listened and hung on every word that was spoken.

But one of the easiest and quickest ways to convey extraordinary belief in what you say is to speak from the heart. It doesn't matter if you are speaking to one person or 1,000 people, speaking from the heart pierces through attitudes of steel. It helps us break through nearly impossible barriers and make a powerful connection with others quickly, even if you are not sure what to say.

For example, in 1968, Senator Robert Kennedy was on an airplane en route to Indianapolis to give a campaign speech when he was notified that Martin Luther King Jr. had just been assassinated. The crowd he was about to address hadn't yet heard the news. Kennedy had prepared and rehearsed a speech, but now everything was different.

When he stepped before the crowd, he asked everyone to please lower their signs. He did not have a prepared speech for these circumstances. All he could do was speak from his heart, holding his rolled-up prepared speech at his side. His speech that day is considered by some as one of the finest impromptu speeches ever given. And Indianapolis was the only major U.S. city that did not riot upon hearing the news of King's assassination.

# 2. Positive Energy

Most people do not have positive energy and are attracted to people with it. When people see others with this energy, they naturally gravitate to them in the hope of getting a small piece of it, for they cannot generate it or are having trouble generating it themselves. Energy is contagious. If you have it, people will come. An important way to become charismatic is to give this energy to others. Non-charismatic people take energy from others.

Ever notice that when you talk to other people on the phone, especially friends, your energy level rises? You could be having a tough day or feeling blah, but when you get someone else on the phone, you instantly smile and say "Billlllllll … hey, what's going on?!" When someone calls you, your energy level quickly rises. You subconsciously know that you need this energy to attract others and come across as "fun." Without this energy, it is difficult to keep others' interest. Energy is an important component to charisma.

Charismatic people have figured out that charisma is an energy game. They have taken the time to master energy. They know how to create it, pull it out of others, and keep it in conversations. And the better they get at this game, the more charismatic they become. Let's take a look at their secrets to continually winning the energy game.

## Secret #1: Charismatic people create the energy they need by pulling it out of themselves.

Charismatic people have the ability to create and hang on to this energy. They know that positive energy temporarily insulates them from negative people and allows them to do and accomplish more. (Review Chapter 1 for how to create personal energy by developing and maintaining the personal power mind-set.)

Charismatic people show this positive energy through their emotions. The more positive emotions they display, the more energy they give and the more strongly they convey charismatic qualities. In his book *Personal Magnetism*, Andrew J. DuBrin says that "people who tightly control their emotions rarely attract the attention of others." He goes on to say that magnetic people show emotional expressiveness. This is seen through their passion for what they do and what they talk about.

## Secret #2: Charismatic people create the energy they need by pulling it out of others.

Charismatic people have the ability to create energy by drawing out positive qualities in others. They use simplified buttonomics (Chapter 4) to find the positive hot buttons in people. They say good things about everyone or nothing at all. They laugh easily and often, giggle a lot, and are sometimes silly. They continually compliment, congratulate, praise, show admiration for others and what they have done, and simply bring out the best in them. And if good people have made mistakes, they help them save face in front of others.

Doing all of these things cranks others' energy up a notch. Charismatic people give people energy by finding and pulling it out of others. Finding this energy positively stimulates individuals and groups and helps them begin to positively contribute to the group. The group begins to find their energy and become more and more positive. They feed off each other. Through the law of attraction, this also draws in other people who want to become positive. People take on the characteristics of the group.

## Secret #3: Charismatic people preserve the energy they created by keeping conversations refreshingly positive.

Charismatic people are a breath of fresh air. What a pleasure it is to get some of the energy they have been losing all day. Charismatic people recharge others. And equally important, charismatic people recharge themselves by feeding off the energy they've helped create in others. This cycle helps to perpetuate positive energy. This is why it is so important to choose positive people to associate with.

Being positive yourself is not enough. With enough negative momentum, other people will undo your positive energy and that of the group. It takes only one person to make a snide remark or negative comment to encourage others to contribute their own horror story. This activates the law of attraction and cancels out any remaining charisma—you cannot be considered charismatic when everyone in the group is negative. To be considered charismatic, people must have positive energy or must convert negative energy.

Charismatic people have the special skill of stopping negative energy before it picks up too much momentum. Once negative energy gets going, charisma is pinched off. But charismatic people are experts at preserving this newly created positive energy by either changing the subject at hand or getting people laughing about the negative situation. If this does not work, they take charge of the conversation and change its conversational focus. Ways to do this include:

- Tweaking conversations. As soon as people begin to show frustration, aggravation, uncertainty, or irritation, charismatic people adjust conversation. They may change the subject, change the focus, mitigate, start to joke around, become silly, tell a joke or a story, or blow the situation so out of proportion that people see how ridiculous they are being.

- Give everything a positive spin. The more positive their spin, the more quickly people want to change. For example, when evaluating someone's speech, a charismatic person wouldn't make any outright negative comments. A charismatic person would spin any negative feedback into something positive, ...
    - "You spoke great tonight, but you will be even better if you ..."
    - "You will dazzle even more people if you ..."
    - "You will be even more effective if you ..."
    - "I challenge you to ..."

Charismatic people show their use of tact, diplomacy and class when they offer this kind of constructive criticism. The person being evaluated and the audience appreciate this. Charismatic people have mastered the art of never talking negatively, but talking with a positive spin instead.

There is clearly an art to keeping conversations refreshingly positive. Kids do it. Teenagers do it. Fun people do it. Charismatic people do it. Although keeping your personal energy level high is essential to charisma, keeping group energy high is equally important.

Charismatic people are good at creating and preserving energy. They have the ability to create the energy needed for charisma by getting into the personal power mind-set. They create still more energy by pulling the good out of others. And as soon as others begin to draw away, steal, or snatch this energy, they change the subject, change the focus, or change the conversational direction. Energy is sacred, and charismatic people do not allow others to take their energy or the group's energy.

## Positive Energy Through Posture

The No. 1 posture mistake people make is not holding their heads over their bodies—they hold them too far forward. Called forward neck syndrome, this is visable when people sit or stand. By pulling your head back over the body, your posture dramatically straightens. This straightened posture visually shows others your positive energy.

A quick way to check your habitual posture, to see if this is a problem for you, is to stand with your back against a wall. Does your head naturally touch the wall? For many non-charismatic people, it does not.

# 3. Passive Likeability

Likeability is a key factor in charisma. The more people like you, the more they are drawn to you. This likeability is passive, meaning that you are not actively praising, flirting, flattering or complimenting others. It is a quiet charm. People who exude passive likeability are warm, relaxed, in control, confident. They are people you feel comfortable with. They know how to set people at ease and build rapport. Examples include Diane Sawyer and Charles Gibson of *Good Morning America* and Matt Lauer of *Today*.

Most passive likeability is created without speaking. It is sitting or standing with a pleasant expression on your face. People with passive likeability just look like pleasant people to be around. They smile with their eyes and cheeks, not so much with their lips. Their face is animated and they look warm and easy to talk to.

While I was writing these words in a local coffee shop, the cutest little girl walked up to my table eating a bagel with cream cheese. Then she put her head on my table in front of me and smiled at me. She, too, looked passively likeable. I asked her how old she was and she held up four fingers. She then moved around the table and carefully touched my face with the palm of her hand (I hadn't shaved that Saturday morning) and then gave me a smile that lit up the room.

Her mom came over and apologized, grabbed her hand, and walked her toward the door. The girl broke free and quickly ran back toward me. She again smiled and said, "Will you still be here when we come back?" I didn't say a word. Then she gave me the cutest smile and said, "Please—for me." I said okay and smiled back. She again started to walk toward the door and turned back and said with her little voice, "We will be back in 15 minutes." Then she dropped her bagel on the floor, picked it up, licked off some of the cream cheese, and walked away.

That was passive likeability. We both immediately liked each other even before a word was spoken. Passive likeability attracts others.

Attractiveness is also a factor in passive likeability, but only a piece of the puzzle. After all, we have all known attractive people whom we have not liked. But generally, the more attractive people are, the more likeable they are, the easier it is to draw people using personal power. What this tells us is that everything we do counts—dressing more neatly, pressing our clothes, polishing our shoes, standing and sitting straighter, whitening our teeth, freshening our breath. It all contributes to passive likeability!

## The Importance of the Face

Uncharismatic people unintentionally send unfriendly signals, negative energy, gloominess, despair, anger, frustration, and resentment to others. They do this silently without saying a word. Most people don't even realize they are doing it. They do it with their face.

When we first look at someone to determine likeability, we pay particular attention to the face. Uncharismatic people have angry and unfriendly habitual facial expressions. In contrast, charismatic people have pleasant habitual facial expressions. These facial expressions are on their faces even when other people are not around. They may be in their car driving and then glance in the mirror and their expression will still be pleasant.

As a side note, I cheat sometimes and look at the wrinkles on other people's faces to see their habitual facial expressions, before I even talk with them, to see how happy a person they tend to be over time (track record). I liked Jennifer, my wife, the first time I met her. She had little wrinkles around the corners of her mouth from where she smiled and laughed over the years. I instantly knew that she was a genuinely happy person and would be a lot of fun to be around (and I was right).

So what else are people looking for when they look at someone's face? They focus on three areas: the eyes, the cheeks, and the corners of the mouth, as follows:

- **Eye contact.** If people don't make eye contact with us, we instantly feel that something is wrong with them or that they are hiding something. And we know that where someone looks is where their attention is. Six-figure communicators have great eye contact with others. They smile with their eyes and cheeks. The eyes of happy people are more wide open than unhappy people. When people have wide-open eyes, we instantly sense that they are genuinely interested in us and it makes us feel good.

- **Cheeks.** Genuine people smile with their cheeks and their eyes. They are connected. When the cheeks rise, the eyes slightly close. Fake people smile only with their lips. You can see a wave of relaxation across the face of genuinely pleasant people.

- **Corners of the mouth.** If the corners of someone's mouth are down, we instantly know that the person probably is not in a good mood or not going to be pleasant to talk to. If the corners are up, the person probably is in a good mood and pleasant to be around. Don't focus on the mouth; focus on the corners.

When we look at people, we naturally start with their eyes and work our way down the face to the cheeks and the corners of the mouth. Each of these areas sends out signals of passive likeability. And we decide right then if a person is going to be pleasant to be around. Too many people destroy charisma before even opening their mouths.

Public speakers understand the importance of the face in setting people at ease. It's difficult for many people to stand before an audience and speak to them. A standard speaker's trick to ease discomfort is to look around the audience while speaking and pick out friendly faces. Look for encouraging faces and people who look like they are supporting you.

Just as speakers may look around the room for faces that encourage them, so do everyday people looking for faces that support them. All of us prefer to speak with someone who is pleasant, encouraging, and supportive. Be that face.

Look at your habitual facial expression now. Study the above-mentioned areas. What message does your expression send to others? Check yourself out at odd times during the day to see what messages your face habitually sends to others. You might be surprised.

## Listening

Passively likeable people are good listeners too. People are innately drawn to people who listen to them. People can always sense if you care about them—really care—and are further drawn to you if you do. The more you let the other person talk in conversation, the more they like you. Good listeners talk only about 20 percent of the time. So what do they do during the other 80 percent?

They show others that they are actively listening. They use gestures and facial expressions to encourage others to talk and to show them that they are actively listening to what they are saying. This is discussed further in Chapter 11.

## Fluidity

Charismatic people speak and move with grace and poise. They take their time and speak carefully and confidently, drawing the attention of others. Harsh tones repel people.

To be more charismatic, walk smoothly without bobbing your head, dipping your shoulders, swinging your arms wildly, or swaying back and forth. Step surely with minimal excess movement. Jerky or sudden movements alarm people or create uneasiness.

Speaking and moving in a smooth, easy style helps others to feel more comfortable and helps you to project confidence, self-control, and composure.

# 4. Ability to Help Others Feel Better

Good communicators know that most people are starved for feelings of importance, validation, and respect. Humans have a built-in craving for these needs to be satisfied. Charismatic people naturally draw others to them by instinctively identifying and addressing these needs. It is as if they soothe the burn. How do they do this?

It starts with talking with others. Charismatic people take the time to connect with people and show a sincere interest in them. They ask questions about how others are doing, what is happening in their lives, how their family is, and so on. Only by taking a little time to chat with people do you learn what is going on in their lives—their fears, excitement, the great things, the tough things, and their longings.

Once you get this information, you can gently address the person's needs by reassuring or praising them, using a bit of flattery or flirting, complimenting or showing appreciation, showing a general interest in what they are doing, or simply offering a smile and support. Sometimes it doesn't take much to help people feel better about themselves or their situations.

The only rule to helping others feel better is to do so genuinely and sincerely. You must come across as believable. If you do not come across as believable, you will lose your charisma and be perceived as a phony. People will feel manipulated. In short, your attempts at being charismatic will backfire.

Helping others feel better is simply fulfilling their basic human needs. Almost everyone wants to laugh, have fun, talk about their children or family, or feel good in some way. This makes life just a little better for you and everyone you come in contact with. Charismatic people do not always know what to talk about during their conversations, but they have an unusual ability to draw others to them by instinctually identifying and feeding basic human needs. And they do it genuinely. Some of these needs are listed below:

- To feel important or significant
- To feel appreciated or recognized
- To feel validated
- To feel connected with someone; for bonding
- To feel pride
- For approval
- For attention
- To feel respected
- For affection
- To feel attractive

# 5. Class

Class can be used in any situation to contribute to charisma. People with class do not go out of their way to please others; they have a quiet, cool professionalism about them. John Curtis, in his book *Operation Charisma: How to Get Charisma and Wind up at the Top,* says that "charismatic people expose the public only to qualities which promote their image." Let's look at the components of class.

- Good manners: Minimum manners don't cut it. People with class always take exceptional care of others by being courteous. They acknowledge the presence of others and make appropriate introductions to others. And if you have forgotten someone's name, simply say: "Please forgive me, I forgot your name."

  If talking with someone in an office setting, ask the other person to have a seat and try to make the other person feel comfortable. Turn off your telephone ringer and let incoming calls go to your assistant or voice mail. Offer your visitor (client) a glass of water or a cup of coffee.

  It doesn't matter if you like another person—be polite and treat all people well. Even if someone is rude, treat that person with respect. You'll find that treating a rude person well will give you instant class.

- Tact and diplomacy: People with class do not embarrass others; they allow them to save face when possible. If they are upset with someone or must tell someone something embarrassing or sensitive, people with class will pull people aside or out of the room to tell them privately.

- Language skills: People with class have outstanding vocabularies and they use colorful expressions, metaphors, and analogies. They clearly pronounce words and clearly articulate thoughts and ideas.

- Purposeful movement and carriage: People with class are aware of their posture, poise, and use of strong gestures. They walk with their heads up, surely, smoothly, and with purpose, rather than bobbing their head, lollygagging, or wandering aimlessly. If you listen to a woman walking down a hallway in heels, you can hear the difference. The walk of a confident woman sounds different. She steps surely and rhythmically, as do men in dress shoes. That's why people often look up when the woman or man comes into sight; people are expecting someone of significance.

- Effective use of timing: People with class use the two- and three-track mind to be aware of the presence of others and to judge appropriately. They use the "golden minute" wisely and effectively.

- Polish: People with class handle themselves smoothly. Certainly experience plays a role in this, but you can take the time to plan a few battle drills (Chapter 1) before important events. Rehearse them in your head before situations arise. This may include your introduction of someone to others, how you will address the host, what you will say, and so on. Visualize and play out scenes before they happen so you will come across smooth and polished during an event. Once you have established battle drills to draw from, you no longer have to plan these drills—they become second nature.

## Chance Encounters

People with class rarely talk business with customers or co-workers during public chance encounters. No one wants to talk business at the grocery store on a Saturday morning. Those who do come across as pushy, annoying, or unprofessional. Instead, simply wave, say hello, or wish the person a good morning, a great weekend, or a pleasant meal. Leave work at work. People with class leave work associates and customers alone during chance encounters.

If the customers or co-workers you see in the chance encounter are with others and you want to say hi and then introduce yourself, acknowledge the other person or the rest of the group, and apologize for interrupting. Doing this shows simple courtesy and respect for others. It's rude to talk with your colleagues and ignore the others they are with. Say your peace and politely excuse yourself from the group. If your colleague wants to talk with you, it is okay, but don't overstay your welcome.

# 6. Humor

Life is tough, and people with a sense of humor lighten the load for the rest of us. Most people are attracted to people who like to laugh and laugh often. Laughter is contagious, and people with a good sense of humor draw others to them. People in the personal power mind-set smile more often and laugh easily around others. They are not stingy with their smiles. They are often on the verge of a laugh.

Funny people are usually good at telling stories and jokes (discussed in Chapter 15). They find the humor in what went wrong. They are playful and even silly at times. But they also realize that they don't always have to be the funny ones. They make other people funny by pushing their fun buttons and "leading" them into laughter. In a group, people will "feed" off each other's laughter and stimulate the group further. This attracts more people into the group.

Paris opera houses in the early 1800s recognized the effect of "leading," when, in 1820, the claque, an organized body of professional applauders, began. Claqueurs not only were paid to sit in the audience and applaud at various times for various singers, but most of them had a fee schedule of charges for various types of applause. In his book *Influence: The Psychology of Persuasion*, Robert Cialdini discusses the power claqueurs had to influence. "So effective were they in stimulating genuine audience reaction with their rigged reactions that before long, claques (usually consisting of a leader, the chef de claque, and several individual claqueurs) had become an established and persistent tradition throughout the world of opera."

Today, the laugh track played on television situation comedies similarly encourages audiences to laugh, and the shows seem funnier than they actually are.

# Chapter Summary

- Charisma is the ability to draw people to you using only your personal power, relentless belief, and uplifting rapport. Uplifting rapport is not about likening or adapting yourself to others, like traditional rapport, but positively differentiating yourself, giving people so many positive feelings that they are attracted to you and want to be around you. Uplifting rapport includes positive energy, passive likeability, the ability to help others feel better, class, and humor.

- Belief. One must have relentless belief in himself, his ideas, a concept, or in others to be charismatic. Find something deep down within you that you can believe in and that you can own. Two techniques that may help you establish a firm belief are to link what you already believe in to what you are doing now, and simply speak from the heart.

- Positive Energy. Most people do not have positive energy and are attracted to people with it. People naturally gravitate to people with positive energy in the hope of getting a small piece of it, for they cannot generate it themselves. An important way to become charismatic is to give this energy to others.

- Passive Likeability. The more people like you, the more they are drawn to you. This likeability is passive, meaning that you are not actively praising, flirting, flattering, or complimenting others. It is a quiet charm. People who exude this passive likeability are warm, relaxed, in control, and confident. Others feel comfortable around these people. This likeability is often created before even a word is spoken. People who are passively likeable set people at ease and build rapport. Components of passive likeability include pleasant facial expressions and appealing personal appearance.

- Help Others Feel Better. The only rule for making others feel better is to do it genuinely and sincerely. Charismatic people first chat with others to get to know them. Then they instinctively address a need and fill it by reassuring, praising, complimenting, and so on. Some of these needs are listed below:
  - Need to feel important/significant
  - Need to feel appreciated/recognized

- Need for validation
- Need to feel connected with someone/bonding
- Need to feel pride
- Need for approval
- Need for attention
- Need to feel respected
- Need for affection
- Need to feel attractive

• Class. The first components of class are good manners, courtesy, and politeness. People with class take exceptional care of others by treating them well. They effectively use tact and diplomacy by being careful not to embarrass others and by allowing them to save face when possible. People with class are skilled with language. People with class are cognizant of how they move, how they carry themselves, and how they walk. They are aware of their posture, poise, and use of strong gestures. People with class use the two- and three-track mind to be constantly aware of others. Finally, they come across as polished, handling situations smoothly.

• Humor. People who can lighten the load of others with their good sense of humor will draw others to them.

## Daily Challenge

Focus on conveying relentless belief today. Incorporate such strong belief into three conversations that you blow the other person away. Believe in something so strongly that the other person can see it in your eyes. Exude more and more belief from the first conversation till the last. Note how your listeners respond to your unshakable belief.

## Executive Challenge

Have at least four conversations with people today and focus on two qualities of uplifting rapport in each conversation. One conversation might focus on passive likeability and humor; another might focus on class and positive energy. Also watch and learn how other people use these qualities.

# Seeing People's True Colors

## In This Chapter:

* Become a better judge of character
* Learn how to spot a phony
* Explore ways to get people to reveal their true colors

The scenario is all too familiar: A colleague seemed clever and charming and seemed to have his act together. You thought you were a good judge of character but later learned how wrong you were. When everything was going well, he was fun to be around. You felt honored to know him. But when things went awry, or when you were not around, he acted completely different. He got angry quickly, was rude to people, became stressed easily, and was simply a jerk. Although you hate to admit it, you were fooled and misjudged this person.

Learning to read people can be challenging. All of us have thought we knew someone, but weeks or years later learned that this person wasn't who we thought he was. Such people put their best foot forward around us and allow us to see only what they want us to see, a "specific" side of them. This scrambles our perceptions and makes it difficult to see others as they truly are.

How much of the real person are we seeing in others? How much do they show us or are they willing to show? Using the two- and three-track mind and other communication skills, we begin to see slight inconsistencies in people. We are given clues. We begin to notice when people accidentally show their true colors. We get a glimpse of their true colors when they "slip."

# Spotting a Phony

Some people laugh and joke around, but change their tune as soon as they turn around (or as soon as you have turned your back). Their smile gives way, almost instantly, to a straight face. Natural smiles do not do that; they linger. So a key to determining if someone is really having a good time and genuinely thinks you are entertaining is in their smile. See how quickly it goes flat.

One day I was in a physician's office and watched a saleswoman talk with a doctor. She giggled and laughed and thanked the doctor for his business. The doctor turned around and started to walk away. I watched this saleswoman a few more seconds and her smile immediately went straight. The doctor had forgotten his clipboard on the counter and quickly turned around after about three steps. That's when the doctor also noticed that this saleswoman, who had been giggling and laughing just three seconds earlier, now had not even the slightest smile on her face. We both quickly realized that this saleswoman was a fake. I'm sure the doctor felt manipulated and used.

Some people's phoniness is revealed unexpectedly when their straight face is reflected in a window or mirror. So watch those smiles a few seconds longer and see how quickly they dissolve. Be aware that this also works in reverse. When you are genuinely smiling and enjoying talking with someone, make sure you hold your smile a few extra seconds after you leave. Let your smile linger.

Another way to spot phonies is to watch how they treat others. Pay particular attention to how people treat those who are not in their group. Do they treat service people, such as waiters and hotel clerks, like second-class citizens? Do they talk down to, talk bad about, or belittle others? How do they treat their family and friends? How they treat other people is indicative of who they really are. They may be treating you better only temporarily, perhaps because they want something out of you. Use the two- and three-track mind techniques to gather more information.

# Getting People to Reveal Themselves

With enough time, energy, money, and emotional resources, the following questions will eventually get answered:
• Does the person get upset easily?
• How does the person act under stress or pressure?

- Does the person complain when the going gets tough?
- Is the person generally negative?
- What does the person really think about certain topics and beliefs?
- Is there important information you should know that others aren't telling you?

But many times we learn the hard way that we misjudged people. By the time we learn this, we feel we have too much invested in someone and just bite our lip, knowing that the person is not right for us or our company. We fret over what to do as we learn more and more unenviable qualities.

What happens, for example, if you date someone for a year and then learn how volatile her temper is or how she treats others? Decisions are tougher when you have invested so much time and energy. You often stick things out when you shouldn't. You hire people who looked good on paper and during the interview, but turned out not to be the person you thought. Deciding to keep people or let them go gets harder and harder as time progresses.

Just imagine how wonderful it would be to have the ability to quickly see people as they truly are before dating, hiring, or trusting them—before your heart gets involved, before you have a legal commitment, or before you hire someone to work for you. The ability to quickly see people as they really are will save you countless hours of pain, misery, and general unhappiness. This section reveals ways that you can accelerate the process of seeing someone's true colors.

## Observing People Under Stress

You can't depend on looks alone to figure people out and see what they are made of. Any situation creating a little stress and strain will quickly show someone's true colors. When people are tired, cold, wet, stressed, hungry, sleep-deprived, angry, or frustrated, you quickly see the true person within.

A week before a major brigade training exercise, I received a long-awaited new soldier into my platoon. This soldier stood 6 feet 4 inches in height, weighed about 210 pounds, had a chiseled face and a high and tight haircut, and was an obvious weight lifter. I thought to myself how great Private Roberts would be when the going got tough during the Joint Readiness Training Exercise.

During this exercise the platoon worked around the clock for almost two weeks. Each of us got no more than a few hours of sleep nightly, if we were lucky. Then one night it happened. About a week into the operation, at 0300 hours we received a mission to unload an aircraft carrying critical supplies. I sent a runner to wake up my new "super soldier" so he could prove himself.

But 10 minutes later, a small, ordinary soldier named Arkwright stood before me. He said the runner tried to get Roberts out of the rack, but Roberts said he was too tired and that it wasn't his turn. Unfortunately, because the aircraft was on the runway and I had no time, I sent Arkwright on the mission. It was Arkwright—who was just as tired, cold, wet, and miserable—who stepped up and made the mission happen. I had words with Roberts later.

## Traveling Together

Whether by plane or by car, taking a trip with someone—or going camping—often reveals a person's true colors. The time together under unpredictable circumstances can be just enough stress for the real person to come out. Miss an exit while driving, get lost, get a flat tire, forget the camera, sit all day in an airport because of a delayed or cancelled flight, lose your luggage, or fail to find a hotel easily—all of these can add stress and unpredictability to our lives.

Spend 24 or 48 hours straight with people and you will definitely start to see their true colors. They may be on their best behavior at first, but most cannot keep up that "charade" for more than a day, especially when stress is involved. A weekend trip often will reveal more about someone's true colors than spending an hour or two a week with the person over the course of a year.

*While tourists discover sights, travelers discover one another.*

## Playing Golf

One of the most fascinatingly aspects of golf is watching people you have known for a long time react under a little stress. I have seen what I thought were some of the nicest people get angry or upset enough to break a golf club over their knee or throw one or more clubs into the woods after a bad shot. Once I even saw a guy throw his driver off a cliff after a bad drive. Some people start off jovial and are a joy to be around, but slowly, after playing worse and worse, become no fun at all.

*In primitive society, when native tribes beat the ground with clubs and yell, it is called witchcraft; in civilized society it is called golf.*
— **old golf joke**

Then again, some people smile and shake their heads when they hit a ball into the woods. Others laugh at themselves and make a joke about how they are playing. One person I golfed with hit a ball at full power almost 150 yards straight up into the sky and yelled, "Hello NASA, come in NASA!"

After 18 holes of golf, you see the real person inside others. It's hard to "fake" your personality for more than an hour on a golf course. After four hours under pressure, people get a better feel for one another. This is quality time together, free of commercials, phones, and distractions. You can talk person to person.

# Drinking Alcohol

One evening I went to dinner with a fascinating woman whom I had known on a casual, professional, and social basis for more than four years. We went to the same church. She was not only a medical doctor, but had taken many vows of the church, though she did not officially consider herself a nun or a Sister.

We went to a beautiful Chinese restaurant and spent the evening talking. She ordered us both saki and later a gigantic Sapporo beer to go with our meal. I jokingly asked her if she was trying to get me drunk. She said she wasn't and smiled. She went on to tell me that people speak much more freely and honestly when they drink alcohol. I asked her what she meant. She laughed and said that alcohol was like truth serum. She said she wanted to see if I was always so nice and wondered if I would slip and let out more about myself than I planned to, my true colors.

Although she made those comments lightheartedly, they are true. People do tend to lose their inhibitions and say more than they ought to when drinking. I am certainly not advocating getting people drunk to interrogate them. But if people are casually drinking at dinner or out on the town, listen a little more closely. They may be telling you a little more than they planned to.

*"Don't Trust Anyone Who Will Not Drink with You."*
— **Old Russian Proverb**

# Chapter Summary

- How much of the real person are you seeing? Around others, people put their best face forward, allowing you to see only what they want you to see, a particular side. This scrambles our perceptions of people and makes it difficult to see people as they truly are.

- Watch someone's smile beyond the laughter and joking around to see how quickly it fades. Natural smiles linger.

- Watch how people treat others as a general rule, especially those outside of their own group.

- Certain questions about people take time to answer, such as the following:
  - Does this person get upset easily?
  - How does this person act under stress or pressure?
  - Does this person complain when the going gets tough?
  - Is this person generally negative?
  - What does this person really think about certain topics and beliefs?

- With enough time, energy, money, and emotional commitment, people will eventually learn who people truly are. But unfortunately, most people learn the answers to these questions the hard way or when it is too late.

- A bit of stress will accelerate the process of bringing out people's true colors. When people are tired, cold, wet, stressed, hungry, angry, or frustrated, we quickly see a side of them that is hidden but always there.

- Taking a trip with people is one way to see them as they truly are. People may be on their best behavior at first, but most cannot keep up that "charade" for more than a day, especially when stress is involved.

- Playing golf is another way to quickly see people's true colors. Pay particular attention to how someone deals with a bad shot. It's hard to fake a personality for more than an hour on a golf course. After four hours under pressure, people will definitely get a better feel for you and you for them.

- Having a drink or two opens people up to speaking much more freely and honestly. Pay close attention to what people say under the influence of alcohol.

## Daily Challenge

Today pay particular attention to how people treat others. See if you can find any inconsistencies in behaviors. Genuine people, showing their true colors, treat all people the same. People who treat others differently are inconsistent and unpredictable. Be alert around such people.

## Executive Challenge

Carefully push someone's negative "warm" buttons. A warm button is not quite enough to make someone angry, but just enough to make the person feel uncomfortable. Take this person a little out of his or her comfort zone by asking a few probing questions or by carefully bringing up topics to get this person to open up. Use caution because of the negative effects of the law of attraction—with one thought stimulating another thought, which attracts still another. As with drinking, playing golf, or traveling with people, your probing questions or comments can reveal how easily upset people get and how they handle themselves under a little pressure.

# The Secret to Great Conversation

## In This Chapter:

- Improve the quality of your interactions with others
- Learn the eight key reasons to let other people talk
- Become more interesting to others
- Establish stronger connections with people

Too many of us are too concerned with what to say when we are around others. We are worried about what to talk about and how to act. Each of us has heard someone talk incessantly about nonsense, and we do not want to come across that way ourselves. We all would like to be considered excellent conversationalists, interesting and funny.

But how many times have you tried to talk to someone and the conversation went nowhere—when it was idle small talk at best and you both walked away feeling awkward? This section discusses conversational basics that are worth considering as you develop or refine your communication style.

## Enable Others to Talk About Themselves

When talking with people, be genuine and show a sincere interest in them. Most people are interesting. You just have to find what makes them tick—find their positive hot buttons. If you show a sincere interest in others, you will no longer have to worry that you'll have an awkward conversation. This principle works so well because:

- The other person's hot button is the right conversational topic
- Letting others talk complements their mood

- Letting others talk allows their energy to flow
- Letting others talk enables them to think out loud, vent, and feel heard
- There is power in simply being with people
- Letting others talk enables them to bond and feel important
- You learn what other people know
- You learn how people process information

You will find that as you continue to get others to talk about themselves, an interesting thing begins to happen: They begin to like you more. This may sound strange but it's true. In fact, the less you say during the conversation, the better a communicator the other person will think you are. Let's take a look at how these points make you a great conversationalist.

## The Right Conversational Topic

For you to be considered interesting or stimulating, you must talk about what is interesting or stimulating to the other person. If the topic is interesting to you but "boring" to the other person, you come across as a bore. So it is a waste of time to worry about how to come across as interesting to others. You are practically guaranteed to be interesting if you talk about what others want to talk about. Ironically, it is their topics that make you interesting, not yours.

A few years ago I was chatting with an old man in the waiting room at a rural West Virginia clinic. I had just gotten back from traveling to Russia and proceeded to tell him about my adventures abroad. Knowing that he would probably never go there, I thought it might be interesting to talk about while we waited. He politely nodded and listened to my adventures. He didn't say a word for 10 minutes and smiled only occasionally.

I then asked the man if he did anything over the summer (my inflection point), and he told me about the family get-together at his house. He was laughing, giggling, and waving his arms as he talked. The more he talked, the more fun he was having. He talked about his grandchildren, his neighbors, his wife, and all of the things they were doing. He was like a different person. The get-together must have been quite an event.

He really didn't care much about the Russian economy, Red Square, or the Cosmonaut museum. He just listened to me. Although my Russia trip was one of the highlights of my life, I came across as boring to him! That's why the other person's topic is always the right conversation topic. It is usually safe ground and of interest to the other person. You can't go wrong.

## Complementing People's Moods

When other people talk, it complements their mood. When we talk, it complements ours! When we approach people, we are usually oblivious to their mood or what happened to them that day. Poor communicators talk about only what they want to talk about and are oblivious to others' needs and concerns. They are usually poor listeners. When they let others speak, it is typically a token gesture.

I've made the mistake of coming across very cheery and later learning that the person to whom I was talking had just lost a loved one. And even if no one died, people have a right to be quiet and relaxed without being overwhelmed by someone's high spirits. Match others' moods and let them do the talking. You can't say anything wrong if they are doing the talking.

I'm reminded of my experience with poor Dr. P. I had just gotten a haircut downtown, the sun was shining, and I felt great. I happened to see Dr. P. parked just down from the barber shop, sitting in his car flipping through some papers. I knocked on the car window, and he rolled it down. "Hi, how are you!" I shouted. I didn't wait for a response and went on to talk about how great everything was going in my life. Months later he told me that when I'd seen him, he was sitting in front of his lawyer's office, shuffling through divorce papers (not his idea) and realizing that his wife was to get the house, the car, everything. I should have used the two- and three-track mind techniques to take Dr. P.'s pulse before talking with him. Remember that when other people do the talking, it is the right conversational topic and it complements their mood.

## Allowing People's Energy to Flow

Think back to a time when you were so excited about something that you couldn't wait to tell someone about it. As you started to tell your news, the other person interrupted you, asked too many questions, and then changed the subject. A parent might have interrupted you to correct your grammar. You were angry! You were so keyed up only moments before, but now you were frustrated that you couldn't share your news, angry that the person wouldn't listen, and stuck in a bad mood. Your energy had gone from pure excitement to resentment in less than 60 seconds!

Six-figure communicators don't kill the energy of others—they feed it! They feed it by asking short questions and making short comments. Ask questions such as "Then what happened?" "Who was he?" "What did you do next?" "What happened?" Responses might include laughter, appropriate body language, or comments such as "Wow!" "No way!" "Really?" Feed other people's energy; don't take it.

## Enabling People to Think Out Loud, Vent, and Be Heard

Many people think and vent out loud. Six-figure communicators realize when people are doing this and let others speak. Women tend to be better at this than men. Poor communicators constantly interrupt, take over conversations, and spout off resolution. One top female communicator I interviewed said that most men don't realize that women are simply venting and thinking out loud. "That is why we get so upset when men interrupt us," she said. "It causes us to lose our train of thought and momentum. We have to get it out of us."

Most people need to feel heard. They need to feel that they are connecting with others. Six-figure communicators are often heard repeating or summarizing what the other person just said. The best salespeople, counselors, and managers do this. They acknowledge comments, summarize, and clarify.

## The Power in Just Being with Someone

Again, too many people are worried about what to say during a conversation. They don't realize that there is incredible power in just being with someone. If we think back to the best times in our childhood, most of us remember the being, not the talking. We remember going to a baseball game with our dad, fishing, camping, and spending time together. And when people we love are troubled, then simply being with them is often the best course. We don't have to say a word, but people feel better just to have someone with them.

## Enabling Others to Bond and Feel Important

All of us want to feel important. When we talk, we feel important. When others talk, they feel important. In fact, the more talking people do, the more significant they feel. And the more important we make others feel, the more important we become to them.

When other people talk, we learn more about them. We build social capital by discovering what we have in common. The more we learn, the more we bond. Relationships strengthen as they move from the superficial to the meaningful. Small talk gets eliminated and we begin to talk about what is truly interesting, making conversations more genuine. Relationships improve.

## Learning What Others Know

When other people tell us what they know about a subject, then we know what they know in addition to what we know! We also know their perspective, what they look for, and what is important to them. Six-figure communicators carefully listen to these valuable pearls of information. They are exponentially better off for listening, for they alone know both sides. They alone fully understand the entire picture. This powerful combination of knowing what they themselves know and what the customer knows or wants makes top salespeople top salespeople. Top salespeople gather as much information as possible by asking questions and carefully listening to customers. Then they tailor that information into their presentation to make it incredibly effective.

While interviewing top salespeople in various industries, I would always ask: What is the No. 1 mistake new salespeople make? One of the most common answers was that they talk too much! "Good listening separates new salespeople from the pros," said one top performer. Several others bluntly said, "Learn to keep your mouth shut." The majority of top salespeople interviewed for this book came across as introverts, which was surprising. You would think they would be outgoing. But top salespeople, including extraverts, have learned to keep their mouths shut and use it primarily to ask questions. They know that the customer should be doing the vast majority of the talking and they the listening.

A top real estate agent was one of the salespeople who told me that new agents talk too much. She said poor agents walk into a house and talk about how wonderful the kitchen cabinets are or how beautiful the view might be. She said her secret was to close her mouth and let the customers get their own impressions of the house. She carefully listens to what is important to the customer and what they want. When she clearly understands what they are looking for, she sells it to them (saving time and energy). There is no arm twisting or pressure closing. She merely matches customers to their wishes.

Michael Feldman, a comedian and talk-show host on National Public Radio, is hilarious interviewing people on his show, *Whad'Ya Know?* If you listen closely to him, however, you realize it is not Michael who is funny, but the things other people say while he talks with them. He is so good at listening that he picks up on all of the funny things people say while they are being interviewed. Then he will ask them a question about those things. It is listening to these interviewed members of his studio audience that really makes the show. Lesson: You don't have to do all of the talking to come across as funny.

## Learning How People Process Information

If you're not doing all of the talking, then you have an opportunity to learn how people process information and what their belief systems are. Intelligent people often are more interested in why someone says something or what beliefs cause others to think a particular way than what those beliefs actually are. But most people get too wrapped up in tidy labels, such as "conservative" or "feminist" or "evangelical" or "environmentalist." What is more interesting is listening to why. You already know all of the answers from your personal belief system; instead, listen to why people believe what they believe. This takes you to a higher conversational plane, plus you might learn something.

A top real estate agent explained to me that it is not just what people say that matters; it is how they process information. She pays particular attention to how people think. She told me that she asks people exactly what they want over the phone, gathering as much information as possible, before meeting with them. She then researches suitable homes. Then when she meets the customers for the first time, she has them tell her again exactly what they are looking for. This does two things: (1) it helps customers refocus on what is important to them, and (2) it allows her to listen to the customer.

While customers are talking, she learns how they think and process information. She listens to hear if the customers are analytical, wanting to see lots of charts and graphs, local school rankings, and crime statistics. Or whether they want to "feel" secure, have nice neighbors, have a sunny open lawn, or a nice view. She listens to how customers want their information, how they process it, who the decision maker is, and what they want. This is advanced listening.

The best salespeople have often been referred to as chameleons. They not only present information the way customers want it, but they adapt themselves to the other person quickly. They instinctively keep their mouths shut, listen, and get a feel for the other person, assessing their mood, energy level, and personality before saying a word. Then they match them by adapting their style accordingly.

# Chapter Summary

- Most people are too concerned with what to talk about with others and how to act. We all would like to be considered excellent conversationalists, interesting and funny. And we become that way by letting others talk.

- Letting others talk works so well because:
  - The other person's hot button is the right conversational topic
  - It complements their mood
  - It does not cut off their energy
  - People think out loud
  - People vent
  - People feel heard
  - There is power in simply being with people
  - People feel important
  - People bond
  - It enables you to learn what they know
  - You learn how they process information.

# Daily Challenge

Most people remember little after their conversations with others. Why? They talk too much. This is one reason people forget the names of others or can't remember much about what others say during a conversation.

Today's assignment is to practice active listening. After your conversations with others, when you get back to your car or other private location, number a sheet of paper from one to five. Try to list five newly learned bits of information. Good listeners will find this easy while poor listeners will be surprised at how difficult this is, even after a lengthy conversation. This exercise will force you to listen to others better and to work on improving your listening skills. This skill is a fundamental communication skill and critical to networking.

If you have trouble starting a conversation, use the magic formula (Chapter 5). If the conversation is not smooth or the other person doesn't talk very much, use simplified buttonomics (Chapter 4) to quickly find someone's core or superficial positive hot buttons.

## Executive Challenge

A successful salesman I know had his boss working with him for two days. The boss carried two stopwatches in his pocket. He used one to time how long the salesman spoke and the other to time how long the customer spoke. At the end of the sales call, the salesman was amazed that he spoke roughly 97 percent of the time. We both learned from that lesson! Any idea how much of the conversation you dominate?

Your challenge today is to get three people to talk fully 90 percent of the time. Keep your introductions and conclusions short. Acknowledge, clarify, and summarize information others provide. Experiment with steering a conversation only by asking questions.

# Part III

Part III of this book is about talking to people—both the psychology behind it and the many secrets six-figure communicators use to improve their daily communication. It is not designed to trick, manipulate, or con people. Nor does it rely on categorizing people into personality types and trying to remember who is in which. Instead, it uses simple, universal principles to help you better communicate.

It's easy to talk to someone when you and the other person are in a good mood. It's easy to talk to someone when there is little stress or few interruptions. It's easy to talk among friends. It's easy to talk with someone you click with or have something in common with. It's easy to talk to people when everything is in your favor. So why then do you need communication skills?

Because people are not always in a good mood! They get tired, angry, disappointed, hurt, fed-up, embarrassed, neglected, and frustrated. We all have bad days; it's just part of being human. And some people are just harder to talk to and approach than others. Or maybe it is you who is not feeling good or feeling worn out at the end of the day. But you still need to talk with people.

Part III discusses techniques and a few "tricks" to improve your communications with others when communicating is difficult. These things are what six-figure communicators do naturally to set people at ease and get others to open up. For them, these are not tricks or techniques, but how they express themselves and talk with others daily.

The goal is not for you to become an insincere person using these techniques, but to learn to give people your undivided attention and put people at ease around you. These techniques have worked for so many six-figure communicators and they can work for you. Remember that the more successful you are at talking with people, the easier and more enjoyable it will be for you. And the more successful you will become at everything you do.

# The Power of Words

## In This Chapter:

- Learn the remarkable power of words
- Learn how words physically change the human body
- Use words now to change people's lives
- Add punch to words using simple delivery strategies
- Discover two listening secrets that will change your life

A great responsibility goes along with opening our mouths, for the words we use, like an arrow shot from a bow, can never be taken back. Words must be chosen carefully. Words die hard and are continually repeated out loud and mentally. "What did he mean by that? Why did he say that to me?" Each word attracts other words, and thus thoughts. And through the law of attraction they begin to snowball, setting off a volatile chain reaction of thoughts and emotions.

## Words Change People

Too many of us take words for granted. We speak without thinking. We put our foot in our mouth. We ramble. We snipe. We insult. We harass. We tease. And we throw salt in people's wounds. We can be careless, unthinking, and shortsighted when speaking.

The saying "sticks and stones can break my bones, but words will never hurt me" is only true in theory. In reality words can maim, cripple, injure, scar, and destroy people's lives. Words are real things that can do real damage to people daily, mutilating and disfiguring psyches for days, if not forever. Words can be like poison, slowly destroying their victims and reducing people's will to endure. Too many people throughout the ages have ended their lives in horrific ways because of words. And countless others quietly have borne the pain.

Fortunately, words also inspire, reassure, and set people at ease. They provide wisdom, meaning, clarification, and direction. They reduce pain and uplift. They show faith, hope, and love; make people feel special; and positively touch people's lives. Words can increase and restore people's sense of well-being. They also help people recognize their gifts, talents, and potential. Words help people strive for excellence and become more than they already are. They help people put their lives back together, reduce their pain, and help lighten the mental load people carry. Words make people feel special.

And if you are a person who does this for people—providing badly needed words when people are at their worst—not only will you never be forgotten, but you certainly will have made a difference to at least one human being.

## Word Permanency

People never forget key words that were spoken to them, positively or negatively affecting their lives. Many people can even tell you the exact time and place that such words were uttered, burned so indelibly into their minds. Many people remember the words so well because the words changed them in some way. Such words never die and are often played back over and over in our minds or bottled up for years in our hearts.

People tend to share with others the immortal words that made a difference in their lives so that others may benefit. Some words have such a profound impact that the recipients feel obligated to travel back, sometimes thousands of miles, to the originator years later. These recipients find meaning in thanking the person and sharing the impact of the words on their lives.

## How Words Change the Physical Body

In his book *The Lost Art of Healing*, Bernard Lown, professor emeritus of cardiology at the Harvard School of Public Health, writes how words can physically affect the functioning of the body, both negatively and positively. "I know of few remedies more powerful than a carefully chosen word. Patients crave caring, which is dispensed largely with words. Talk, which can be therapeutic, is one of the underrated tools in a physician's armamentarium."

## The Effect of Words on the Heart

In his first example, Dr. Lown reports about making hospital rounds one morning with his colleague Dr. Levine and other physicians. After a rapid examination, Dr. Levine told the doctors that the patient they were seeing had TS. Then Dr. Levine hurriedly moved on to the next patient. But some doctors stayed behind to listen to the patient's heart. Dr. Lown was one of them, and he heard the woman murmur, "This is the end. Dr. Levine said I had TS." Dr. Lown replied, "Yes, of course you have TS. What do you think TS means?" The patient responded: "It means terminal situation."

Dr. Lown tried to explain to the patient that it was an abbreviation for tricuspid stenosis. But she was no longer listening. All attempts to reassure her failed. All of a sudden her breathing became labored and rapid. She could no longer lie back on the bed. "Only minutes earlier her lungs had been completely clear. A chest X ray confirmed that her lungs now were flooded with fluid …"

Later that evening the woman was "overwhelmed with pulmonary edema" and died. But what was interesting, Dr. Lown wrote, is that "patients with tricuspid stenosis waste away and die slowly, not with frothing congestion of the lungs. Such congestion is invariably the result of a failing left ventricle, but her left ventricle was not diseased."

Words physically changed this patient's normal body functioning and set off a sudden chain reaction rippling through her body, quickly killing her.

Similarly, words and beliefs can heal patients as well. The following account is about a different patient, on his death bed. Dr. Lown had already written on the patient's chart "do not resuscitate." This man had had a heart attack and since then had experienced "every complication in the book." Nearly half of his heart muscle was destroyed and his lips were a purplish blue from lack of oxygen in his blood.

Then one day the man mysteriously started to get better and within a week improved so significantly that he was discharged from the hospital. Six months later the man walked into Dr. Lown's office looking to be in "remarkably good health." The doctor was amazed and convinced it was a "miracle." Lown reported that "while this patient's heart was badly damaged, he was free of congestion and largely asymptomatic."

The patient said it was no miracle, that he could name the exact time he started getting better—when the doctor made the comment that he had a "wholesome gallop" to his heart. The patient said, "I figured that if my heart was still capable of a healthy gallop, I couldn't be dying, and I got well. So you see, Doc, it wasn't a miracle. It was mind over matter."

What the patient didn't understand—fortunately, as it turns out—was that a gallop was a bad thing, an "overstretched and failing ventricle straining ineffectively to pump blood," to be exact.

Dr. Lown's accounts show that the words doctors use can physically change human physiology, both positively and negatively. There is clearly a link between what patients hear and how they respond. Words can physically affect the human heart.

## Words and Placebos

In all large drug trials, some patients will be healed by placebo, regardless of the disease or condition. A placebo is merely sugar disguised as a pill with no healing properties. It must be said that there are not many patients healed by placebo, but there are always some. Why? The sugar pill cannot scientifically heal, so healing can't come from the pill directly. Then what is it? It comes from the belief in or expectation from the pill. And what created this belief or expectation? The words the doctor used while prescribing the pill to the patient.

*"Words are, of course, the most powerful drug used by mankind."*
—**Rudyard Kipling**

Let's take a look at the healing rates of one of the most common medications for gastro esophageal reflux disease, Prilosec.[1] In one arm of a small clinical trial comparing the healing rates of patients with erosive esophagitis (inflammation of the esophagus), clinicians compared Prilosec 20 mg, Prilosec 40 mg, and a placebo at week four and week eight to find the number of patients healed on each pill. Almost a third of patients were healed with the sugar pill at week eight! (In comparison, 89 percent and 86 percent of patients were healed on Prilosec 20 mg and 40 mg, respectively, by week eight.[2]) This study is one of many that provides important clues into the power of belief and expectation created by words.

Patients can be healed by believing that a placebo is an active drug, but they also can be disfigured. Of patients with hypercortisolism (excessive production of the hormone cortisol), a placebo caused some of them to experience adverse reactions.[3] Of the 107 patients taking placebo, 14 developed acne, 12 bruised easily, six developed swollen ankles, and two developed skin striations. Most striking, two patients developed what is called a buffalo hump on their back and four had their face so swollen that they developed what doctors call a moon face.[4]

How did words cause people to grow humps on their backs or make their faces swell so dramatically? It couldn't have come from the inactive sugar pill. And the odds are that the physician didn't say anything negative about the medication if he or she was prescribing it. No, perhaps the negative words came from the patients themselves, through their own negative thoughts. Maybe these patients didn't get the symptom relief they had hoped for and became pessimistic or even cynical about the "medication." Or perhaps they were treated poorly by the physician, hospital, or others participating in the clinical trial.

Our internal thoughts and the words we habitually think probably have a greater impact on our physical bodies than we realize.

## Words and Depression

Depression afflicts 19 million American adults annually. This disorder affects body, mood, and thoughts. It can disable people or keep them from functioning or feeling well. People afflicted with depression often feel sad, hopeless, helpless, worthless, and tired. They may have difficulty sleeping or concentrating and may experience significant weight loss or gain.

Although scientists are still unclear about the causes of depression, they do know that critical neural circuits in the brains of depressed people do not function properly, and that neurotransmitters—chemicals used by the nerve cells to communicate—are out of balance.[5]

Regardless of its cause, the two primary treatments for depression are drug therapy and psychotherapy, commonly referred to as "talk therapy." Talk therapy alone can be effective in treating patients with mild depression, and more effective when combined with antidepressant medication in treating patients with moderate to severe depression. The three primary types of talk therapy focus on changing negative styles of thinking and behaving, working on disturbed relationships, and helping patients resolve conflicted feelings.

Scientists know that talk therapy has been proven to help restore critical neural circuits in the brain and rebalance important neurotransmitters that help nerve cells communicate. Can talk therapy also help prevent these chemical imbalances by reducing stress and improving psychological well-being? This remains to be seen.

# Words of Wisdom That Change Lives

Life-changing experiences come from the resolution of conflicts. You cannot have a "life change" without a resolution, which means you must have a conflict first. And when you are concerned, troubled, or worried, you actively seek answers. From whom do you find the words of wisdom you seek? Research has shown that the words that change your life come from whomever or whatever is with you at your time of trouble.

In her book *The Right Words at the Right Time*, Marlo Thomas compiled 109 stories that famous people sent to her about the words that changed their lives. The stories came from such luminaries as Lance Armstrong, Walter Cronkite, Bill Cosby, Rudolf Giuliani, Steven Spielberg, and Barbara Walters. Ninety-eight percent of the respondents told of life-changing words from sources other than themselves, such as teachers, parents, friends, strangers, mentors, movies, books, or songs.

We can learn two important lessons from this about changing people's lives with words:

- Everyday people like us have the greatest impact on others. This is primarily because we are the ones who are around during people's times of confusion and can offer our humble or inspiring words while they are making important choices about their lives.
- If people don't get the inspiring words they need from people like us (everyday people who are close to them), they will get them from strangers, books, songs, movies, psychologists, or a higher power.

In the absence of quality conversation during times of trouble, people will go elsewhere for ideas and solutions. What makes this unfortunate is that troubled people frequently are not in a positive or solid state of mind when they look for answers, making them more vulnerable to poor advice or solutions. This is especially true for children in conflict, not only because children are impressionable, but also because, in the absence of high-quality conversation with their parents, children will get answers elsewhere. And those may not be good solutions.

# Helping Others with Your Words

Words that change people must be tailored to the individual and must be exactly what is needed at the time. But how do you know when is the "right time"? You can't talk to people about a problem before the problem is even uncovered. Simply spouting off resolutions without a connection to a specific problem is preaching.

Six-figure communicators know how to either find problems or expand concerns into problems. They realize that life-changing words don't start with them. They start with the other person, with his conflict. In other words, six-figure communicators don't teach until the student is ready.

This section helps you read people and situations so you can give them good, accurate advice in their times of trouble.

## Keeping in Touch

Being able to offer words of wisdom to people in need requires frequency of communication. Frequency is far more important than how long you spend communicating at any given time. Short phone calls weekly or monthly, just to say hello and check in are more important than hour-long phone calls once in a blue moon. Six-figure communicators talk frequently to people they care about. That is why they always seem to have great timing, calling when someone is going through a tough time.

If you communicate infrequently and superficially, it is easy to miss when others are going through a tough time. Of course people don't always ask for advice, but if you just happen to call when someone is going through a tough time, you can have particular influence. If you call often, you will be more likely to catch others at "just the right time" or when they are in the midst of tough choices.

## Reading People Accurately

Frequency of communication also helps you know people better—their background, history, strengths, weaknesses, tendencies, and so on. This makes your words particularly credible. Communicating infrequently makes it difficult to know people well enough to give them advice tailored to their particular situation.

• Six-figure communicators are extraordinary at reading people and their situations. They do this using both the two-track and three-track minds (Chapter 3). They hear what people say and see what they don't say. This helps them better detect trouble, discover concerns, sense uneasiness, and put more accurate words into their mouths.

- Six-figure communicators know how to find or draw out conflict in people constructively through conversation. Without talking to people, they cannot draw out their conflict or trouble to know what words to use. Poor communicators may recognize that something is generally wrong, but they may be unable to identify it, so they throw out random words and thoughts in the hope that something they say helps. But the way to draw information out of people and achieve conversational depth is by probing and asking good questions.

## Using Core Messages to Make Your Point

Six-figure communicators use a core message to keep their counsel on track. This message focuses and simplifies their point. It is a small morsel that is easy to understand and makes sense, something that the other person can apply right away.

Poor communicators, by contrast, ramble too much, offering too much useless information. People stop listening when they are overwhelmed with inappropriate or irrelevant verbiage.

To do this, boil your message down to its essence, knowing that any more will dilute or cloud its meaning. Use as few words as possible. Core messages are always fewer than a dozen words. The fewer words in a core message, the more effective it will be. The core message is the take-home message. Examples of this include: it will pass, we will survive, let it go, what do you want?, at least you tried, stay the course, let it be, focus is power, I'm proud of you, skate the ice, always look forward—never back, time will heal all, the sun will rise tomorrow, bring it on, life is good, finish the race, finish the job, etc.

Sometimes this core message is in the form of a punch line, ending a story with a point. This is not a joke, but a core message used to drive home a point. It is the take-home message that people remember.

Zig Ziglar, the legendary motivational speaker, cleverly uses this technique in a story he tells about processionary caterpillars. He ends his story with the question: "Do you know why the caterpillars died from starvation and exhaustion, with food literally inches away?" His punch line and core message: "Because they confused activity with accomplishment."[6] Ziglar understands the power of a good story and uses its core message as the story's punch line.

# Eight Strategies to Make Your Words Count

What are the best ways to penetrate someone's thick skull, touch their heart, or impart words of wisdom? What are the best ways to make messages stick with people? The key lies in the delivery. The more effective the delivery of the message, the more likely it is to get through. Let's take a look at eight delivery strategies.

1.  Set people up to really listen and take heed before you impart your wisdom, advice, or counsel to others. Too many people speak before the other person is really ready to listen. Here are a few ways six-figure communicators put others in the receive mode to get their attention before delivering their message:
    *   Smile before giving the message.
    *   "Please sit down; I want to tell you something that I have never told anyone else ..."
    *   "Just remember this ..."
    *   "Look at me; I am only going to say this once ..."
    *   "I want to say one thing to you that is very important ..."
    *   "I never say this to anyone, so I want you to listen good ..."
    *   "I have been wanting to tell you something for a long time ..."
    Regardless of how you phrase it, the general idea is to get people's undivided attention before making an important point. This enhances delivery.

2.  Tell a short story and back it up with a reminder gift or token. Marlo Thomas recounts advice from her father at a tough point in her career:
    "I raised you to be a thoroughbred. [core message] When thorough-breds run, they wear blinders to keep their eyes focused straight ahead with no distractions, no other horses. They hear the crowd but they don't listen. They just run their own race. That's what you have to do." The next night before going on stage, Marlo was handed a white box with a red ribbon around it in her dressing room before the show. Inside was an old pair of horse blinders with a little note that read, "Run your own race, Baby."[7]

Reminder items work really well after a story. For example, if your core message was "I raised you to be the leader of the pack," a dog tag with the name of the message recipient would reinforce the message. If it was a story of survival and perseverance under adverse circumstances, then perhaps an old pocket knife that got you through a tough situation would be a great reminder to reinforce your message.

Keep reminder items or tokens inexpensive, small, and linked in some way to the story. Sentimental items can add special significance. As its name implies, a reminder item, vs. a token, often works best if you wait a short time before giving or sending it.

A twist on using reminder items or tokens is to start with the object in mind and then create a story around it. For example, you could start with a flower and create a story around it that would incorporate your core message of "forget the past and enjoy the present." The following day, you could send a single flower with a note attached, repeating that core message to reinforce it in the person's mind.

3. Deliver a core message in an unusual way, such as by telegram, letter, card, note (handwritten or email), picture, film, or personal delivery. The fun of cards and notes is in their placement, such as in lunch bags, on the seat of a car, on the windshield, or in a purse, coat pocket, or shoes. Sometimes the core message alone is enough for a card or note. Another advantage of notes and cards is that they are tangible and meaningful and can be saved. Ever send someone a telegram?

4. Use body language to add an extra punch to your message. This would include sending silent communication to others to show genuineness, concern, confidence, or other meanings. You might touch someone on the arm or shoulder while talking with them, squint a little to show added sincerity, smile before or after you say something, hold someone or squeeze their hand while talking with them, or clutch your heart while talking sincerely.

5. Deliver your core message and then leave the room quietly. This is not intended as a way to get the last word in, but to give others time to think about your words and to let them soak in. When you stay in

the room, by contrast, people are tempted to question or rebut what you said. The idea is to deliver carefully thought-out advice to inspire, motivate, or get people thinking. If done carefully, this delivery strategy can intensify your words.

6.  Use the law of reciprocity to enhance your delivery. Do something for others and they will feel a sense of obligation to do something for you. At the very least, they will give you a few moments of their time. Taking them to dinner (and paying for it), inviting them to your house for dinner, or giving them a gift will usually make them more receptive to your ideas and information. They feel a sort of obligation to at least listen to what you have to say.

    People who sell time shares or pyramid marketing schemes often use this tactic. They give prospects a "free dinner," set of kitchen knives, or Disney World passes just to "listen" to a presentation. They know that people usually will sit through a presentation to "pay" for their meal. And then the people will take in the sales pitch more easily. The bigger the "something," the greater people seem to listen.

7.  Talk with people in a different environment or atmosphere and your words will make a more profound impact. The same message given over coffee at a café, instead of a boardroom, will not only set people at ease better, but also increase the penetration of your message (see Chapter 5). People usually listen better when they are relaxed and in a positive state. Their habitual defenses go down. Talking by a lake, for example, without other people around, can ensure that your words will be better received than if they are delivered in front of family, friends, or strangers. This is because people often act differently around others. Although praise in front of others can increase the effectiveness of words, admonishment in front of others can diminish their effectiveness.

8.  Use a verbal shock to motivate someone to action. Many people don't like to be told what to do. They don't like to be told that they are not cut out for something, that they will never make it, that they will never go anywhere in this world, or that they will never amount to anything. Teenagers, especially, do not like to be told what to do. Something must be their idea for action to take place. All we can do is to gently "shock" and paint a different picture for others.

The idea is to shock people into seeking action—sort of a wake-up call. They must make the choice to change. This is not a time to tell others how to change, or what needs to be done, but to "wake" them up. That is all that is required. If they get "woken up," they will take the required steps on their own or be motivated to seek help.

My friend Matt offers an example of this strategy. The words that changed his life came from his high school guidance counselor. She sat Matt down in the office and closed the door. She took out his file, looked him in the eye, and told him not to go to college! She told him he was not cut out for it. Instead, she told him to go to a technical school or into the Army. Matt said that as soon as she told him not to go to college, he had to go to college!

A good way to use this technique is to build up the situation and then deliver the shock. Invite someone to lunch or dinner, wine and dine them, and build up good feelings, trust, and rapport—and then deliver the shock. Pull someone aside into your office, close the door, build up a little fear, and then deliver the message.

Or do the opposite. Catch people feeling great, having a great day, in a great mood, and then shock or challenge them to action. This uses positive energy to motivate. People make better decisions when they are in a positive state of mind—the personal power mind-set. But both techniques work.

A word of caution about the negative-challenge delivery strategy: Use it for people who don't like to be told what to do. Don't use it for people who might listen to you and heed your advice.

Proceed by building up the other person slightly and then negatively challenge him to step up. You could start, for example, by saying that you were impressed with the way he handled a particular situation and that you have noticed he has a flair for people. But because he can't get his grades up, doesn't have the ability to concentrate, and is constantly getting in trouble, you have to recommend that he drop out of school and seek work as a busboy or whatever job he can find. "You just don't have what it takes here, and I think that line of work is best for you."

When a restaurant customer told my former boss Vijay that he had a nice smile, "for a waiter"—that was enough to challenge Vijay to get his MBA!

# Don't Let Negative Words Get You Down

Every one of us, like it or not, is the recipient of thousands of negative words during our lifetime. But these negative words need not tear you down. The truth is, words have no meaning except the meaning we give them. It's what we do with words that separates the real winners and losers in life.

## Turn Negative Words into Fuel!

Winners don't take negative words to heart or ignore them. They turn negative words into fuel and use them to their advantage to propel them to greater heights.

When the president of CNN called the assignment desk and said "I never want to see her on the air again," Katie Couric was not destroyed by these words nor did she disregard them. She took her father's childhood advice that "even the most critical words can bring about the most positive results. My boss's bleak forecast of my future only fueled my ambition." And she later got to enjoy a bit of "I told you so."[8] Couric learned at a young age to use other people's words to her advantage and to turn their negative comments into fuel to fire up her ambition and drive.

Muhammad Ali did the same. His most inspiring words came from a teacher who thought he was nothing but "another loudmouth." He said that she kept putting him down and did not believe in anyone's potential. What inspired him was when she said: "You ain't gonna be nuthin." Here is an excerpt from his letter in *The Right Words at the Right Time*:

"I won the Golden Gloves in Louisville when I was seventeen. And then the next year, it happened: I won the Gold Medal at the 1960 Rome Olympics. I was the greatest in the whole world! First thing I did when I got home was to go straight to that teacher's classroom. 'Remember when you said I wouldn't ever be nuthin'?"[9]

Learn to turn words to fuel and it will change your life too!

## Be a Little Deaf

Bob, one of my good friends and co-workers, had a different strategy. He once told me his secret to his 25-year marriage to his wife, Tammy. He looked at me, and with the slightest smile on his face, said: "Selective hearing!"

The Honorable Ruth Bader Ginsburg, Associate Justice of the U.S. Supreme Court agrees. She said that the morning she was getting married, her fiancé's mother put something into her hand and said, "I am going to give you some advice that will serve you well. In every good marriage, it pays sometimes to be a little deaf." She had placed a set of wax earplugs into Ruth's hand (core message/reminder gift).

Ginsburg writes that "sometimes people say unkind or thoughtless things, and when they do, it is best to be a little hard of hearing—to tune out and not snap back in anger or impatience."[10] She knows that we all get upset sometimes, rightly or wrongly. We all have good days and bad days. But sometimes it is best to be a little deaf, for all of us occasionally say things rashly out of fear or anger.

Whether you are getting married, are married, or never want to get married, this advice works with all people. Whether you call it "selective hearing" or purposefully "being a little deaf," ignoring other people's words can prevent anger, frustration, and misery. Put another way: take everything with a grain of salt.

## Chapter Summary

- Words Change People: People never forget key words spoken to them, which positively or negatively affect their lives. And then they pass the immortal words on to others so that others can benefit.

- Words Change the Physical Body: Words can kill, heal, depress, cure, and disfigure people.

- Words of Wisdom That Change Lives: Everyday people like us have the greatest impact on others, so it's important to keep in touch so we can help people in their time of need.

- Helping Others with Your Words: Six-figure communicators talk to people regularly, read people and their situations extraordinarily well, uncover constructively any conflict that people are going through, and boil their counsel down to its simplest form using a core message.

- Eight Strategies to Make Your Words Count:
  - Set people up to really listen and take heed before imparting knowledge.

- Tell a short story and use a reminder gift or token to back it up.
- Use an alternate route of communication, like a telegram, card, note, poster, song, or delivery.
- Use body language such as a touch on the arm or a squint or smile to show sincerity, warmth, or understanding.
- Leave the room quietly after delivering the core message. This is not to get the last word in, but to give the other person time to think about the message, rather than rebutting, and to allow time for the words to soak in.
- Build in a subtle obligation to listen by using the law of reciprocity.
- Talk with people in a different environment or atmosphere. People will think and act differently in different surroundings. The same message might be better received, for example, out of the office over a cup of coffee at a nearby café.
- Use a verbal shock to motivate someone to action. Build up the person slightly and then deliver the "shock" of saying that the person can't or shouldn't do something. Use this strategy only on people who don't like to be told what to do. The goal is to wake them up, not to tell them how to do something.

- Don't Let Negative Words Get You Down:
  - Turn negative words into fuel and use them to your advantage. Use negative words to rocket yourself to greater heights.
  - Be a little "deaf" around others. Ignore the negative comments people make rather than quibbling over petty comments.

## Daily Challenge

Inspire someone today! Make your words the highlight of their day. Chat with someone to get a sense of what they're going through. Then create a core message and use one of the delivery strategies outlined in this chapter.

## Executive Challenge

Inspire four people today using four delivery strategies from this chapter. Then create your own delivery strategy and use it to inspire someone else.

# Listening Techniques for Enhancing Conversations

## In This Chapter:

- Learn five techniques to enhance or expand conversations
- Make conversations less awkward and feel more natural
- Discover how the pros make feel people listened to and understood

The techniques in this chapter will help you keep conversations going by letting people know that you are staying with their story as they speak. They help people keep their momentum going during a conversation.

If you interrupt someone on a roll, you break the person's energy flow. Thus, the fewer words you say, the better. Imagine a kid sharing his excitement about something while someone constantly interrupted the story. You don't want to do that. Instead, apply these techniques to let the speaker know you are listening without interrupting.

## Parroting

Parroting[1] is a powerful technique for bonding with people, showing that you are listening, and helping any conversation move along smoothly. Six-figure communicators use this technique to build rapport and enhance conversations. But few people pick up on it. It is easy to do, and with a little practice, anyone can experience the power of parroting.

Parroting is merely saying back to someone the same thing they just said to you or repeating back the last few words of what the person just said. For example, if someone said that he was feeling pretty tired, you would parrot back, sympathetically, "You're feeling pretty tired." If someone said she enjoys Mozart, you would respond, "Mozart?" If someone said he was going to Hawaii this weekend, you would say, "You are going to Hawaii this weekend?"

I taught this technique to a physician's girlfriend, Lisa, who once told me that she felt inferior at many social gatherings. She told me that she was not a world traveler as many doctors seemed to be, she didn't know much about history, wasn't college-educated, and had few of the experiences she thought others had, such as sailing. So Lisa learned to parrot and was exceptional at it, dramatically changing her experience. She said, "When I used that technique, I felt that I was now part of the group and didn't feel so stupid," and then she laughed.

Parroting is a natural way to get others to clarify or expand on their statements. It is a kind of hot button. You are acknowledging what people have said, which shows them that you are listening and that you are interested in what they are talking about.

## Parroting Without Mocking

Although it seems that it would be obvious that you were parroting people, if done correctly, others will not pick up on it (even if they're familiar with the concept of parroting). The key is parroting correctly. You can parrot a lot of what someone is saying, but speaking verbatim or too often will lead people to realize what you are doing and they will feel mocked. Instead, choose occasional words and phrases to parrot. Or make a small change in what people have said.

For example, try putting a short, exclamatory word in front of the parroted phrase to come across warmer and more genuine. See how this would work if you were going to parrot the statement, "I am going to Hawaii this weekend," as follows:

• Oh, you are going to Hawaii this weekend?
• So, you are going to Hawaii this weekend?
• Ah, you are going to Hawaii this weekend?
• Say, you are going to Hawaii this weekend?
• Wow, you are going to Hawaii this weekend?

This approach softens parroting and makes you come across more casual and personable. These small words are dabs of "grease" that help lubricate the rusty gears of conversation.

# Paraphrasing

Similar to parroting, paraphrasing is saying back to people what you heard them say, but in shorter sentences. Unlike parroting, paraphrasing is using your own words.

Let's say someone was talking about the great seats he got at a football game, saying, "We had unbelievable seats on the 49-yard line, right behind the players at the Dallas game. It was amazing!" To paraphrase, you might say, "You sat right on the 49-yard line?!" or "You sat right behind the players at the Dallas game?!"

Paraphrasing is better than parroting when a person is giving a lot of information quickly, as when telling a story. By rephrasing in your own words, you will not come across as parroting or mocking others.

Some of the best communicators use paraphrasing with an analytical twist. They carefully listen to the other person, think about what was just said, and then paraphrase it back, adding some thought.

Let's say your neighbor was talking about renting a pressure washer to wash pine tar off the driveway this weekend. You might listen carefully to the other person and then paraphrase, "A pressure washer might get that tar up, but what size pressure washer are you going to use, a 150 p.s.i. or a 300?" You might also say, "That pressure washer will do a great job, but how did that tar get on the driveway in the first place?" Lastly, you might reply that a pressure washer will get the tar off and they are on sale this week at Sears.

This technique keeps the conversation moving and progressing in a possibly different direction.

# Summarizing or Rephrasing

Another technique to show people that you are listening and that you are following the conversation is summarizing and rephrasing what was said. It helps clarify what is being said and helps people feel they are connecting (clicking) with you. When done well, like parroting and paraphrasing, people do not pick up on your use of this technique. But unlike paraphrasing, it involves using only a few words to summarize and rephrase—not whole sentences.

Let's say someone is telling you about the traffic jams on Harper Road. You shrug as you say, "It does get pretty congested" (rephrasing). Then she tells you about how busy it was shopping at the mall. You say, smiling, "It's packed" (summarizing). She goes into great detail describing a great new car she saw on the way home, and you reply, "Cool car" (summarizing). (Or if she called it a "rad car," your reply would be a rephrase!)

Summarizing is speaking a few words to sum up what you heard the other person say, and rephrasing is using a few different words to mean the same thing the person just said. Both techniques let people know that you are listening and that you understand the gist of what they are saying. Saying "cool car" acknowledges to the other person that you heard her description and that you are with her during the conversation. Summarizing and rephrasing feed people's energy, help them speak, and untie the tongue-tied.

## Piggybacking

Some people are really tough to talk to. You may want to converse with each other, but you don't have much to say or you run out of things to say. The conversation is dying fast. You may even try using buttonomics, but the other person makes finding these buttons difficult. When this happens, piggybacking will work especially well. This technique will help you get the other person talking and help you expand the conversation.

In his book *Selling for Dummies*, Tom Hopkins describes this conversational technique. If someone said, "Yeah, I learned how to do that in the Army," then you would say, "So, you were in the Army," or "So, what type of work did you do in the Army?" You would key off the word Army. If someone said, "That's because Jennifer and I went to school together," your piggyback response might be, "So, what school did you go to?" or "I didn't know you and Jennifer went to school together." Get the idea? Just turn what the person said back into a question or a statement.

# Chapter Summary

- The listening techniques in this chapter help keep conversations going. They show others that you are with them and that you understand, while not taking away their momentum.

- Parroting: Repeating back what someone just said to you or repeating the last few words of what the person said.

- Paraphrasing: Picking out key points or phrases of what the person said and then putting them into your own words. Paraphrasing is better than parroting when people are giving a lot of information quickly, such as telling a story, or when they feel tongue-tied.

- Summarizing or Rephrasing: Helps clarify what is being said and helps others feel they are making a connection. Both techniques involve just a few words. Summarizing "sums up" what you heard the person say. Rephrasing uses different words to mean the same thing as what the person said.

- Piggybacking: Turning what someone said back into a question or statement that the person can respond to. You pick up on a key word in the other person's statement and then make a follow-up statement or ask a question that follows up on that key word. This gives you a way to expand the conversation.

## Daily/Executive Challenge

Try each of these three techniques at least once today. Notice how conversations become easier, less awkward, and more enjoyable.

# Using Body Movement to Enhance Communication

## In This Chapter:

- Learn to use your body more effectively while talking to others
- Discover the hidden power of nonlinguistic body movements
- Learn to read people better
- Create stronger rapport
- Use body positioning to more effectively communicate
- Learn techniques to connect with almost anyone

Kinesics is the systematic study of the relationship between nonlinguistic body movements (blushing, eye movements, etc.) and communication. Six-figure communicators are masters at using body movements to enhance communication. They use these movements to build rapport, increase likeability, become more charismatic, add more impact to presentations, and communicate their message more effectively.

Many researchers have studied the highly clinical aspects of body language to scientifically record spatial distances. For example, one researcher tested people's comfort zones by continually walking forward during a conversation with someone and noting how many inches of distance that person maintained between the two of them as he continually backed away. Another researcher divided this space into eight categories and specifically designated how many inches each category consisted of. Still another continually put objects into an individual's personal space to see how the person reacted.

Other researchers have studied unique extra verbal communication between world cultures to see how they vary. One researcher, for example, went to India and found regions where its people communicate "yes" by moving their head in a back and forth motion and "no" in an up and down motion. In Puerto Rico, not looking your elders in the eye is a sign of respect, instead of dishonesty.

Many books on body language teach readers how to interpret and pick up on what people's bodies say that their mouths do not. Sitting with your arms crossed, for example, might be interpreted as not being open to others. Some experts believe the same is true of crossing your legs. These experts say that crossed arms and legs signal that you are defensive, guarded, or closed to interacting, and they advise to "unlock" your posture to communicate openness.

Unfortunately, however, interpreting body language can be tough, particularly if you do not know precisely what to look for. This is because people often sit or stand a certain way merely because it is more comfortable or even habitual. People switch which leg is on top to let the other leg rest; they are not intentionally sending mixed signals. And it is just natural for some people to cross their arms when they are a bit nervous. It doesn't mean that they are not open to others.

This chapter does not focus on the highly clinical, the unique cultural differences between people, or body language that can be too easily misinterpreted. Instead, it examines realistic, reliable, and useful techniques that six-figure communicators use and look for while conversing with others. It looks at how you can purposefully and intentionally send body language to others to create stronger connections and relationships and to increase the effectiveness of your message.

# Connecting Through Nonlinguistic Movements

Some of the smallest, most reliable building blocks of body language are picked up only on a subconscious level, while others are larger and are picked up on a conscious level. Either way, they change how people see and feel about others, building rapport or generating charisma. In essence, these nonlinguistic body movements (NLMs) are a great communicator's "sixth sense" for understanding people and a secret weapon in communicating with them.

NLMs include pupil and eye movements, subtle movements of the fingers and hands, and facial expressions. They send vital information to others critical to establishing and increasing rapport. They make people feel comfortable around you and encourage them to talk. They show others that you are actively listening.

While simplified buttonomics is connecting with people on a mental level, NLMs enable you to connect with people on a physical level. Salespeople, politicians, negotiators, and many other people who connect with others for a living use these techniques consciously or unconsciously to strengthen their interactions.

I first discovered the power of these NLMs using the two- and three-track minds. When I was in the Army, I had a young warrant officer working for me who was an extraordinary listener. Somehow, for some reason, I always felt that I connected with him. He didn't say a lot, but I always felt a lot of conversational energy while communicating with him. I felt that I was connecting to his very soul when I spoke. At the time I couldn't put my finger on exactly how this powerful connection was being created.

But after many years I began to understand exactly what made that and other connections with people so powerful. I began to understand how others created these connections, and I started to incorporate those skills into my personal and professional life. I learned to make connections faster, stronger, and better than I ever had before, and I was enjoying the results as never before. The results have been extraordinary.

After personally making more than 7,000 professional sales calls and interviewing scores of six-figure communicators in different industries, I can say without batting an eyelash (body language?) that NLMs are real and they are powerful. And they will dramatically help you improve the quality of your interactions with others too.

It is important to reemphasize that using NLMs is a natural behavior for people who genuinely care for and have a genuine interest in others. They are what six-figure communicators naturally pick up on and send to others during conversations. Natural communicators instinctively do this; using NLMs is one of the things that makes them six-figure communicators.

Self-taught communicators, on the other hand, have to learn, over many years of trial and error, how to communicate their thoughts and ideas more effectively. For them, incorporating new ideas and techniques, like NLMs, into their communicative style is a way to enhance their communication.

# Understanding NLMs

By understanding NLMs, you will become a better judge of character and a superior communicator. You will begin to notice the power in the smallest body movements, for there is power in the minutiae when we communicate. When others speak, you will start to notice their NLMs and will learn how to send them to others. Let's take a look at the NLMs from the list that follows.

## Common NLMs

| | |
|---|---|
| Darting Eyes | Face People |
| Eye Point | Very Slight Head Cock |
| Squint | Head Nod |
| Big Eyes | Hand Flip |
| Pupil Dilation/Constriction | Shoulder Shrug |
| Lean Forward | Finger Over Mouth |
| Smile | Chin on Palm of Hand |

## Eye Movements

When people are truly connected, especially people of opposite sexes, their eyes dart back and forth while looking at each other. Because it is difficult to look at both eyes at the same time, you will look at one eye, and then the other eye, and then back to the first eye. This creates an intimate connection between you and the other person.

Darting eyes exist at both the physical and the subconscious level when two people bond. Other people do it to you or you do it to others, and neither of you realize what is happening. You just know that you both are connected.

You will see the eye dart in movies, particularly romance movies (people very connected). The couple's eyes will dart back and forth as they gaze at each other.

If you see this phenomenon in another person, then you know that the person is truly interested in the conversation at hand and rapport is established. If you are speaking and your listener's eyes begin to dart, you have created a true connection. If the other person is speaking with eyes darting, then he or she is genuinely getting into the conversation.

Try the eye dart while speaking. It will amplify whatever emotion you are trying to convey. If you are being genuine, sincere, and down-to-earth, this technique will intensify your emotions. You don't have to shout your emotions; this technique is far more effective than shouting.

Apply the eye dart when speaking to the people closest to you. Tell them how lucky you feel to have them in your life, all the while looking at one eye, then the other, and then back to the first eye. Your loved ones will feel your comments in their soul.

Darting eyes are equally powerful for communicating negative feelings. If you use the eye dart technique as you tell others how disappointed you are in them, they will feel those words right down to their core. You will never have to yell or scream.

Another NLM to observe is the eye point. Wherever people's eyes are pointing is where their attention is temporarily. The location may change frequently during a conversation. Good salespeople, for example, notice when someone is looking over their shoulder, peeking a look at a clock, or simply focusing somewhere else. They quickly recognize distracted people and either skillfully redirect their attention to the conversation at hand or they yield to the distraction and either stop the conversation or offer to talk at another time.

When people squint their eyes, they are usually conveying sincerity and speaking from the heart. When people squint their eyes as they are talking, usually they really mean what they are saying.

Like all NLMs, squinting can be abused once people understand its power. Former President Bill Clinton used to squint his eyes on television to show his sincerity when he spoke—including in the famous video clip of his saying: "I did not have sexual relations with that woman!" Although he later revealed he was lying as he uttered those words, he knew the power of squinting while he spoke to try to convey extraordinary sincerity.

Another NLM to watch for when others are speaking is big eyes. This does not refer to the size of one's pupil, but rather the white space between the eyelid and the iris (colored part of the eye). When people are really surprised, shocked, and excited, they open their eyes more than usual, revealing a wider sliver of white above the iris. You may see this when someone answers "No way!" People with big eyes during a conversation are usually genuinely excited.

Watch for pupil size during conversations. Pupils are the easiest to see in blue or green eyes. You may see them dilate and constrict during different topics of a conversation. When people are excited, their pupils dilate, similar to the "big eyes." But when people are offended, the pupils immediately constrict. Pupil dilation is an involuntary response. This means you have struck a nerve or quickly turned someone off.

Expert salespeople know that if their prospect's pupils dilate during a particular part of a presentation, then this is a point that is important to the prospect. So the salesperson will stay on that point. By the same token, if you see your prospect's eyes constrict during a presentation, you may have hit a nerve (such as price point). Then you should quickly move on to the features and benefits of what you're selling. Severe, acute eye constriction may call for you to quickly backpedal, apologize, or excuse yourself and leave.

## Whole-Body Movements

The way people lean toward or away from you and the direction they face during a conversation are usually indicative of their conversational interest. It really doesn't matter if people sit at the edge of their chair or the back of it; what matters is which way they lean. Leaning forward shows interest. Leaning back shows a lack of interest or a hesitation.

Similarly, notice how people face you while sitting or standing. Focus on their shoulders first and then on their hips—both pointing toward you is best. If only their head is pointing toward you and their shoulders and knees are pointing elsewhere, they have lost interest in the conversation.

Even the slightest head movements during conversations with others are noticeable. A slight cock of the head while listening to someone is perceptible and shows your interest in what is being said. Moreover, nodding your head while the other person is speaking shows that you are listening and receiving what is being said.

## Hand and Finger Movements

Small movements of the hands or fingers are also perceivable. The previously mentioned warrant officer was great at encouraging me to talk and showing me that he was staying with me. One way he would do this was with the hand flip. He would casually flip his hand over and nod his head ever so slightly while I was speaking. His extended hand started out palm facing down and he would then flip it three-quarters of the way over while I was making various points. Sometimes he would even throw in a shrug as he would do that.

These NLMs were ways he would silently and consciously or subconsciously send me signals that he was actively listening to what I was saying and encouraging me to state my views. As a result, I liked, trusted, and felt comfortable around this officer—and I wrote him great comments on his officer evaluation report!

Most NLMs can be used while speaking or listening, but the final two are specifically for listening. Both of them subconsciously show others that you are going to let them speak freely and not interrupt them. One technique is placing a finger over your mouth while the other person is talking. Another is propping up your head in the palm of your hand while sitting at a table. Because the lips are immobilized in the first technique and the jaw is immobilized in the second, you clearly put yourself in "receive" mode. You clearly show the other person that you are giving your undivided attention. And people will love you for giving them that gift (see Chapter 8).

Watch for NLMs and use them while speaking or listening. Understanding what each one is and its meaning will make you a better judge of character and help you more effectively deliver your message.

A way to maximize NLMs is to combine them. By using an eye dart and a slight eye squint, you can dramatically increase the effectiveness of your message. By smiling and slightly cocking your head after someone asks you a question, you can project even more warmth. Similarly, by leaning forward, nodding occasionally, and propping up your head while someone is speaking, you will subconsciously send the message to others that you are really listening to them, and they will love you for it.

NLMs help you physically click with people even when you are not in the best of moods. By knowing how to act differently with NLMs, you can use them to your advantage to help you more effectively communicate during tough days or when you are not in the mood to talk with others. You can use them as a crutch to strengthen your connections with others and communicate more effectively, helping you get back into a better mood and back into the personal power mind-set.

## Noticing Others' Body Language

It is amazing how much information people send with their bodies without realizing it. Expert communicators are watching and absorbing as much body language as possible during their interactions with people. They are intensely aware of others and are using both two- and three-track mind techniques. One track is paying attention to everything the other person is saying and the other track(s) is focusing intently on what the other person's body is doing or who else is in the room, continually determining congruency.

Because many six-figure communicators know about NLMs, they notice these very fine changes in body language. Picking up on NLMs helps you differentiate those who fake interest in a conversation from those who genuinely and sincerely enjoy talking with you.

Six-figure communicators know that people who are actively listening move to some degree. People who don't move tend to be daydreaming, zoning out, falling asleep, or thinking of something else. Watch people to see how alert they are. Are they bouncing their leg, brushing their hair aside, chewing gum, scratching, or twirling or shaking a pen? You can see this in the classroom. Have you noticed that excellent students are moving while they are listening? The leg bounce is a sure sign someone is alert.

Six-figure communicators also know that people who actively listen have active faces. Their faces fluctuate often. They smile or pout, their eyes move or get bigger, they squint, their eyebrows move, or their tongue may stick out a little. These facial expressions and NLMs fluctuate on their face to show interest, disgust, envy, excitement, and disbelief. People who are not actively listening (daydreaming or disinterested) do not have active faces.

Good judges of character notice lines around people's eyes and the corners of their mouths. These lines are indicative of habitual expressions on their faces. Are people usually smiling and happy or are they habitually frowning? The lines will tell.

Remember to pay particular attention to where people's eyes point. If their eyes start looking over your shoulder or behind you, you have lost their attention and they are faking interest.

## Sending Body Language as You Speak

Six-figure communicators know the extraordinary power of sending NLMs to others. Sending NLMs is how they physically "click" or make connections with people on a physical level. They send signals to encourage others to talk and feel comfortable. These signals are imperceptible to most, but are essential to establishing and building rapport.

Many public speakers have told me after their speech that they appreciated my listening to them and encouraging them to speak. I genuinely enjoy listening to speakers, and I know that I consciously and even unconsciously send NLMs of interest to others.

I have noticed that I unconsciously (and sometimes consciously) send out NLMs in groups too. I have seen other people in groups fight to get my attention, like little kids trying to get my attention to hear their stories. I would guess this is because I keep my mouth shut and listen, send NLMs to people speaking, and ask occasional short questions or make short comments to keep their energy flowing.

Another aspect of sending NLMs is doing it consciously when you are tired or not really in the mood to talk to people. This happens to all of us from time to time. Perhaps you have been traveling all day or received some bad news at work, but you still have to deal with important customers.

In times like these, NLMs will help you fake a state of mind until you get a better hold on it and get back into a powerful mental state. When you are not in a powerful state, NLMs will help you close the gap and make you a stronger communicator. They will help you get through the tough or even "blah" times. And when you begin to use NLMs, other people will lighten up and respond better, further helping you get back into a positive state. You can use NLMs as a temporary crutch.

# Other Ways to Use NLMs

Now that you understand what NLMs are, what to look for, and how to send them, how else can you use them? An important question to ask is whether you want to create sameness between you and others or whether you want to differentiate yourself. Let's take a look at each.

## Creating Sameness

The essence of rapport is to be like the other person (sameness). If the other person talks fast, you talk fast. If the other person talks slowly, you talk slowly. If the other person speaks quietly, you speak quietly. If the other person uses facts and figures, you use facts and figures. If the other person sits while speaking, you sit while speaking. If she stands, you stand. If she sits at the edge of her chair, you sit at the edge of your chair. If she is rigid and formal during a business meeting, you are rigid and formal. If she uses a lot of gestures while speaking, you use a lot of gestures.

This is called matching. Matching is a natural phenomenon between connected people who have already established rapport. They match each other back and forth through their conversation without realizing they are doing it. They match dialect, tone, words, body language, and so on. Matching other people is a key to building sameness, and six-figure communicators consciously or subconsciously do this all the time. Often they adjust themselves to others to build rapport more easily.

Other times communicators will "lead" the matching by, for example, taking off a suit coat and hanging it on the back of their chair to intentionally help others feel at ease. The goal is that others then will take your lead and "match" your comfort level.

Many books teach readers to go a step further and to match others precisely. For example, if the other person puts her hands on her head while speaking, you would put your hands on your head to copy her body language. If you were sitting at a table across from a friend and the friend reached for the salt with his right hand, you would wait a few seconds and then reach for an object with your right hand.

Mirroring is using the opposite hand or foot from what the other person uses, as if looking in a mirror. If the other person is sitting at a table across from you and he reaches for the salt with the right hand, you would grab the salt with your left hand, for a mirror effect. If that person props his head up using his left hand at a table while talking or listening, you would mirror him by propping up your head using the opposite hand, the right.

A good rule of thumb is to match the other person in a general way only. If the other person is sitting comfortably, you sit comfortably. If the other person is standing, you stand. Matching precise body movements is mimicking the other person, and mirroring is taking things a bit too far. To precisely sit the same way someone else sits may be uncomfortable to you and this may be obvious to the other person. She will be able to tell you are sitting in an unfamiliar or uncomfortable position and feel a bit uneasy about why you are doing it. If you get caught mimicking the other person precisely, not only will rapport suffer, but the other person will feel mocked.

## Differentiating Yourself

So why would anyone not want to match others and build rapport? Why would anyone intentionally send out opposite or different body language signals? The answer is that by using different body language, we differentiate ourselves and send specific messages to others. Let's take a look at some of the ways to use our bodies to show difference.

- To be charismatic. Charismatic people stand straighter, smile more, and display other distinguishing characteristics. Using NLMs and other body language when others are not using them can project power, importance, and uniqueness.

- To show you are listening. Six-figure communicators are good listeners and consciously or unconsciously use NLMs and listening cues, whether others in the group are listening or not. This is a primary reason that people almost always talk to or look at anyone who seems to be listening to them. A well-known public speaker's trick is to scan the audience and look for friendly faces that seem supportive. It's easier to talk to a few smiling and friendly faces than blank stares. These faces encourage and support the speaker.

- To show disinterest. Women often intentionally face a different direction to avoid men they do not wish to talk to or encourage. When men are part of a group with women, they often close off their group to "outside" men by standing in such a way as to "block out" other men from joining.

So ask yourself if you want to create similarity or differentiate yourself from others with your body language. There is a time and place for each. Six-figure communicators consciously or unconsciously match or differentiate themselves from others as situations arise.

## Positioning Yourself with Others

Body language literature includes many terms to describe the space between individuals in conversation: comfort zone, social distance, personal space, personal bubble, territory, and so on. But six-figure communicators think of this simply as *positioning*. Positioning is a more inclusive term and puts people in charge by making conscious and deliberate decisions. Six-figure communicators constantly ask themselves: Where and how do I want to physically position myself during a conversation?

Let's first take a look at the where. Too many poor communicators who really want to socialize with others unintentionally isolate themselves. They hope to meet exciting people but rarely do. They have trouble striking up conversations with people at company functions or out on the town. They are in the mood to talk and they get all dressed up to do so, but they have a hard time of it. They just find it difficult or awkward. Why?

The primary reason is isolation. They go out with friends and find the "last two chairs" in the corner of a bar. At social functions they stand in a corner or sit at a table out of sight, out of mind. They want to "get out of the way," and they do. Few people venture to that corner of the room, the end of the bar, or to that out-of-the-way spot.

Six-figure communicators, by contrast, walk into a room and momentarily stop in the doorway to survey the room. They look around to find key traffic areas and where groups and people are located. In her book *Little Tricks of Big Winners*, Leil Lowndes says that this is one way big winners make an entrance and get noticed.

Six-figure communicators also position themselves in key areas in a room, like in high-traffic areas and near a main entrance or exit door—to see everyone twice. People who stand or sit in high-traffic areas see more friends and have more chance encounters. They are more visible and more accessible to others. This makes it easier to meet people, find people, and socialize. It also makes it easier to get introduced early to new people, instead of on the way out or not at all. It makes it easier for people to circle back to you or run into you multiple times, particularly if you maintain your position. Maintaining a key position in a room also makes it easier for people to tell others where you are, increasing social contact.

One trick six-figure communicators use in positioning themselves at a table or in a waiting room is to sit at a right angle to others when possible. Sitting directly across from someone can be cold and awkward and sometimes confrontational. When you sit at right angles, though, you are close to the customer but you don't have to worry about uncomfortable eye contact. This also makes it easy to share information and point out specifics when going over paperwork or a sales presentation. Conversations with people should feel comfortable.

## Mr. X's Masterful Use of Body Positioning

I once knew an extremely talented military officer, Mr. X, who frequently used body positioning to his advantage. He would walk senior officers out of his office by carefully walking forward (toward them) during conversations. As he moved forward, other officers moved back (toward the door) to maintain their personal distance. Mr. X essentially "asked" people to leave without even uttering a word. He also carefully used this technique on key people whom he couldn't pin down. He would carefully back them against a wall, in essence pinning them down.

One day a major from another unit wanted to complain to Mr. X about a problem while he was standing in a parking lot in the middle of a bright, sunny day. Short on time, Mr. X positioned his back to the sun the entire time the major spoke. He knew that the major wouldn't stare straight into the sun for very long to complain, and he was right. The major never realized what was happening, but ended the conversation quickly and left. Mr. X , using his body, quietly, without saying a word, forced an end to the complaining.

Mr. X was a tall man who knew the importance of keeping his eyes level with people he was talking to. Often he would invite shorter people to have a seat with him to make them feel more comfortable. If he was talking to a very short person on or near a stairway, he would stand a few steps lower to keep his eyes level with the other person. He might even squat down to talk to a child.

## Positioning and Group Dynamics

In group dynamics, the closer the proximity of people, the more group energy is increased. When people spread out, group energy dissipates quickly and is difficult to generate.

This is why most people prefer booths to tables at restaurants. This is why it is more fun to ride together in a group than take separate cars. This is why the more people you can fit in the car, the more fun people have.

Notice how "fun groups" position themselves in restaurants, coffee shops, or school cafeterias. You will notice that they crowd as many people as possible around as few tables as possible. Groups that are not particularly social logically string more tables together so that they can "spread out" and be more comfortable. There seems to be something about having shoulder-to-shoulder contact with people and occasionally bumping elbows with them that energizes people's "fun" buttons.

The same is true when socializing at home. Houses with seating that is separated or spread out (maybe in different rooms) lose group energy. This is why people love to congregate in the kitchen. Certainly food attracts people to some extent, but gathering in the kitchen is also an excuse for people to get tight.

Conversational energy is also increased in groups. The extroverts come alive in groups and keep group energy high. They love to be in groups and they feed off others, tying the group together. And the introverts don't feel the pressure of speaking with the person right in front of them to break the silence, but can speak as they feel comfortable. They can be part of a conversation if they choose or sit back and be a part of a larger one.

The closer people are to each other, the easier it is to move in and out of conversations. More conversational topics emerge to appeal to more people. You don't get stuck in endless conversations because there are other people near to interrupt or change the subject. And with more people, there are more side conversations that appeal to more people, helping to better match people with similar interests.

# Body Language That Breaks Rapport

The focus of this chapter has been on using body language to create stronger connections and relationships and to increase the effectiveness of your message. But some body language can have the opposite effect, causing you to break rapport with another person. Let's look at the body movements that are most likely to alienate others.

- Scowling Face: The most common way people destroy rapport with their bodies is with their face. Without realizing it, most people walk, sit, and drive with habitual scowls on their faces. Charismatic people, on the other hand, are passively likeable and draw people to them by having a pleasant expression on their face. This promotes rapport and charisma. Check for scowls on your face by looking at the corners of your mouth to see if they are habitually pointing down.

- Crossed Arms: Some people cross their arms because it is more comfortable, and others do it to give the illusion of power. But either way, people who cross their arms make talking to and working with others difficult. It destroys rapport and shows others that you are not open to approach and are insecure in a particular setting.

  Charismatic people, by contrast, usually are moving their hands and arms around as they speak. They use their fingers to count off key points and emphasize important information. Arm motion creates enthusiasm and interest in what you have to say.

  If you don't know what to do with your hands, hold something in one or both of them. Hold a pen, calculator, notepad, or a drink. Or simply put a hand in your pocket.

- Pointing Fingers: "Don't point that at me; it has a nail in it!" Most people don't realize when they literally point their finger at someone during a conversation. This often irritates or offends others. One might be pointing a finger saying, "You need to … You better … You didn't … You always …" Finger pointing can be risky, especially if you are angry or upset.

  On the Fox News Channel talk show *Hannity and Colmes*, Sean Hannity once pointed his finger at a guest he was debating, and his guest started to freak out emotionally. The guest even said, on national television, how much the finger pointing bothered him. Most of us don't realize when we point at someone as we speak, but the other person is astutely aware of it. Finger pointing is rude and destroys rapport.

# Chapter Summary

- Nonlinguistic body movements (NLMs) are universal distinctions in body language that change the way people see and feel about other people, building rapport or creating charisma. NLMs make people feel comfortable and encourage them to talk. They show others that you are actively listening. Simplified buttonomics is connecting with people on a mental level, and NLMs are for connecting with people on a physical level.

- Common NLMs

| | |
|---|---|
| Darting Eyes | Face People |
| Eye Point | Very Slight Head Cock |
| Squint | Head Nod |
| Big Eyes | Hand Flip |
| Pupil Dilation/Constriction | Shoulder Shrug |
| Lean Forward | Finger Over Mouth |
| Smile | Chin on Palm of Hand |

- Notice Others' Body Language. Use the two- and three-track minds during conversations to absorb as much information as possible. People who are actively listening move. People who don't move tend to be daydreaming, zoning out, falling asleep, or thinking of something else. Watch people for body and facial movement that conveys interest, disgust, envy, excitement, and disbelief.

- Send Body Language as You Speak. Send NLMs to physically "click" or connect with people on a physical level. Encourage them to talk, feel comfortable, and speak out.

- Use NLMs to Create Sameness or to Differentiate Yourself. Matching others in a general way is a key to building sameness. Avoid precise matching or mirroring, which mocks others. Use different body language to differentiate yourself or to send specific messages, such as to project power, importance, and uniqueness. Show disinterest by turning your back to others or facing the side.

- Positioning. Six-figure communicators are constantly aware of their positioning in a room and around others. Many people unintentionally isolate themselves from others. But six-figure communicators survey a room to find key traffic areas and where different groups and people are located, and then they position themselves accordingly. When sitting one-on-one with someone, a key position is at a right angle to the other person. Positioning also includes being able to have level eye contact.

- Body Language That Breaks Rapport. Scowling face, crossed arms, and finger pointing are examples of body language that tend to alienate others rather than help you connect.

## Daily Challenge

Spend the first half of today watching people and picking up on as many NLMs as you can. See how many you can spot from the common NLM list. Pay particular attention to the face and eyes when people speak.

Spend the second half of the day consciously and deliberately sending NLMs to other people when you speak and when you listen. Experiment with NLMs to strengthen your messages when you're speaking and to show others you understand them when you're listening.

## Executive Challenge

Notice how and where people position themselves in rooms and while talking to others. Are they leaning against a door? Are they sitting at a corner table in a cafeteria away from others? Are they leaning forward? Do they stand close to you or others when they speak? Where do people in the room seem to congregate?

Practice walking into a room and momentarily hesitating at the door to see where traffic patterns are and where people and groups are positioned. Make a quick scan of the room and then move to the area of your choosing.

# Asking Good Questions

## In This Chapter:

- Learn to start conversations using questions
- Discover the power of open-ended questions
- Make conversations real by using five simple principles
- Learn how to use questions in business

The ability to ask good questions is one of the most powerful skills that six-figure communicators possess. They ask questions to clarify, gather information, focus conversations, show interest, show intelligence, show concern, start conversations, keep conversations moving, and stimulate thought. And the better they are at doing this, the more effective they become.

The greatest communicators ask questions in a state of curiosity, interest, happiness, helpfulness, or caring. When you ask questions in a positive state, others instinctively respond in kind. People pick up on your state and then decide how they will respond to you. Questions asked from negative states, such as selfishness, anger, fear, aggravation, jealousy, desperation, and frustration, almost always come out wrong and do more harm than good. The only question people should ask in a negative state is how they are going to get out of their negative state!

Asking questions to build rapport is essential. Ask questions to show an interest in others, find out how they are doing, get to know them, and show concern. All the body language you can muster can't do what questions can.

# Talk-Show Host Technique

Talking to people is often like hosting a late-night talk show or *Good Morning America* or even a radio show. You can direct the conversation and bring out different traits in people.

Art Linkletter had fun asking children questions during his "Kids Say the Darndest Things" segments on his 1960s television show *Art Linkletter's House Party*. Although it was his show, he made the children the stars. Like Art Linkletter, you can make other people the star of your own "show," bringing out wonderful qualities and stories in them. Think of talking to people as a three-minute spot in which you're the host. Talking to people in this way takes a lot of the awkwardness out of the conversation and it becomes fun.

As a pharmaceutical salesman, I talked with countless people genuinely and sincerely, particularly in doctors' offices. I have a real interest in people and know that most people have something interesting to say. You just have to find it and pull it out of them. While talking to people, my dominant state is one of curiosity and interest. When I'm in this mind-set, questions come out naturally and don't come across as an interrogation.

> *"Ask another question."*
> — **my Uncle Bill, retired salesman, when asked for his secret in talking with people**

Of all of the conversations I had in clinic waiting rooms, I found the ones with high school students most interesting. We might have started out talking about the weather and then naturally progressed to a slightly more personal conversation. Soon, these high school students were telling me about their favorite teachers, the ones they didn't like, what they did during lunch, what things they learned in Spanish class, their circle of friends, their dates, if they played sports, what they thought about different subjects, school politics, and on and on.

The parents were either reading a magazine or working on something, intermittently listening to the conversation. Then something interesting would happen. The parents would put down their magazine and begin listening intently to our conversation (using the three-track mind). They realized that I was learning more about what their children were going through than they were! But all I was doing was pleasantly asking questions and showing a genuine interest. I was making the kids the star.

One December I was sitting in a physician's waiting room where there was a Christmas tree in the corner. A woman about 80 years old, accompanied by her middle-aged daughter, was sitting next to me. I commented how beautiful the Christmas tree was, and they agreed. Then I turned toward the older lady and asked her if she liked Christmastime. She replied that she loved that time of year. I commented that it was a beautiful time and then smiled and asked her what her all-time favorite Christmas was. She started telling me a wonderful Christmas story. Then I asked her about her all-time favorite gift. And she told me. And her daughter didn't even know about that unique gift or that blissful Christmas.

All I had done was asked occasional questions and then listened. I felt bad that I knew about some of the woman's favorite Christmas memories, while her own daughter hadn't a clue. The moral of the story: Ask questions!

# Starting Conversations with Questions

A great way to start conversations with people is to pay them a compliment and then follow it up with a question. People love sincere compliments. And by asking a follow-up question, they will be gently persuaded to answer. This is because of their feeling of pride and the law of reciprocity. A few examples are:

- That is a lovely scarf—did you buy it locally?
- That is an unusual pin—is it very old?
- What a beautiful watch—what kind is it?

Regardless of someone's starting mood, this technique starts conversations well. It gently flatters the person's ego and then nudges the conversation into a positive direction. (It's hard to be mad at someone who likes your grandmother's pin.) Even if the person was angry before she met you, you carefully redirected her thinking.

A slight modification of this technique is to make a general statement and then follow it up with a question. This technique often works best if you're looking straight ahead as you make the statement, and then turn toward the other person to ask the follow-up question. For example:

- Those clouds outside look black. Do you think we are going to get hit hard?
- Last night I saw the movie [fill in the blank]. Have you seen it?
- I'm going to the circus tonight. Have you been?
- You seem like you are in a good mood. Want to tell me about it?

Management guru Tom Peters adds a simple "isn't it?" or "doesn't it?" at the end of his statements to gently induce a response, as in "It's a beautiful day, isn't it?"

# Using Preparatory Questions

Six-figure communicators use preparatory questions to prepare people to hear important questions. It gives people a few moments to stop their thinking and quiet their minds to listen to your question with their undivided attention. Preparatory questions help important questions get the attention they deserve.

One of the most effective preparatory questions is "Can I ask you a question?" As soon as you ask that question, people automatically answer yes in their head and usually say aloud, "Sure" or "Okay." Perhaps 99 percent of people answer in the affirmative because they have been asked only if they can be asked a question—they still don't know what the question is. Now they're mentally ready to receive your question.

Play around with different wording for your preparatory question. Changing the wording prepares listeners differently to respond to your question. As soon as they agree to hear your question, mentally or verbally, they will give you their attention. And it shows manners and class to ask permission to ask a personal or sensitive question.

A few examples of preparatory questions are the following:

- May I ask you a technical question about engines? (The other person is now thinking about engines.)
- May I ask you a question about computers? (The other person is ready to be asked a question about computers.)
- May I ask you a personal question? (The other person automatically respects that you asked his permission to be personal, and the question will be taken better than if you did not ask.)

Preparatory questions can also prepare someone for a change in conversational tone or subject or to be asked a serious question. Preparatory questions help important questions to come across more effectively and to be received more easily.

Note: Preparatory statements, such as "I need your help on something" work the same way. The other person mentally or verbally gives you her permission to ask for help and gives you her undivided attention. She is now ready to listen to your request. People are also gently flattered that you need their help with something, and most people will help you if they can. Few people will look you in the eye and refuse help if they are able to help.

# Asking Open-Ended Questions

Most people struggle through conversations because they ask closed-ended questions. Closed-ended questions kill conversations because they do not give people the latitude to expand on ideas, talk about how they felt, share what interests them most, or relate what they learned. People who ask closed-ended questions restrict conversational flow.

**Closed-ended questions include the following:**
- How long have you lived in Seattle?
- Does it rain there a lot?
- Do you ski?
- Which ski resort do you prefer?
- Have you been skiing this year?

Answers to close-ended questions are usually only a word or two. Where were you last night? Who was there? Why did you go there? Closed-ended questions often come across as an interrogation. They are not conversationally friendly.

Closed-ended questions are okay, but they must be followed up with open-ended questions. Open-ended questions are what excellent conversationalists use. These questions get people talking and they expand conversations. They take much of the awkwardness out of the conversation and encourage people to talk about what they find interesting. Open-ended questions show an interest in others.

**Examples of open-ended questions are the following:**
- Then what happened?
- Why do you think he did that?
- How did that happen?
- What made you decide to do that?
- What do you do for fun when you aren't working?
- What are your thoughts and feelings about ...?

Questions that begin with "why," "how," and "what" are usually open-ended. It is easy to keep conversations moving smoothly by asking several open-ended questions.

# Making Conversations Real

All too often I see and hear people trying to talk with others, but their conversations come across as awkward and uneasy. They want to talk with others, but they don't know what to talk about. Out of desperation, they grudgingly talk about the weather or some other banal topic for an extended period. Their conversation is difficult and frustrating. Neither person really wants to talk about the weather for 15 minutes, but they are seemingly stuck talking about it. Each person knows the conversation is going nowhere fast but doesn't know what to do about it. Usually one person finally puts the dying conversation out of its misery and tells the other person that he needs to be running along.

Here are five suggestions to improve awkward conversations and make them real.

- Start conversations and guide them using open-ended questions. Let the other person talk most of the time.

- Use open-ended questions to get people to expand on what they are talking about:
  - Why?
  - Then what happened?
  - What did you do after that?
  - What did he say then?

- Get slightly personal and ask open-ended questions. This makes the conversations real and eliminates the small talk. Ask the other person questions like:
  - What made you say that?
  - What made you do that?
  - How did that make you feel?
  - Were you scared? (closed-ended)

- Pretend you are interviewing someone for a radio audience. Ask the other person to describe what the house looked like, how someone was dressed, how something was decorated, what color something was, and so on.
- Use piggybacking (Chapter 10) and simplified buttonomics (Chapter 4) to find people's positive hot buttons. Ask questions to bring out colorful stories and adventures in others.

# Phrasing Your Questions for Quality Answers

People who are asked questions feel obligated to answer questions. Questions stimulate thought and drive conversations and discussions. But the key to getting the conversations and discussions you're looking for is in how you ask questions.

What you ask is what you receive. Ask a good question; get a good answer. Ask a poor question; get a poor answer. The quality of the questions usually influences the quality of the answers. For example, a vice president of public relations for a local Toastmasters club asked new members to answer a few questions so their answers could be posted on the club Web site. It was a good way to get to know new members. She asked three questions:

- Why did you join Toastmasters?
- Why did you join this club?
- What do you do in your free time?

Everyone responded to the first question that they wanted to get over their fear of public speaking and improve their speaking skills. They answered the second question that they wanted to learn to organize their thoughts and become more comfortable speaking with a fun and supportive group. The only question that differentiated new members was what they did in their free time.

People usually answer questions exactly as they are posed. This is why it is important to think about the way you phrase questions. By phrasing questions differently, you change not only the answers, but also the conversational tone and direction.

I asked a podiatrist one time what he did for fun. He took offense at the question and responded that podiatry was fun and that he chose to be a podiatrist—he didn't want to be an M.D. This question certainly started a conversation but not the one I had intended. My phrasing changed the conversational tone and direction.

Changing one word of a question can dramatically change the way a question is received and the way people respond. If you are not getting the right answers, or if your conversations do not go the way you want them to, try changing the wording of your questions.

I now imply that all jobs or pursuits are fun, and I ask people, "So, what do you do for fun when you are not [fill in the pursuit]." This is a more powerful question. By implying that they are having fun at whatever they are doing allows others to feel more comfortable and takes away their need to defend their job, lifestyle, or hobby.

Ask a homemaker what kind of work she does and she may feel a need to justify or defend her job. But ask her at a social event how she spends her time or what she does for fun when she is not attending social functions, and she will take the conversation in a direction she feels most comfortable. (This open-ended question gives her lots of directions to go in.)

## What to Do After Asking a Question

After asking a question, shut up and listen to the other person. Hearing is not listening. Keep your mouth shut and let the other person answer. If you need clarification, ask for it, then shut up and let the other person answer. Resist the temptation to interrupt.

While someone is talking, use the two- and three-track minds to watch the person. If the person is with someone, notice who fields the question, who is in charge, how they process information, how they answer questions, and if you can better understand their decision-making process. But the most important thing to pick up on is their personalities.

Then try to customize your information and adapt your style to the other person. This builds rapport and improves communication more effectively. People who can do this are more successful communicators.

# Using Questions in Business

Top businesspeople credit their ability to ask good questions as one of the most important skills for success. They use questions to gather information, find out what customers want, guide discussions, and stimulate thought. And the better they do this, the more successful they become. Learning to ask good questions comes with time and practice.

This section discusses only three areas of business in which asking good questions can make a huge difference. Use this section to help you ask better questions in not just your professional life, but your personal life too.

## Interviews

The secret to asking questions is to be curious and conversational. This approach will set people at ease. Asking open-ended questions will help get the other person talking and take some of the interviewing burden off yourself, whether you are the interviewer or the interviewee. This will also help you get a better feel for the other person. Asking good questions shows an interest in the individual and the company.

In his book *201 Best Questions to Ask on Your Interview*, John Kador hits the nail on the head when he writes, "Asking questions also enables you to break down the formal interviewer-candidate relationship, establish an easy flow of conversation, and build trust and rapport." This is one of the greatest reasons to ask questions, particularly in interviews.

Kador asks readers, "Of the following five candidate behaviors in the job interview, what behavior do you think recruiters find most unforgivable: poor personal appearance, overemphasis on money, failure to look at interviewer while interviewing, doesn't ask questions, or late to interview?" The answer is that the failure to ask questions is what causes recruiters to "lose confidence," based on a survey of 150 recruiters, job coaches, and hiring managers. Kador says that questions are not an option because they show interest, intelligence, confidence, personal appeal, and assertiveness. Questions are a must.

Interviews are all about asking and answering questions. A hiring manager and job seeker should be probing each other and asking questions to gather information. In his book *What Color is Your Parachute*, Richard Nelson Bolles says that each side should be asking five primary questions to see if the other is a match, and the questions for each side are essentially the same.

**Hiring Manager:**
- Why are you here?
- What can you do for us?
- What kind of person are you?
- What distinguishes you from 19 other people who can do the same tasks that you can?
- Can I afford you?

**Job Seeker:**
- What does this job involve?
- What are the skills a top employee in this job would have to have?

The next section will address how top salespeople use questions to interview customers. These interviews are less formal than job interviews, but they still take place. Some salespeople even interview while standing or walking with customers. Keep in mind that all of us are salespeople, selling our ideas, products, and services.

## Sales

Top salespeople sell themselves first, building trust, credibility, and rapport. They make the time to get to know customers and their needs before ever mentioning product. Do not talk product until you first sell yourself and build trust, credibility, and rapport. Too many salespeople start a conversation talking about products. If this happens, customers will usually humor you or pick your brain, and then shop elsewhere.

After establishing yourself, start selling. In its simplest form, selling is merely finding the needs or wants of people and then filling them with a service or product. You can do this in two questions: What are your needs, and how can I be of help? A common mistake that new salespeople make is trying to sell something before finding the need. So how do you find a need? Do it conversationally with a sense of curiosity and by asking questions.

### How We Got Sold an Expensive Pair of Shoes

A few days before Christmas, my brother Nick and I went shopping for running shoes. At the first store, the salesman recommended three expensive pairs. He said they were the best shoes and that we would be happy with any of the shoes he recommended. Nick and I, however, had planned on buying the cheapest pair we could find. We didn't like the salesman and we didn't like his shoes, so we left the store.

At the next store we met a salesman about 19 years old. Before ever mentioning shoes, he made it a point to get to know us first. Then he asked us what kind of running we did—on the road, cross-country, or both? He asked us how far we ran per week. Then he asked if we preferred a heavier shoe with more cushioning and support or a lighter, faster shoe with less support. Were we pronators or supinators? I wasn't sure and then he explained the differences. It turned out that I was a supinator, and my brother was a pronator. With that established, he found three shoes that would be best for me and then three shoes that would be best for Nick. He told us that the most expensive shoes weren't necessarily better for us; what mattered was how well the shoe fit.

We both selected a pair of shoes and spent almost twice the money we had planned, but we walked away feeling that we had picked the perfect shoe—a "custom" shoe, carefully selected for each of us. Checking out, I told the sales manager how much we appreciated his salesman's taking time to really, really help us find a shoe that we would be happy with.

This salesman used questions to get to know us and our running needs. He built rapport and clearly identified our individual needs before ever picking up a pair of shoes. He asked us questions about what we wanted that we hadn't even asked ourselves. He did this with a pleasant conversational tone. After clearly identifying our needs, he gave us shoe choices that would be best suited for each of us. After he took the time to identify our perfect shoe (what we needed), it only made sense to purchase them.

## "Based on What You Told Me ..."

Selling is far easier for people who ask questions. A yellow pages salesman told me that he asks what customers want and then carefully listens. If he doesn't exactly understand, he clarifies the customers' wants or needs. Then he gave me his magic phrase: "*Based on what you told me*, I recommend ..." He gives his customers three choices to let them decide what is best for them. The choices might be divided into three packages, A, B, and C.

After explaining his technique to me, the salesman asked me rhetorically, "How could customers not want one of the three choices when they are all based on exactly what they asked for?"

> *I have found the best way to give advice to your children is to find out what they want and advise them to do it.*
> —**Harry S. Truman**

## Closing the Sale

Ironically, top salespeople are not "hard closers." Instead, they zero in on exactly what customers want, listen carefully to their criteria, and then help them get it. They find out what people want and then give it to them. There is no arm twisting. People buy because they are happy with the service or the product.

Salespeople do not earn the right to close a sale until after they take the time to "interview" customers and learn their needs. Poor salespeople try to force product. They pressure customers by saying things like the following:

- Doctor, will you put your next 10 patients on this drug?
- Sir, I will take you around all day to look at houses, but I want you to sign a statement that you will buy a house if we find the perfect one at a reasonable price.
- This is a great car—what will it take to put you in it today?
- Ma'am, based on what I have shown you here today, will you buy some advertising from me?

Selling should be just a natural progression of discovering customer wants and fulfilling them. When you find prospective homeowners the house they have been looking for, in the kind of neighborhood they feel comfortable in, at a price they can afford, you don't have to close them. They are naturally ready to buy it. One top salesman told me it is as if the salesperson is simply standing between the customer and the product—"they want it."

Find out what people want (by asking questions), and then give it to them. You don't have to *sell* people; they already know that they want to buy a house, a car, or running shoes, particularly if they sought you out. The hard work and the skill comes from asking questions to find out exactly what they want, and then finding (or producing) it for them. Almost all top salespeople with whom I spoke said that they always "interview" customers first to find out exactly what they want (asking questions) and then try their darnedest to deliver it. If you do that, why would the customer go anywhere else to find it?

A real estate agent in the top 1 percent of certified relocation specialists shared with me how she uses questions to help first-time customers find exactly what they are looking for. Asking questions allows her to do her homework and gives customers the greatest service and the best information tailored to them. It also gives her the time to eliminate obstacles before she meets with customers. Then when she does meet with them for the first time, she has the most accurate and pertinent information gathered. This way she is most likely to find her customers a house they will be happy with the first time out on a home tour.

When she eventually sits down with the customers for the first time, she again asks them exactly what they want before she shows them properties. This firms up in their minds exactly what they want so that when they see it, it becomes an easy decision. Throughout the process, she reconfirms with the customers what their wants are because they may change slightly as they go along. This ensures that she and her customers stay focused and know exactly what they are looking for.

**Top salespeople sell more and more every year for two reasons:**
* Happy customers keep coming back. They continually upgrade or replace their product with the person who initially sold it to them. They like that person. They keep coming back year after year, enabling the salesperson to make repetitive sales.

* Happy customers tell everyone they know about "their" salesperson. They like this person enough that they keep sending her referrals. Entire families often buy from the same real estate or car salesperson. Top salespeople have the top referral rates. One salesperson I spoke with told me that 90 percent of her business came from referrals. Another told me that he made the most money from his happiest customers—they send their family and friends to him.

When you force a sale, customers will loathe you for it. If they buy from you, often they will have buyer's remorse. If they don't buy from you, they will feel bad will toward you and may tell others to stay away from you.

# Facilitating

Adults learn best by looking inside themselves for answers. Don't *tell* adults—draw the answers out of them instead. The best facilitators know how to use questions to stimulate group and individual thinking. They know how to ask questions to help organizations better focus discussions and come up with their own best solutions.

Good facilitators know and understand the end state. Their job is to guide groups to an objective by keeping them within boundaries. They lead groups to problems or areas that may need attention and let them come up with their own solutions. They help groups tighten their focus and prevent them from running off track. Poor facilitators may have a delightful time talking but do not move the group purposefully forward.

Good facilitators move groups forward by asking purposeful questions. Questions are usually thought out ahead of time and have an objective. Good facilitators ask open-ended questions to stimulate thought and discussion. They usually don't tell the group what to do, but lead them in the right direction to draw their own conclusions and come up with their own solutions.

Good facilitating is like using a global positioning system. A GPS doesn't care where it is; it just notes where it is and sets a course to where it needs to go. If it gets off course, it simply recalculates to get back on track. Similarly, good facilitators redirect the group's energies to help them stay on course to achieve their desired end state.

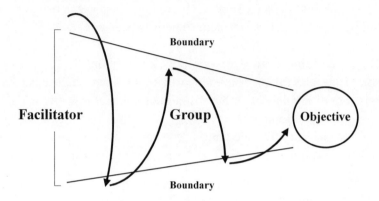

I have had the pleasure to learn from many great military facilitators. They knew how to keep a group focused, engage the group, stimulate thought, and move toward an endpoint. Some of their discussion comments and questions are listed below to give you a better feel for how they facilitate and run meetings:

- All right, what do you want to improve?
- Here's what I heard ...
- Interesting you said that. What caused you to say that?
- What is that going to allow you to do?
-  Is it a procedural problem or a systemic problem?
- This indicates that someone hasn't solved a problem.
- We are losing our focus; we need to focus our efforts.
- We will talk about that after this meeting.
- Is that a feasible solution?
- Let's go back to ...
- Where do you think that ___ will come from?
- We are doing a lot of things well; we are doing x, y, and z. But here are some things we are not doing well ...
- I want to talk about three specific areas. After that I will take comments from other areas.

- Would that cause a significant emotional event?
- Okay, what do we need to make that better?
- Maybe when ...
- What if ...
- I'm coming to that.
- It's an issue, and we have to come to terms with it.
- How would we do that?
- Let's not say it was your fault, though it was your fault. What we need is a system in place.

**Here are four general questions helpful for facilitators:**
- Where are we now?
- Where do we want to be?
- How do we get there from here?
- How did we do?

Always have someone recording comments, points, and ideas—preferably on flip charts. This frees the facilitator to engage the audience and focus on where the group is and where it needs to go. This way the facilitator can stay focused on the larger picture.

> *"Meetings are great, but the reason we have them is to fix the problem and fix the long-term system."*
> — **Army Colonel Robert Dail**

A common mistake that new facilitators make is arguing with an individual or complaining along with the group. Don't do this, and if you do, have a definite point you are driving at. If the group is not moving toward an objective, discussions can easily turn into a "bitch session." Remember to move the group forward to an endpoint.

# Chapter Summary

- Ask questions in a positive state. People immediately pick up on your state, and then decide how they will respond to you. The greatest communicators are in a state of curiosity, interest, happiness, helpfulness, or caring when they ask questions.

- Use the talk-show host technique. Acting as if you're host of your own talk show, direct the conversation and bring out different traits in people, making them the star. Do this by showing an interest and curiosity in them while asking them questions.

- Use follow-up questions to spark conversations. Pay someone a compliment and then follow it up with a question. By asking a follow-up question, you will gently persuade people to answer because of their feelings of pride and the law of reciprocity. A variation of this technique is to make a general statement and then follow it up with a question.

- Ask preparatory questions as a prelude to important questions. These help people give you their undivided attention and transition into different subjects.

- Ask open-ended questions to keep conversations moving smoothly. In contrast, closed-ended questions can be answered with a simple yes or no. Closed-ended questions are not conversational; they come across as an interrogation.

- Make conversations real. Start and guide conversations using open-ended questions. Let the other person talk most of the time. Get slightly personal to eliminate the small talk. Pretend you are interviewing someone for a radio audience to get the person to provide description and detail. Use piggybacking (Chapter 10) and simplified buttonomics (Chapter 4) to find people's positive hot buttons. Pay attention to how you phrase questions, to help direct the conversation and achieve the tone you want. Use the two- and three-track mind to adapt your style to the other person.

- Use questions in business:
  - Interviews. Questions are not optional. Be curious and have a conversational tone while asking questions. Ask open-ended questions to get the other person talking. Asking questions shows an interest in the company and the individual.

  - Sales. Sell yourself first, building trust, credibility, and rapport. Take the time to get to know customers and their needs before ever mentioning product. Then find out exactly what the customer wants by asking questions, and then match your products and services to those needs or wants.

- Facilitating. Good facilitators know and understand the end state. Their job is to guide groups to an objective by keeping them within boundaries and on track. They help groups tighten their focus and prevent them from running off on a tangent. Good facilitators move groups forward by asking purposeful questions. They usually don't tell the group what to do, but lead them in a positive direction to enable them to come up with their own conclusions and solutions.

## Daily Challenge

Think of yourself as a talk-show host during a conversation today. Start the conversation by either complimenting someone and then following up with a question, or making a general statement and then asking a question. Try to make your conversation genuine by finding the person's positive hot buttons and asking good questions.

## Executive Challenge

Improve the quality of at least three conversations today by making them more real, genuine, and down to earth. Try the five suggestions listed under "Making Conversations Real." Experiment with getting people to expand on what they are talking about and their feelings.

CHAPTER 13:

# Influencing People

## In This Chapter:

- Learn three remarkable techniques to subtly influence others
- Get other people to agree with you without even realizing it
- Become more persuasive in your daily interactions with others

It seems some people just won't take no for an answer. What drives our powerful impulse to comply with the pressures of others? Whether you're a mere consumer or someone weaving the web of persuasion to urge others to buy your product or service or come over to your way of thinking, this chapter will help you understand some of the most common ways that you can influence others.

## Understanding "Click-Whirr" Responses

Thousands of small shortcuts are already programmed in each of us to keep us from overwhelming ourselves with common everyday decisions. In most cases, this is an advantage. But because we no longer think about and analyze every little decision, we occasionally find ourselves prey to masters of influence.

In his book *Influence*, Robert Cialdini writes that we all have "click-whirr" responses to save us time. These are "fixed-action patterns," or reactions, that automatically play when triggered, like popping in a prerecorded cassette tape every time you receive a particular stimulus. This reduces, as Cialdini puts it, "brain strain," preventing us from "standing frozen—cataloging, appraising, and calibrating—as the time for action sped by and away." A beggar reaches out for a handout and we either give or keep walking—

173

we've already decided our course of action ahead of time. In his book Cialdini describes other fixed-action patterns such as "expensive = good."

Often, without even thinking about it, we find ourselves agreeing with others. Try subtly nodding your head up and down in the affirmative as you ask someone toward the end of the day, or someone who is tired: "You are pretty tired, aren't you?" Nine times out of 10, the person will nod back and agree with you, without consciously thinking about it.

Then try the opposite. Subtly shake your head in the negative and "tell" someone that he is not tired as you "ask" him. Nine times out of 10 he will agree with you that he is not tired. Experiment with your own variations of this technique.

## The Jelly Donut Girl

So there I was, driving through scenic downtown Beckley, West Virginia, and I decided to stop in at the Dunkin' Donuts for a cup of coffee. I had eaten breakfast earlier and all I wanted was a cup of coffee. Incredibly, however, I walked out with a cup of coffee and a jelly donut—that girl was good!

I remember sitting in my car with the coffee to go and the jelly donut, wondering how in the world I had gotten suckered—I didn't even want the donut! What happened was, I had fallen victim to the donut nod, the whisper, and the secret selling technique—all used together on me.

The following day I went back for another cup of coffee and complimented the young woman behind the counter on her fine job of selling a salesman. She just grinned and innocently said that she had no idea what I was talking about and went on with her business. Whether she knew what she was doing or not, it certainly worked.

Here is what had happened. I had walked in and ordered a cup of coffee and then kept my mouth shut until after I'd paid (so the waitress couldn't up-sell me). Just before walking out of the store I had made my mistake. I asked her which donut, out of all the donuts in the store, was her favorite. She replied that every morning when she came in, she loved to eat a warm glazed donut. She said they were unbelievable.

Then she turned the question around on me and asked me what my favorite donut was out of all the donuts on the shelf. I told her that I was partial to the jelly donuts. Then she did her magic. She looked to the left, then to the right. Then she carefully leaned in toward me, as if to tell me a secret. I naturally leaned in, too, to "get in on it." She whispered (so I would pay particular attention to what she was saying), "Would you like a jelly donut?"

When she asked me this, she slowly nodded her head ever so slightly in a familiar "yes" motion. Without realizing it, I nodded my head back at her. I didn't know if she was giving me this donut or selling it to me; I just nodded. She picked up the donut, put it in the bag and rang it up for 63 cents! I just smiled at her, knowing that I had been had. She was good.

Waiters in restaurants frequently try to up-sell us because the more they sell, the higher the overall bill and the more their tip. The largest profit margin and greatest potential for wait staff to increase your bill is in the drinks. Waiters tend to mention the most expensive drinks at the end of their "ask." They might ask, "Would you like this drink, this drink, or would you like the fireball?!" When they say, "the fireball," they might subtly nod their head. Without thinking, we often nod back in agreement, "I want the fireball."

## Using Third-Party Examples

Salespeople are trained in sales courses to be "consultants." The trainers advise, "You know more about your product, your competitor's products, and the industry than your customers do, so think of yourself as consultants." Then salespeople go into the field and find that they are a dime a dozen. Salespeople seem to be everywhere! Salespeople even complain about being treated like salespeople!

But six-figure salespeople differentiate themselves from the pack with their extraordinary communication skills. They know to establish trust and credibility up front, or else all of their technical knowledge is useless. But here is the secret of salespeople who are more of a consultant than a salesperson: they use third-party examples.

Salespeople have the unique advantage of talking with countless people in various industries. One pharmaceutical salesman told me that he talks with about 135 doctors every month. So he uses third-party examples to discuss his product. He relates discussions and conversations with other doctors to position himself as a resource—a consultant—for the physician he's calling on. He will say something like: "A doctor I was talking to this morning in Beckley was having the same problem you are having and this is how he handled it." Or: "You are doing the same thing that a physician in Marlinton was doing, but he found that …"

Using third-party examples shows people your experience level, gives you more credibility, and helps you position yourself as a resource (consultant), all of which helps you persuade people to your way of thinking or to what you have to sell.

# Offering Choices

People like choices! They want a decision to do something to be theirs; they don't want to be told or sold. So if you offer them a choice between two items, and they pick one, then the decision is theirs. And you just "made the sale" without even asking if they wanted what you were selling. This is another click-whirr response—we are conditioned to choose one of the choices we are offered.

I saw this in action at a dinner at which I ate way too much. I don't believe I have ever eaten as much food. Not only is Stacy Underwood an unbelievable cook, she is an unbelievable salesperson! She cooked up one of the finest meals I had ever eaten. She apparently did not like leftovers and wanted us to finish all of the food during dinner. She did it with one remarkably simple, but effective technique, the "rather."

Stacy would say, "Pete, would you rather have more steak or potatoes?" Then she would give me the one I chose. Then she would say, "Would you rather have more beans or corn?" Without realizing it, I would always pick one of her two choices. Note that she cleverly didn't give me the "choice" to have more food or not to have more food! Yet she never came across as forcing me to eat more; she was just giving me choices. She was so nice and fast about it that I didn't realize how much I was eating.

Something similar to this happens to all of us, all of the time, without our realizing it. Once at a local bar and grill, my brother Steve and I ordered something to drink and were thinking about ordering a little something to eat. The waitress recommended the deluxe nachos. Steve said that sounded good and ordered them. The waitress asked, "Would you prefer the chicken or the beef?" Without thinking, Steve replied "chicken." Later we realized that the nachos were a $1.50 more with chicken or beef added. The waitress had cleverly "up-sold" us by giving us a choice.

In his book *Selling for Dummies*, Tom Hopkins recommends this "choice" method. He said he might make a statement, such as "It sure would be a pretty day to play golf." When the other person agreed, he would say, "Let's play golf. Would you rather play at 2 P.M. or 3 P.M.? He said people would pick a time and never realize that they had never even said they wanted to play golf.

My editor said the man who became her husband used this technique when he asked her out on their first date. At that time she was a salesperson and his company was a customer. He said, "We should go out to dinner some night after work. Would you prefer a Tuesday or a Thursday?" She answered "Thursday" without even thinking about whether she really wanted to go out with him or not!

Experienced moms use this technique to "sell" their children on doing what they need to do. They give their children choices: "Would you rather clean your room or go to bed?" Either way, the mother wins. "Would you rather clean out the garage or brush your teeth?" Children, like adults, don't often think about it and just pick one of the two choices out of conditioning.

My brother Nick always gives a choice of what to do, including the pros and cons of each, but he's secretly weighted the choice he wants you to choose. When he went to Ukraine with my other brother Steve, he asked: "Would you rather take a train to Kiev or Odessa?" He added that Odessa would be fun, but it would be a full day there, full day back, and they would have only a day there at best. But he said it was Steve's choice. Without Steve realizing it, Nick had gently swayed Steve to his way of thinking simply by offering him the choice. Steve chose Kiev and was happy they were going there, for it was "his" choice.

This choice technique works in business as well. I know a salesman who used this technique and up-sold 90 percent of his accounts by 30 percent on average. He would give each customer a choice. He said it didn't even matter how good the choices were; it worked simply because customers were given a choice. When it came time for customers to renew their advertising for the next year, the salesman would increase the price 30 percent for Package A. He created a Package B by throwing in a few bells and whistles and charging $15 more. If either package sold, the salesman was happy, for he increased his orders 30 percent, so he came across relaxed and not pushy. He said most people chose Package B for only $15 more because it was a better choice!

# Flattery Will Get You Everywhere

An Army warrant officer I worked with, Chief Swearingen, influenced people with flattery. One day I wanted to shorten the weekly motor stables (scheduled maintenance), in which we would do preventive checks and services on our equipment. I suggested to Chief that I was going to shorten the maintenance period so we could get other things done.

He countered with, "Sir, as a good officer you know how important this equipment is to our daily missions." I thought to myself, "I am a good officer; he is right." He would say to the battalion commander, "As a good commander, you know that …" He would say to soldiers, "As a new leader you know …" If an older sergeant didn't want to perform maintenance, he would pull him aside and say, "Sarge, as a couple of guys that have been around for a while, you know how important good maintenance is …"

He would bond with you and then subtly appeal to your ego. Since you're a good communicator, I'm sure you can see how valuable this technique might be to you …!

## Chapter Summary

- "Click-Whirr" Responses. Thousands of small shortcuts are programmed in each of us to keep us from overwhelming ourselves with common everyday decisions. These "fixed-action patterns," or reactions, automatically play when triggered, like nodding your head in agreement every time people ask you something while nodding their head.

- Third-Party Examples. Relate how others have addressed the point you're bringing up, which will help you position yourself as a consultant or resource. This will show people your experience level and give you more credibility as you try to persuade them to your way of thinking.

- Offering Choices. People want a decision to do something to be theirs; they don't want to be told or sold. So if you offer them a choice, and they pick one, then the decision is theirs. And you just "made the sale" without even asking if they wanted what you were selling.

- Flattery Will Get You Everywhere. Chief Swearingen would bond with people, compliment them, and subtly appeal to their noble side.

## Daily Challenge

Ask someone to lunch today. Ask them if they would rather meet you at 11:30 A.M. or if noon would be better. Next practice asking someone a question and nodding either in the affirmative or the negative while you ask it. Nod your head slightly and say to someone, "You are pretty tired, aren't you?" Practice the secret/whisper technique.

## Executive Challenge

Today, practice appealing to someone's ego and flatter them a little. Imply how noble they are and then appeal to their sense of nobility. If you were selling advertising, for example, you might appeal to someone's business sense by saying something along the lines of, "As a successful businessman, you know how crucial advertising is to an organization in competitive markets." Appeal to their good business sense.

# Talking Like a Politician

## In This Chapter:

- Discover the secrets to bringing people and groups together
- Learn how winners unite people, not divide them
- Find common ground and shared values with people
- Use three easy tricks to talk with people on difficult subjects
- Talk with people on politically charged subjects safely
- Learn to tiptoe your way through difficult situations and build goodwill

**A**lthough many people can't even get along with their family or neighbors, they are often able to come together under the leadership of a successful politician. How do politicians accomplish this enormous feat?

This chapter is not about politicking or speaking with political correctness. Nor is it about how to lie! Instead, it looks at specialized communication skills to help you unite people, build solidarity, and strengthen relationships—in short, how to be politically savvy.

> *"When he is against you, it's tough.*
> *When he is with you, it's a great feeling."*
> **—President George W. Bush, January 2002,**
> **speaking about Senator Edward Kennedy**

When people are with us, life is good. And when they are against us, life is more difficult. Doesn't it simply make good sense to take the time to learn how to find common ground and shared values with people? Isn't it more enjoyable to find how much you have in common with others and not argue over the few points where you differ? Doesn't it just make sense to talk about what you both agree on and build solidarity? The more people you have on your side, the easier life becomes.

## Unite People, Don't Divide Them

Politicians know the power of uniting people. They understand the power of the masses. They know that none of us is as strong as all of us. They know that the only way to change legislation is by rallying people behind them. They understand the power of numbers and use it to their advantage.

Poor communicators have not learned these lessons. They divide and segregate people in many ways. They judge and categorize people during their conversations by finding faults and areas of disagreement. This approach shatters their base, like a mirror thrown from a cliff. It scatters countless people into a myriad of directions. They lose their core group of family, friends, and work associates. This causes people either to never build a base or to destroy it continually over time.

One way to unite people is to use inclusive language. Use words like "we" and "our." Talk about the great things "we" do. Talk about what "we" have done as a company or team. Talk about "our" goals, "our" state, and "our" country.

People who divide groups create what one of my colonels in the Army called a "we/they thing." They instantly separate people and categorize them into groups. People who create a "we/they thing" often talk about how "they always," "you never," or "she constantly." It is an "us" against "them" attitude. This destroys or diminishes the effectiveness of teams, organizations, friends, and families that share common goals or common roots. Put another way, partisan politics always creates a winner and a loser.

Here is an example. In April 2003 I was watching an interview with Michael Reagan, popular radio talk-show host and son of the former President, on the Fox News Channel program *Hannity and Colmes*. Reagan started out talking about how great it was that Iraq was being liberated in the war, but soon began tearing apart groups and individuals that didn't support the war from the start. His comments started out as teasing but soon became a shouting match, instilling feelings of hate and resentment on one side, even though some of his points may have been valid.

Later that night Joe Scarborough, former congressman and a talk-show host on the MSNBC cable channel, had a completely different show on the same topic. It was very uplifting. Scarborough didn't divide or separate groups or single out any individuals. He used words to unite all viewers. "It's a great day for America …, we did something great, the United States…, our country…, our president …," and the like. He united people; Michael Reagan divided people. Both men said the United States and coalition partners liberated Iraq, but one elicited anger and one elicited pride. Would you rather feel proud or angry?

## Close Conversations on a High Note

Politically savvy people are great conversation closers. They always leave others on a high note, regardless whether they had a 20-second conversation or a three-day meeting. They leave people feeling a little better than they did before the conversation or meeting. They may be helpful, complimentary, and even charming. They reassure people and make them feel good about a decision they made. They do it sincerely and genuinely.

Listed below are a few conversational closes that I have heard six-figure communicators use:

- "Terry Gross, you have no idea the thrill it's been to converse with you." —Bill Russell, NBA Great, concluding an interview on National Public Radio, 2002.
- "Pete, what a pleasure it was to see you again. If there is anything in the world that I can ever do for you, please don't hesitate to let me know." —Dr. Gary Poling, Family Practitioner
- Doug, you have certainly been a big help; thank you.
- It has certainly been a pleasure meeting you. Have fun kayaking this weekend.
- (Smile) Thanks.
- I wish you the best of luck with _____.
- I hope you enjoy your _____.
- Have a great day (flooding smile and eye dart)
- This has been the highlight of my day, talking with you. Have a safe trip back.
- You are going to do terrific in the championships; have fun!
- Carrie, it sounds like it will be quite a weekend; enjoy the wedding.
- You have nothing to worry about; you are going to be great!

# Create Allies

Politicians shake a lot of hands, pat people on the back, and meet people wherever they go. They have outgoing personalities and have never met a voter that they didn't like. They meet people on the spot and enlist their help if needed.

Like politicians, six-figure communicators introduce themselves easily to others. They come across as warm and genuine to everyone they meet, wherever they meet them. They build rapport with people before asking anyone for anything. Because of this, they create allies wherever they go. If they need real help anywhere, they have a new group of people who will genuinely and sincerely help them. These allies are willing to go out of their way to help, offering to do special favors or offering advice. Six-figure communicators get further in life with less effort because they have more people helping them along the way.

## Break the Ice Quickly

When you're in a place where you may want to have allies, then break the ice quickly with those you encounter. This is of particular help when you are far from home or the office. When you're traveling, break the ice with the flight attendants or the hotel staff. Have them on your side from the start. Then if you ever need their assistance, you have an ally.

The first time I flew to Detroit, I had a horrible headache, maybe because I had hardly eaten all day. My "ride" was not there to pick me up, and I was exhausted from many hours of travel. I went to an information booth and asked the woman behind the counter about a special shuttle and other questions about Detroit. We hit it off immediately. She offered me her apple, an aspirin, and entry into a show she was managing downtown later that week! How thoughtful of her. It was great to have an ally in unfamiliar territory. And it certainly made traveling easier and better.

If you avoid the opportunity to make that initial contact, but then later need help from the person, don't expect her to be your ally. You will get marginal advice or none at all. Creating an ally might be as simple as a compliment, such as "nice hat." You deliver the compliment genuinely and sincerely, and then if you ever need the person's help, the ice is broken and usually she will reciprocate with honest and sincere help.

## Use People's Names

One tip in creating allies is to get the person's name and use it periodically throughout your conversation. This not only helps you remember your new ally's name, but it makes him feel flattered that you made the effort to learn it. Use his name to say good-bye and to leave him on a high note: "John, it was certainly a pleasure to meet you. Good luck on your competition this weekend." If you ever need to speak with John again, you are on a first-name basis.

**Note:** Call the person by the name he used to introduce himself. If someone introduces himself as Andrew, do not call him Andy. If you are introduced to a couple as Mr. and Mrs. [last name], address each with Mr. or Mrs., unless you are corrected otherwise.

# Thank People!

Surely you have seen politicians walking around thanking constituents for their hard work and support? Politicians actively get out there and work the crowds. They know how important it is to thank veterans, volunteers, and other voters. They send cards and congratulate people on their accomplishments. They even thank people for asking them questions. This gratitude makes constituents feel good and helps politicians stay in office. Politicians have learned over the years how important it is to recognize others.

Politicians always have something positive to say. They not only congratulate people, but also compliment them whenever they get the chance. Although a constituent may be yelling about something, the successful politician will turn the objection around and thank the constituent for his concern, telling him how much she appreciates his interest in the matter and how important the issue is. Then she will quickly address the question and then speak to a more general statement. She makes the other person feel listened to and heard.

Like politicians, professional fund-raisers are profuse in their thanks. One professional fund-raiser told me in an interview that his organization's goal is to thank donors at least seven times. He and other people within his organization thank donors on the phone, by letter, at the start of a social function, at the end of the social function. They may also thank them with a small gift. It is a group effort that has raised literally millions of dollars for the betterment of others.

You, too, can thank your "constituents" or "stakeholders" by telling them how much you appreciate their support and service. Tell people when they did well. When was the last time you thanked your employees, or even your dry cleaner, for all of their hard work and for taking the extra time to do the job right? Taking a minute out of your week to do this not only will be the highlight of their day, but will get you far better service and more loyal employees.

Six-figure communicators know the power of telling others how much they appreciate their help and how they made their life a little easier. They give people encouraging words when they need them, tell people how much they love them, let people know how proud they are of them, and simply congratulate people on their accomplishments. They always take the time to let people know.

## Cards and Notes

Don't underestimate the power of a card or note. Six-figure communicators usually have a box of blank cards available at the office, in their car, or at home. They typically use the two- or three-sentence technique (TST)—just two or three sentences on a note card and delivered in person or dropped in the mail. Always use the TST to thank people for hosting, sponsoring, or coordinating an event. It is surprising how many people come to an event, eat the food, talk to their friends, and leave without saying a word to the people who made the event possible.

The TST takes only a minute and means a lot to the person who put a lot of work into something, such as hosting you at dinner, preparing a speech, planning a social function, or doing something for others. It is far more important to get the cards out than to have every card perfect. This simple action will win you more friends, loyalty, and respect, simply and easily.

**Here are a few examples:**
- Thank you for having us over. We really enjoyed ourselves.
- Thank you for taking the time to put together that presentation. I learned a lot.
- You did a great job today. Keep up the good work!

Politically savvy people also use cards to keep their networks strong. They often send cards to contacts to keep their relationships alive and contacts current. They know that what's important isn't what they say, but that they send something periodically. The advantage of cards is that people can target several people quickly without spending time chatting on the phone.

> Always ask people for their business cards after meeting and then send them a thank-you note. Top communicators use the TST to write cards quickly and mail them the same day.

## In-Person Thanks

Another way to thank people who "did good" or to keep in contact with others is by doing it in person. Pull them aside if you can, invite them into your office, or have coffee or lunch with them, and then use the opportunity to say "good job," to congratulate them, or to thank them for their help. As with the written TST, you don't have to say a lot. Just say your two or three sentences aloud. That is enough. Anything more is icing on the cake. To make it even more powerful, use a nonlinguistic body movement (Chapter 11).

> Use the TST when giving gifts of books. Write two or three sentences just inside the front cover. For example, "I saw this book on having your first child and thought of you. I think you are going to make a great mom. Congratulations!"

# Agree with People

Politicians strive to make themselves likeable when they are working a crowd or speaking to groups. They always seem to tell you what you want to hear.

We could argue about the value of this in politics, but the fact remains that people would rather agree with you than disagree. It feels better to say yes than no. It feels better to talk about common ground and areas where you see eye-to-eye than to find the areas where you disagree. You, too, can build this kinship and bonding by agreeing with everything you can.

The incremental model below illustrates that more people find unity and agreement on a general level rather than at a specific level. No one agrees perfectly on every issue, on every course of action, or on every response, even within families. It is impossible. So how do you find common ground with others on things you disagree on? Through the techniques discussed in this section: zooming, notching, and setting aside.

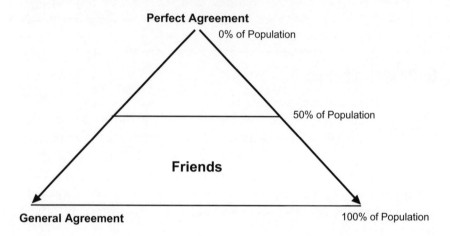

**Perfect Agreement**
0% of Population

50% of Population

**Friends**

**General Agreement**

100% of Population

## Zooming

As soon as you start talking "out of synch" with someone, stop. If you cannot agree on a specific, "zoom out" a little and agree with a more general statement. If you can't quite agree on that statement, zoom out a little more and agree with a broader subject. Keep zooming out until you find agreement. This is the place to spend most of your time.

For example, let's say that you are in a clinic waiting room and someone strikes up a conversation with you. He starts complaining about the long wait and then moves into a diatribe against the U.S. health care trend toward managed care. He is getting really upset and becomes outraged at what he sees as the insurance companies' interfering in the doctor's business (law of attraction).

Some people in a situation like this might try to "out debate" the other person. It starts off fun but soon turns ugly. You have almost no chance of changing someone's entrenched opinions in five minutes in a doctor's office. People are set in their ways and rarely change. Disagreement, particularly on highly charged topics, only builds animosity and anger.

Instead, focus on what you both agree on and talk about that. If you can't agree specifically on what to do, or if he has told you his opinion without yet knowing yours, zoom out of the specifics and find more general areas to agree on. Talk about how important it is to have health insurance. If that doesn't work, zoom out more and talk about wellness in general, or the good that has come from advanced medical technology.

If you zoom out enough, sooner or later everyone must agree. All too often, when we disagree with people, we are wasting time talking about specifics. Talking about specifics does more harm than good. Then through the law of attraction, we or they get angrier, more frustrated, and more irritated. Avoid no-win arguments by zooming out to general topics or changing the subject. A wise person does not talk in specifics.

## Notching

Another way to work toward agreement with people is by finding out where they stand on an issue on a Likert scale (a rating scale used to measure the strength of agreement with a clear statement). You might say, "On a scale of 1 to 10, with 10 being the most adamant, how do you feel about [fill in the blank]?" If someone is at a level 10, then you know that she is immovable and you can avoid arguing over the subject. A person at a level 5, however, would be easier to move a notch or two toward your way of thinking. This is called notching. Don't try to get 100 percent agreement all at once.

By asking people where they stand on a Likert scale, you not only learn their stance, but also you give yourself a starting point to work with to better understand how ingrained they are in their beliefs. You instantly take some of the subjectivity out of the conversation.

If you're a salesperson, you might use the incremental model to pinpoint a customer's current satisfaction with a competitor's product or service and then point out how your product or service would increase satisfaction by a notch or two. For example, you might ask a customer, "On a scale of 1 to 10, how happy are you with the performance of your suppliers?" Few people will give a 10, no matter how pleased they are. They will be conservative and give an 8. They admit the suppliers aren't perfect, thereby opening the door to discussion about why or what can be done to improve performance. This helps you pin down specific problems, such as late deliveries, and address real concerns. You simply move the customer up a notch or two by showing how your product or service can reduce delays and save the customer money over the long run.

If a customer is pretty satisfied with his present situation, then you can zoom out and talk more broadly to try to find an opening for your product or service. You're looking for areas of agreement on how your product or service could improve the customer's situation. Too many salespeople try to get 100 percent of a client's business all at once. Move slowly if you must, a notch at a time.

Likewise, in issues discussions, if someone says he is a 7 on a scale of 1 to 10, with 10 being an unchangeable position, then begin zooming out and talking more broadly on the subject. Move him down only a notch or two and get a more general agreement. You can rarely change another person's thinking and lifelong beliefs all at once.

## Setting Aside

Another technique to find or maintain agreement with another person is to set aside issues that you disagree on. Don't let these issues cloud the larger picture and stop momentum in a conversation. Diplomats as well as salespeople know to tell others, "Let's put that [obstacle] aside for now." By doing this, the two of you can stay focused and build agreement without letting temporary distractions impede progress.

## Use Safe Statements

Politicians know all too well how difficult it is to talk with some people. They know that no matter what they say, they just can't make some people happy. They know that some people are easily offended and that some subjects are no-win. They know that some subjects radically divide people and create hostility and bitterness. And because of this, politicians and others have learned to use safe statements.

When Bob Barker, the host of the *Price is Right* game show, was interviewed on the *Today* show, the interviewer asked him about being an animal rights activist. I thought to myself at the time that the interview had gone so well, it would be a shame to blow it talking about activism. Barker answered the question by saying, "Ohhhh, I just love animals!" He said this with a huge smile and a real love in his voice. Who could disagree with that? Few people really dislike animals. He didn't stay on that subject for long but his love for animals shone through, making you feel warm inside. What a pro!

Without going into the details, you can agree with people by using safe statements, like Bob Barker's. Safe statements don't really say a lot but they make people feel good, they let people feel that you understand them, and more important, they do not offend. One of my favorite statements is "You need to have balance." You can use it in almost any situation to talk about anything, building solidarity. Come up with your own, but the following are a few examples of safe statements and comments:

- Well, sure
- Absolutely
- What's important is the safety of our citizens/children/seniors/highways/parks/transportation system/food supply
- I'm not thrilled with it, but …
- I don't know all the specifics of what transpired, but I do know that …
- It's not perfect, but we are probably better off with it than without it
- It's not ideal, but in all honestly, you are probably better off doing it than not doing it
- We are looking forward, not backward
- It's a good first step
- You are both right, but you are each looking at it from your own perspective

# Bring Out Different Sides

Politicians understand that we all wear many hats—such as parent, brother, friend, soccer coach, manager, laborer, student, alumnus—so they will address the crowd as these different roles. They'll address crowds as parents when they're talking about school initiatives and as veterans while talking about issues of national defense.

To be more politically savvy yourself, bring out different sides of people when talking to them to help them see things from a different perspective. Asking someone how he feels about a subject as a father, for example, might elicit a different response than asking him how he feels about that subject as a military officer. As a grandparent, what are your thoughts on …? As a woman, what do you think about …?

# Tell the Good with the Bad

Politicians are diplomatic. They know the importance of telling the good with the bad. Many of us make the mistake of telling only the bad! Most people have feelings, especially on sensitive topics involving pride and ego and are just trying to do the best they can.

Telling the good with the bad makes it easier to tell anyone anything. It softens the blow and helps people feel more comfortable communicating. It also puts things into a better perspective. You'll get the idea from these examples:

- Son, I'm really proud of how you brought up your grades this semester, but we still have some problems in geometry.
- Beckley is a wonderful town and the people are so nice—but the traffic is terrible!
- Plum Orchard Lake is a beautiful lake—thank you for taking me— but the fishing is not worth a nickel!

Toastmasters teaches club members how to evaluate one another's speeches. Evaluation is important to becoming a better speaker, for if you don't hear feedback, you will not learn how you're doing or how to improve. One technique Toastmasters recommends is called sandwiching:

1. Tell speakers what you liked about their speech.
2. Suggest improvements or challenge them to do something different next time.
3. Conclude with something you really liked.

This technique sandwiches the bad between two pieces of good into a "palatable" evaluation. By hearing the good with the bad (2-to-1 ratio of good), people are more open to constructive criticism and they will learn more quickly.

# Resolve Conflicts at the Lowest Level Possible

People with political savvy handle problems and situations at the lowest level possible. Only as a last resort do they escalate problems or situations. They know that the higher the problem goes, the more ill will is created and the more people will be forced to justify their actions, regardless of how right or wrong they were.

Poor communicators escalate situations too quickly without giving people at lower levels a "fair shake." Even when you find that the higher-ups agree with you, often you still have to go back and face the original person with whom you had the conflict. This creates ill will and bad feelings, not to mention the loss of time, energy, and perhaps money. Working relationships and possibly even friendships are lost.

A couple I know got into an argument with an Internal Revenue Service agent who sent them a bill for $9,500. Of course the couple was outraged, and they started yelling and screaming at the agent. Unfortunately, they also told the agent that they were going to go way over his head and not work with him to resolve the problem. Once they did this, they left no other options on the table for the agent. The agent couldn't, or wouldn't, go out of his way for them and take another look at the situation. He felt forced to stand firm and justify his initial position to his supervisors. The outcome: Many years and $110,000 in attorney fees later, the couple won and didn't have to pay the $9,500 to the IRS agent. But what did they gain?

Six-figure communicators prevent situations from escalating by talking and working with people at the lowest level possible. They are polite to everyone and take exceptional care of people at all levels. They make people feel respected, and they solve as much as they can at the lowest level possible.

## Engage Others

Politicians know how to engage others in conversation and bring people together. This is one of the ways they form groups of people around them, unintentionally raising their own popularity or status. They use the three-track mind to notice other people in the immediate area whom they want to pull into the conversation. They realize that quiet people or introverts usually get ignored by extraverts in groups. Extraverts have been known to monopolize conversations unintentionally. But six-figure communicators include others by asking:

- What do you think about that, Joe?
- Ann Marie, what are your thoughts on ...?
- Jennifer, how do you feel about ...?
- Do you know what I mean, Nick?

Using someone's name and then asking what she thinks about a particular subject gently flatters her. Six-figure communicators know that it is okay if people don't want to talk or participate in a conversation, but they at least make an attempt to check in with others. They give other people a chance to participate, feel part of the group, and feel valued. Do you know what I mean?

A top auto salesperson once told me that his greatest mistake when a couple came in to buy a car was talking to the husband and ignoring the wife. He said he didn't mean to, but the husband was asking all of the questions. He never realized he was doing that until one wife angrily jumped into the conversation and asked why the husband was getting all of the questions when the car was really for her!

The next day (lesson learned), a female customer thanked him for talking with her about the car by saying: "You were the only person at a dealership to actually talk to me." She went on to say that she didn't know what questions to ask, but "you talked to me." The salesman says that now, when he's working with a couple, he spends two-thirds of the time talking to the wife and only one-third talking to the husband.

# Choose Your Battles

Politicians know that they cannot take on the entire world. They know that some people will always disagree with them. But they don't fight everyone on everything. Instead, they choose their battles. They know that a victory at any cost can be ruinous.

Like politicians, great generals know the importance, literally, of choosing their battles—or at least most of them. When King Pyrrhus of Epirus was called on by the Greek city-state of Tarentum (located in the "heel" of southern Italy) to protect it and other Greek city-states from the Romans in 280 B.C., he jumped at the opportunity. Pyrrhus was a distant relative of Alexander the Great and always envisioned himself as "Alexanderesque." This was his chance to take on the Romans and expand Macedonian power and glory.

Pyrrhus certainly had reason to believe he could do this. He had the most modern and advanced army of the day. And when he stepped off his ship onto the shores of Italy, he had 25,000 men, including 3,000 cavalry and 2,000 archers. He also had 20 trained war elephants he would use to stampede through Roman lines.

His first battle was in Heraclea. Though he technically won this battle, he suffered great losses. He lost at least 4,000 soldiers and one source put it as high as 13,000. He lost so many soldiers in that battle that he had to stop his campaign to protect other Greek city-states and wait till the next year for more reinforcements.

The following year he fought another major battle, this time in Ausculum. Pyrrhus again won the battle, but suffered heavy casualties—3,500 casualties to the Romans' 6,000. According to Plutach, when congratulated on winning this battle, he replied, "One more such victory and I am lost."

Pyrrhus set sail to Sicily to aid Greeks there and stopped the Carthaginians from attacking Syracuse, his logistics base. There he liberated Syracuse and captured Eryx and Panormus. But again he sustained heavy losses.

He returned to Italy to learn that while he was in Sicily, the Romans moved back into Tarentum and southern Italy with reinforcements. Pyrrhus caught up with the Romans in Malventum for one last battle. There he and his army were utterly defeated.

The term *Pyrrhic* describes something achieved at excessive cost. It was coined after the battle of Ausculum. Though Pyrrhus won all of his major battles (except for his last), we must ask, at what cost? What did he accomplish? Was it worth it? Were he and his kingdom better off for it?

We must not forget King Pyrrhus or his Pyrrhic victories. We must remember that we probably can win battles with our 25,000 soldiers, 3,000 cavalry, 2,000 archers and 20 war-trained elephants. We must remember that we may have the most modern, best-equipped, and greatest soldiers in the world. We might even have the backing of other Greek kingdoms. But even if we win all of our battles, every time, are we losing the war?

If we win the "battle," what have we won? Was it won at too high a cost? Was the victory really worth it? Were we better off before or after the battle? How much damage was done? How did the battle improve our position or situation?

The lesson here is to choose your battles. You don't have to take every hill in life to be successful. You don't have to burn every bridge in battle either. There are times we must stop and assess where we are, what we are doing, and what is happening in the larger scheme of life. As tough as it may be, we have to know when to stop. From the days of Pyrrhus to modern times, winning battles can be costly.

Six-figure communicators avoid battles whenever possible. But if they do fight them, they choose their battles and keep the end state in mind. And only then, they fight using adroitness, tact, and diplomacy.

# Chapter Summary

- Although many people have trouble getting along with friends and neighbors, people with political savvy not only can get along with large numbers of people, but also can get large numbers of people to come together. When people are with us, life is good. When they are against us, life is more difficult. The more people you have on your side, the easier life becomes.

- Unite people, don't divide them. Use inclusive language to unite people. Use words like *we* and *our* to avoid creating "a we/they thing." Talk about *our* company, *our* family, and *our* group.

- Close conversations on a positive note.

- Create allies. Politically savvy people introduce themselves easily to others and create allies wherever they go. Then if they need real help, they have a group of people who will genuinely and sincerely help them.

- Thank people! Most people are in need of sincere, honest appreciation. Take a minute to thank people for their time, service, and the job they are performing. Use the two-sentence technique (TST)—simply write down two or three sentences on a card and either mail or drop off the card. Phone calls and thanking people in person are also effective.

- Agree with people. Agree with everything you can when talking to others. Talk about what you both agree on, not your differences. This builds kinship and bonding. As soon as you start talking "out of synch," stop.

- Zooming. If you cannot agree on a specific, zoom out a little and agree with a more general statement. If you can't quite agree on that statement, zoom out a little more and agree on a broader subject. Most of a conversation should be about what you both agree on, not what you disagree on.

- Notching. Identify people's position on a subject or issue on a Likert scale and then try to move them up or down a notch or two on the scale. Often this is more effective than trying to completely change someone's views.

- Setting aside. If you can't agree, don't let this cloud the larger picture and stop momentum in a conversation. By doing this, the two of you can stay focused and build agreement without letting temporary distractions impede progress.

- Use safe statements. Some subjects are no-win and radically divide people. Instead of going into details of a divisive issue, use safe statements. These don't really say a lot, but they make people feel better, help them feel understood, and do not offend.

- Bring out people's different roles. Ask people to see things from a certain perspective by asking them to put themselves into a specific role, such as "As a parent, how do you feel about …"

- Tell the good with the bad. This makes it easier to tell anyone anything, softening the blow and helping people to feel more comfortable communicating. Sandwiching the bad between two "goods" also puts things into a more optimistic perspective.

- Resolve conflicts at the lowest level possible. Only as a last resort do politically savvy people take a problem to a higher level.

- Engage others. At least make an attempt to check in with others, and give other people a chance to participate, feel part of the group, and feel valued.

- Choose your battles. Know that you may be able to win some battles, but the cost of victory may be high. If you must fight, choose the battles you can be successful at, keeping the end in mind. Unlike Pyrrhus, consider the cost of winning the battle.

## Daily Challenge

You are going to have a great day! Your goal today is to find reasons to thank people. Thank them for their hard work or their support. Thank them for all they have done for you over the years. Try the TST in person or write it in a card or note. Thank a least five people before you go to bed. Notice what this does to you and your relationships with others!

## Executive Challenge

Use simplified buttonomics (Chapter 4) and the incremental model today to quickly find common ground with people. If you can't find it, zoom out
until you can find it. Use inclusive language and words like *we* and *our* to
find solidarity. Don't be afraid to bring out people's different roles to do this.
This may help people shift their mental gears more easily.

# Storytelling

## In This Chapter:

- Learn the importance of telling stories
- Draw people into your stories and capture their attention
- Add impact to your stories by using 11 simple tips

W hether you call them parables, anecdotes, fables, illustrations, public speaking, dinner conversation, telling a joke, managing employees, selling, or simply recounting your day, stories have a unique ability to capture people's attention, simplify complex information, and teach others in a way that lecturing never could. Six-figure communicators have learned that storytelling is a shortcut to building rapport and effectively getting their message across to others. Even Christ taught with stories.

David Brooks, the 1990 World Champion of Public Speaking, says that public speaking is merely telling a story and making a point— telling another story and then making another point—telling still another story and making still another point. One new hospital CEO told me that he starts every meeting with success stories from various departments on how well they are implementing his plan. He said stories and testimonials build energy, solidarity, and belief that his restructuring plan works. Spencer Johnson, M.D., sold more than 12 million copies of his international best-selling business book *Who Moved My Cheese?*, a story of how two mice and two people deal with change.

Though story telling is extremely important in business, it is also important in our personal lives. Have you ever gone to a restaurant with a group of friends and seen another group in the corner laughing and having a good time? Although you liked the people you were with, you may have secretly wished you were in the "fun group"! Groups that have lots of energy always have people with good social skills telling stories. It is an important way we interact with others.

I've know people who have traveled to some of the most remote corners of the world and seen spectacular sights; but when asked to relate their travels to others, they made their experience sound barely out of the ordinary. And I have heard others tell a group of people about their weekend trip to the park and made it seem like one of the most interesting trips ever. It was the person who went to the park who had everyone's attention, not the guy who just got back from Istanbul! Why?

# 11 Tips for Telling Great Stories

Remember this: it is not where you go or what you do that makes the story—this has little to do with it. It is how well you tell it! It's how well you tell the joke or describe your day that interests people and draws them into the conversation. Good storytellers grab people's attention and hold it.

Learning to tell good stories is a skill like anything else. It is one of the most valuable of all people skills. Employers ask job applicants for stories and examples when they interview for a job. Friends and family also enjoy the richness of stories. All of us, children and adults alike, love to hear stories. And the better people are at telling stories, the more popular they will be and the more fun they and their group will have. Storytellers are always in the "fun group"—because they created it.

Storytelling could be simply describing your day, talking about your weekend, telling others about a movie you saw, or simply telling people about something that caught your attention. It doesn't have to be a formal story as such. Good storytelling is the art of *telling* "stories," not necessarily what you talk about or what happened.

## 1. Choose a Subject the Audience Can Relate To

Remember that the speech or story is for the audience, not you. If possible, choose a universal theme that the audience would enjoy hearing about. This helps to build rapport with the audience quickly.

If the audience can't relate to your story or topic easily, your first job is to build rapport for this topic. "Sell" the importance of the topic or relate it directly to them. This might be as simple as starting out with, "As fellow parents, you know how children manipulate us ..." Then talk about how you outsmarted your son.

## 2. Start Stories in the Middle of an Action

Regardless of what anyone says, don't start your story from the beginning! Most people don't care what time you got up, that you took a taxi to the airport, spilled coffee on your pants or arrived two hours late. Instead begin in the middle of an action, conversation, incident, or argument:

- I was fixing the radiator of my truck when all of a sudden a car...
- I was just standing there in the street when a man...
- I was talking to the latte lady at the airport when I...
- The teenager that was standing behind me all of a sudden...
- There were fourteen of us eating fondue when we heard the knock at the door...

## 3. Don't Tell us What Happened, Take us There!

The No. 1 mistake people make while telling stories is listing what happened in chronological order. "First we landed in Paris, then we took a bus to the hotel, then we took a tour of Notre Dame, and finally we had lunch in a little French cafe. Boring!

Instead, tell the story as it is happening and take us there with you. We want to be along with you on the police foot-chase, we want to be with you in that taxi, we want to be part of the excitement!

## 4. Incorporate the Five Senses

Tell us what we are seeing, smelling, feeling, hearing and tasting! You got us excited about what was happening, now we are craving sensory information. What is happening to us now? Describe the people, the scenery, and atmosphere. We want details!

Describe the exhilaration of strolling down the Champs Elysees, smelling the freshly brewed coffee in sidewalk cafes, hearing people laughing and speaking French, and seeing the elegant fashions in colorful store windows. Tell people what you were feeling as the sun rose on the French Riviera or set on the blue-green Mediterranean. Make us feel as if we are with you, dining in that cafe with you, or exploring with you. People want to feel as if they are there too!

## 5. Smile and Have Fun Telling Your Story

Charismatic people have figured out that, consciously or unconsciously, smiling while talking warms people up. This magical technique draws people toward you and pulls them in to whatever you have to say, whether or not you are telling a story. Smiling is so powerful that researchers have found that listeners can tell when you are smiling while you talk on the phone. It somehow comes across in your intonation.

But you need not stop at smiling. Crack up when you get to different parts of your story. Laughing and giggling your way through a story will draw people into it. Storytelling needs to be enjoyable. It's okay to have fun and laugh while you are telling it; it's your story.

## 6. Express Emotion as You Tell Your Story

When you're telling a story, express your emotions through your words and through nonlinguistic body movements (see Chapter 11), such as squinting, opening your eyes widely, hunching down, and so on. The stronger the emotion you express, the more powerful your stories will become.

Noncharismatic people typically have a "dead face" rather than an active face when they tell a story. They lack emotion and kill their stories with "information-dumping"—talking in facts and figures and merely listing what they did or what they saw. You'll have a much better story if you instead describe your impressions of what you did or saw.

## 7. Put Your Whole Body into the Story

The more you move with your story, the better it will be. Wave your arms and hands. Use your fingers to describe how crooked a road was or to imitate snow falling in your eyelashes. Touch your heart when telling about a sweet thing your child did, how wonderful your wife is, or how good her double-fudge chocolate chip brownies are. Rock back and forth or jump up and down if these movements will help you "act out" the story.

## 8. Use Colorful Language

Colorful language can spice up any story. Use various expressions, similes, and metaphors to draw in listeners and hold their attention. Talk about getting beat like a piñata, your term paper looking like Swiss cheese when your professor got through with it, or your boss having a temper as explosive as a volcano.

## 9. Take Poetic License with Exaggeration

Your story is sure to be funnier if you exaggerate the details. For great storytellers, the more they tell the story, the better it gets. They add at least one new detail every time they tell it—like a fish story. Even though it may seem a little unrealistic or outrageous, it does no harm and spices up the story. This is called poetic license—a deviation from fact to create an effect. Make something taller, bigger, smaller, louder, more dangerous, more spectacular, or more courageous than it might have been.

You could say that you were driving and saw the Weiner Mobile on the highway (statement). Or you could describe how you were adjusting a few buttons on the radio and glanced up to see what appeared to be a 65-foot-long hotdog on wheels. For example: "I mean, that 65-foot-long hotdog was flying down the interstate like a bat out of hell. I'm lucky to be alive! It was a speeding rocket that could have killed me! Killed by a hotdog! What would they have put on my tombstone?"

## 10. Build Up the Story with Details

Continually build up the story by adding more and more details. Most people just state the facts of what happened (statement) and jump right into the conclusion, without leading up to a punch line. But the longer you can keep the suspense, the better. Great storytellers use specifics and talk about the details, using similes, metaphors, and colorful language to build the suspense.

## 11. Use a Punch Linc When Possible

Although you don't always need a punch line, building up to one is a great way to top off a story. Here's an example:

At a gas station in West Virginia, I saw perhaps the most beautiful woman I'd ever seen. I walked into the store and there she stood—a vision of loveliness. I don't know how I got so lucky. Perhaps it was the alignment of the planets or the stars, or maybe it was my good clean living. This woman was an angel standing there behind the checkout counter. It was in the summertime, and her hair was blowing in the wind from a fan behind her. I don't know how long I stood in the doorway looking at her. It could have been just a second or it could have been a minute; I lost all sense of time. I slowly got in line and asked the good Lord to put the right words in my mouth to seem personable and charming. As I worked my way to the front of the line, she spoke the first words to me. "It's $13.93," she said with a great big smile.

She had one black tooth on the top and two on the bottom! I was petrified; I stood there for what seemed like an eternity, with my jaw dropped, trying to figure out what had just happened …

The story continued, but the punch line stuck. I smiled while telling this story, waved my hands and arms, built it up, used a metaphor, and delivered a punch line. I told this story as I experienced it at the time and made people feel that they were with me at the gas station. The fun, of course, is just trying to top your story with more details each time you tell it.

## Chapter Summary

• Six-figure communicators know that telling stories is a shortcut to building rapport and effectively getting their message across to others. The best managers, salespeople, physicians, and others use stories in both their professional and personal lives.

• It is not where you go or what you do that makes the story; this has little to do with it. The secret is how well you tell it! It's how well you tell the joke or describe your day that interests people and draws them into the story. Good storytellers grab people's attention and hold it.

• **11 Tips for Telling Great Stories**
    1. Choose a subject the audience can relate to
    2. Start stories in the middle of an action
    3. Don't tell us what happened, take us there
    4. Incorporate the five senses
    5. Smile and have fun telling your story
    6. Express emotion as you tell your story
    7. Put your whole body into the story
    8. Use colorful language
    9. Take poetic license with exaggeration
    10. Build up the story with details
    11. Use a punch line when possible

## Daily Challenge

Tell the same story today many times. Every time you tell it, add a few details and improve upon it. See how much you can build it up by the end of the day. Try to incorporate as many of the 11 keys to great storytelling as you can. And most important, enjoy telling the story.

## Executive Challenge

Practice reading excerpts today from at least three books. Concentrate on using enthusiasm to convey the story. As you read aloud, pay particular attention to your intonation, speaking speed, and style. Smile while you read and throw in a few hand gestures. With this exercise you don't have to worry about the words you use; just practice your delivery.

# Establishing Rapport Through Representational System

## In This Chapter:

- Understand how tuning in to a representational system can help you become more charismatic
- Learn the hidden secrets that visually charismatic people aren't telling you
- Hear how auditorily charismatic people use sound to establish rapport
- Develop the warmth and charisma of kinesthetic communicators

Neuro-Linguistic Programming (NLP) is a field of study that examines the structure of how humans think and experience the world. Among its teachings are that although people take in information using all of their senses, they tend to be dominant with one—visual, auditory, or kinesthetic. NLP terms this dominant sense a *representational system*. It is through your representational system that you interpret much of your world.

You will find it easier to establish rapport with someone if both of you have the same representational system. Then you communicate in the same "language." For example, if you and another person are both visual, it will be easier for you to establish rapport than if one of you is visual and the other is auditorily dominant. But rather than try to figure out in which representational system another person is dominant, become as charismatic as possible in all three.

This chapter divides rapport into these three component systems—visual, auditory, and kinesthetic. The more charismatic you become in each representational system, the more easily you will be able to establish rapport with a broader range of people.

## Developing Charisma

The quickest way to develop charisma is to focus on visual and auditory traits. Research shows that in a presentation before a group, 55 percent of the impact of your presentation is determined by your body language—posture, gestures, and eye contact; 38 percent by your voice; and only 7 percent by the content.[1] In other words, it's not what you say as much as how you say it that matters. Focus on communicating visually and auditorily for impact and charisma, and then focus on the kinesthetics.

The goal of this chapter is to give you simple, practical methods to increase charisma now! It is not designed to cover charismatic theory, its origins, history, speech-writing techniques, or scientific principles. Many books have been written on just these components. This chapter introduces how to connect with people's representational system on an interpersonal and conversational level. It will give you practical techniques to put to use right away.

## Visual Charisma

Visual people make up about 60 percent of the population. They communicate much more quickly than auditory or kinesthetic people. Their eyes are constantly scanning their environment, looking for movement, color, or anything else that catches their eye. Visual people tend to lock eyes quickly with other visual people as if to say, "Did you see that?" or "What did you think of that?" Wherever visual people's eyes are looking is where their attention is. They notice clothing, facial expressions, and posture much more quickly than others, for this is their dominant sense.

Visual people don't necessarily feel the need to talk a lot for they absorb most of their information through their eyes, not their ears. Words are secondary or tertiary to a visual person. Often visual people use gestures instead of talking. For example, if they walk by someone, they might nod their head or smile at the other person in acknowledgement without feeling the need even to say hello. For them, such a greeting is just as good as or even better than speaking.

Visual charisma consists of anything that can be picked up by the human eye. Much of the time this type of charisma is done subtly, as with nonlinguistic movements (see Chapter 11). Other times it is done on a larger scale, with grand gestures. What follows are the core and secondary traits of visually charismatic people. This section will look at each of these in more detail.

| Core Traits | Specifics |
|---|---|
| Presentation | well groomed, neatly dressed, well put together |
| Pleasant/Active Face | NLMs (smile, eyes, cheecks, eyebrows, etc.) |
| Deliberate Movement | NLMs (facial, hands, fingers, head), gestures |

| Secondary Traits | Specifics |
|---|---|
| Posture | head back over body, fig-leaf stance, correct sitting |
| Focus | one-track mind (while speaking and listening) |

# Presentation

Presentation is how we look when we leave the house and our appearance throughout the day. "Never leave the house a mess," is the way one mother phrased it to her daughter growing up. You never have a second chance to make a first impression. Presentation consists of being well groomed, neatly dressed, and well put together. Everything we do counts.

One Saturday morning I decided to walk to the dry cleaners, about two blocks away, to drop off several suits. At the house I was wearing khaki pants, shoes, and a white undershirt. At first I thought, "I'm just going to the cleaners; I don't need to put on a nicer shirt." But as I started toward the door, I caught myself and went back to put one on, to look more put together.

To my surprise, I ran into two people I knew at the cleaners and struck up a fascinating conversation with a man who had just bought a brand-new Porsche and climbed the Himalayans and other mountains around the world. I was glad I had taken the extra time to put on a better shirt.

For people who have never met you before, a large part of their three-second first impression comes from your presentation. And the more put together you look, the better this impression. The more drawing power you will have.

It is important to point out that you don't have to overdress or wear expensive clothes to look put together. But there are a few basic rules for dressing. Being neatly groomed also plays an important part in presentation. There are many excellent books for helping men and women with their appearance, and a few of these are included in the bibliography.

## Pleasant, Active Face

The second core trait most people look at is your face. People are looking for two things when they look at the face—a pleasant expression and action. People don't want to talk to or approach anyone with a scowl. People subconsciously know that habitual facial expressions are just that, habitual. This tells them that the person who scowls is usually down and depressed and no fun to be around. Some people are just "heavy." Most people like to be around uplifting people. Your face must be inviting and pleasant.

Visually charismatic people also have active faces. They move a lot, showing alertness and emotional expressiveness. They move their faces using nonlinguistic movements. Their eyeballs move a lot, their eyes open wider or squint, their eyes dart, and so on. People who do not show this emotional expressiveness are almost always not listening, do not care about what is being said, or are thinking of something else. People who do not have visual charisma do not show emotional expressiveness; they have dead faces. Use NLMs to combat dead face. Use them to talk and to listen.

One way charismatic people do this is with their smile. They don't have a big, goofy smile, but they soak in people's personas and then give a slow, warm, confident smile. In her book *Talking the Winner's Way: 92 Little Tricks for Big Success in Business*, Leil Lowndes calls this the "flooding smile," which slowly spreads across the face. She says that the smile should reach your eyes. Smile first with your eyes, then your cheeks, and then the corners of your mouth. Smiling softens your face and makes you look warmer and more confident, putting people at ease quickly.

Smile before you say something. If someone asks you how you are doing, for example, smile broadly, wait a second or two, and then answer (unless you are not doing so well). It is almost like rewarding someone with a smile for asking about you. Great speakers also smile after making a comment or emphasizing a point, similarly warming up others.

Women can draw more attention to their smile by wearing lipstick. Beauty pageant contestants and even belly dancers understand the power of the smile, and smile continually through their performances.

## Deliberate Movement

Fidgeting is distracting, but deliberate movement is charismatic. Use your fingers to emphasize key points. Coordinate your fingers so that you use them at the exact moment you make the point. It is as if you are saying to the other person: "Here comes the second point ... watch me ... okay ... now!" This technique increases the effectiveness of that point by auditorily telling listeners the point and then visually showing them that you are making the point (focusing their attention).

Have you ever watched an old Cary Grant movie or any other movie with the volume muted? You will particularly notice how people move, gesture, smile, and so on. You won't know exactly what they are saying, but you will get a pretty good sense about the characters. If the movie is on video, you can hit fast-forward and watch how people move a little more quickly. You may be surprised to see how many hand and arm gestures people make.

If you were to videotape most noncharismatic people telling a story and then watched them while fast-forwarding the tape, they would hardly move. You might see them occasionally shifting their body weight or scratching or slightly moving their head. But you would see nowhere near the hand, arm, and body motions you would see watching visually charismatic people.

When I was at the local school track running some laps after work, I noticed a group of five women who had just finished walking their laps. They were stopped in the parking lot to talk for a while before getting into their cars and going their own separate ways. Although I was jogging around the track listening to my radio with headphones, I could see one woman telling an unbelievable story to the group.

I have wondered what the story was about because I couldn't hear a word of it. But I saw the woman wave her arms around as she spoke, squat with one hand over her eyes, and then make a lassoing gesture. Every time I ran around the track, I saw her use her body to tell this story. Not surprisingly, she drew a crowd and told the story for at least nine of my laps. I regret not hearing it myself. How about that for using visual charisma?

When using gestures, remember that there are one-handed and two-handed gestures. Some of these gestures are small and close in and others are big and all-encompassing. Small gestures use subtle finger, hand, and arm movements. Big gestures include extending both arms or using the entire body such as squatting. Regardless, the deliberate use of gestures increases visual charisma.

Many six-figure communicators talk with their hands over a note pad. Usually they have a pen or a pencil in one hand when they do this. Bill O'Reilly, of the Fox News Channel's *The O'Reilly Factor*, does this nightly on camera. He uses the pen in his hand to emphasize key parts of his argument or what he is trying to say. I have seen many intelligent people doing this in a boardroom as they are asking questions. They talk with one or both hands. The pen or pencil subconsciously says they are organized, taking notes, referring to notes, and taking the subject seriously.

## Posture

If you go to any Internet dating Web site, you will see that most women are looking for tall men. Almost every single woman in Yahoo.com's personal ads, for example, says that her ideal mate's height is between 5'10" and 7'11". Seven-foot-eleven cracks me up, but the point is that every inch taller is seemingly better and more attractive. And the more attractive you are, the greater your drawing power. Most people slouch and cheat themselves out of two or three inches of charisma!

When standing, the most significant posture mistake most people make is having their head too far forward and not "atop" their body. This creates a hump in the back. If you pull your head back, your body will straighten itself out. To diagnose your posture, stand with your heels and back against a wall in a normal posture. The key is to have both shoulder blades and the back of your head touching the wall simultaneously. This usually gets rid of the hump in your back if there is one. Your buttocks should slightly touch the wall too. Notice how different this feels and how out of line your posture may have been. Now add a confident smile and look out!

Another technique to feel for correct posture is to stick a ruler exactly halfway down your shirt at the collar. Ensure the back of your head touches the ruler and slightly pushes back against it. If your head is too far forward, the ruler falls down your shirt (move the shoulders forward or button another shirt button if the ruler slides down the shirt too easily). Sitting or standing like this will show you what the correct head position feels like.

The second posture mistake people make is standing in the fig-leaf stance, as if you are covering yourself in the Garden of Eden. Stand with your arms at your side, with a hand in one pocket, or with one hand holding something. Holding something in one of your hands can significantly soften your image and make you more approachable.

When sitting at a table or desk, scoot your buttocks to the back of the chair, put your elbows on the table, and straighten your back. The chair should be close to the table. This posture shows interest, energy, and confidence. Leaning back or sitting straight sends signals of disinterest, stiffness, or awkwardness. Most important, such postures will make building rapport more difficult.

## Focus

*The greatest enemy of visual charisma is time.*
*The more tired people get, the harder it is to maintain charisma.*

Visually charismatic people do not look around when they are speaking to others. They may be aware of their surroundings, but they don't glance around because others can sense on a conscious or even subconscious level when your attention is elsewhere. Charismatic people instead focus all of their energy and attention on speaking and listening. They give others their full and undivided attention. Charismatic people go into the one-track mind when speaking with others and ignore the rest of the world, often for 45 to 90 minutes at a time. You can see this concentration on their faces while they speak and listen, drawing people toward them.

## Auditory Charisma

Auditory charisma involves primarily the voice and sound. Many visual people rarely pay attention to the sound of their voice. Instead, they are overly concerned with word choice, persuasiveness, and logical arguments. They don't think about the impact of voice. But remember the study, mentioned earlier in this chapter, that showed 38 percent of people's impact before a group is conveyed auditorily. This section looks at how you can convey auditory charisma.

- **Speak clearly and smoothly**
    What does your voice sound like? How choppy is it? Does it squeal? One way to tell if people are auditorily dominant is to listen to the quality of their voice. They have a soft but confident voice. Often they speak so smoothly that they almost hypnotize people, lulling them, as they speak. This puts people at ease quickly. Masters of this are Charles Gibson and Diane Sawyer of ABC News.

- **Take your time when you speak**

    Don't rush your words. Noncharismatic people speak faster and faster when time is short, as if they were trying to get everything in, in just a few sentences. But when you rush, you lose charisma. Instead, savor your words. Jean Hamilton, a professional voice coach, says that each voice has a "flavor" to it, and that we should "taste each word" as we say it.[2] She advises clients to read nursery rhymes, listening carefully to their voice as they read them, modulating tone, tempo, vocal variety, and so on.

- **Work on your voice**

    Some of highest-paid public speakers today (those making more than a million dollars a year) still use a voice trainer to smooth out their voice and work on their inflection. Let me repeat that: People making more than a million dollars annually still pay people to help make their voice even better. What does that tell you about the importance of voice?

    Another way to work on your voice is to read stories aloud. Read an entire short story or just a few pages, paying attention to how your voice sounds. Experiment with modulating it.

- **Use interesting words and phrases**

    Charismatic people use fewer clichés and trite phrases when they speak, which immediately differentiates them from others. Noncharismatic people continually use the same tired, worn-out, one- or two-word expressions.

    For example, instead of simply thanking someone for inviting you to their party, consider saying something more lively and original, such as, "You made us feel so welcome," or "Did we have a fabulous time, or what?!"

    At a bookstore one time, I held a door open a few seconds longer for an elderly lady who was walking in behind me. She commented: "What perfect timing, running into a nice guy like you. Thank you." (By the way, this is an example of a TST.)

- **Speak people's names**

    People love the sound of their own name. It is music to their ears and they open up.

When you use "I" statements and talk about yourself, however, people close up. People don't care about what you want; only what they want. It is a turnoff when you talk about yourself, particularly in front of a group. This is why public speakers have other people introduce them before they walk on the stage.

- **Pay attention to the sound of your walk**

    People can hear you when you walk, so step surely and smoothly. Take your time, but don't walk lackadaisically. Confident walkers sound different, especially when wearing high heels or dress shoes on a hard surface. That is why people look up when someone comes into sight; they have been listening to that person confidently walking down a hallway for some time. They are expecting someone attractive, of stature and importance—because this is the way that confident people walk!

- **Adjust your voice to warm people up to you**

    Once you have people's attention, don't speak too loudly at first. Slowly warming people up to you increases your likeability and helps you establish rapport.

# Kinesthetic Charisma

Kinesthetic charisma is all about making other people *feel* good. Charismatic people do this with charm, personality, and a sense of humor. The most powerful way to use kinesthetic charisma is through emotion. This section discusses ways to connect with people on a more emotional, or feeling, level.

- **Find people's emotional hot buttons**

    Use simplified buttonomics to find people's positive emotional hot buttons—and then dig in! Keep asking questions about this button. If someone were asking me, for example, about my book (positive hot button), they might "dig in" by asking about my favorite chapter, the hardest chapter to write, or the top two or three skills in the book. Finding people's positive emotional hot buttons is a quick way to get to their soul and bring out the best in them. Kinesthetic charisma makes people feel good, special, important, or flattered; and simplified buttonomics is an important tool for doing this.

- **Smile**

   A kinesthetic nurse once told me that a smile is the first thing she notices about people. She "feels good" when she gets a smile and subsequently feels good around that person. She instantly likes a person who smiles readily.

- **Keep your posture open**

   Too many noncharismatic people walk or stand with clenched fists or crossed arms. Better to sit or stand in a more open and approachable stance, ready to welcome a kinesthetic person. Leaning on a wall, doorway, or table can help people feel a little more comfortable around you.

- **Touch people lightly when you talk**

   If done appropriately, touching can increase your charisma. It may be a touch on someone's arm, a hug, or a pat on the back. If you touch kinesthetic people slightly on the arm or shoulder when you greet them or when you are making a point, they will respond positively to you. Touch is powerful. As Leil Lowndes writes in her book *Talking the Winner's Way,* "We live in a touch-starved society."

   Many professionals know the importance of touch to people who need it. Politicians walk into a crowd and try to shake as many hands as they can and let people slap them on the back. Celebrities, especially rock stars, also know the importance of reaching out to fans and touching them by slapping hands, for example. Television evangelists touch people on the foreheads after preaching. I once saw an evangelist preaching on television who, knowing that he couldn't touch everyone on the forehead, called for backup and asked two other ministers to touch people as he preached.

   My neighbor once told me that she didn't like her doctor's new physician assistant. She said the PA didn't do a very good job. I knew my neighbor couldn't know specifically what tests and examinations were needed, so I was curious why she thought the PA was not good. She replied that she felt "ripped off" after her appointment. After a little probing, I found out that the PA had never touched my neighbor. Even though my neighbor had gone in for a rash, she thought the PA should have listened to her heart or listened while she breathed! My neighbor felt that she wasn't being taken care of because she had not been touched!

   Kinesthetic people want to be touched, particularly at the doctor's office. But heed this word of warning: make sure the person you are touching is receptive to touch. Because this can be hit or miss, it is recommended that you touch only those you know well, like close friends or family members. Don't touch strangers or work colleagues. If so, you may get punched, slapped, or worse. This charismatic technique can be extremely powerful with the right person, but risky with the wrong person. In general, women can get away with touch more easily.

When people don't feel comfortable around you, or when they say they don't like you, it is most likely that you did not take the time to build rapport with them. Kinesthetic people pick up on this immediately, and they particularly need a little warming up, verbally or nonverbally.

# Chapter Summary

- Neuro-Linguistic Programming teaches that though people take in information using all of their senses, they tend to be dominant with one—visual, auditory, or kinesthetic. NLP calls this a representational system. You don't have to identify people's representational system to establish rapport with them. The goal is to be charismatic using all three systems.

- Visual charisma is the most common representational system and consists of anything that can be picked up by the human eye. The three core traits of people with visual charisma are presentation; pleasant, active face; and deliberate movement. Secondary traits include correct posture and focus.

- Auditory charisma involves the voice and sound. Auditorily charismatic people speak clearly and smoothly, almost in a hypnotizing lull. When you rush words, you lose charisma. Instead, savor and "taste" your words. Speak in livelier and original phrases rather than clichés and trite statements. Use the names of other people frequently and use few "I" statements. Walk with a confident sound to your step. When you talk with people, warm them up to you with your voice to build rapport and charisma.

- Kinesthetic charisma is all about making other people feel good. You can achieve this with charm, personality, and a sense of humor. A powerful way to use kinesthetic charisma is through emotions. Find people's positive emotional hot buttons by using simplified buttonomics. When you find one of these buttons, dig in and keep asking questions about it. A smile sets people at ease and builds positive emotion in them, thus making you more charismatic. Sit or stand in an open position to appear approachable and warm. A slight touch on kinesthetic people when emphasizing a point can be powerful, but should be reserved for close friends and family. Take the time to build rapport.

## Daily Challenge

Pick the representational system that you are weakest in and work on developing that today. Whichever it is, go back to that section in this chapter and reread how to become more charismatic in that system. Use these suggestions in at least three conversations today to become more charismatic.

## Executive Challenge

Pay particular attention to any visually, auditorily, or kinesthetically charismatic traits you see in people today. Notice how they use that specific representational system. Write the qualities and techniques you observe in a notebook. Incorporate a few of these techniques into your own conversations before the day is over. Think about how you could incorporate others.

# Part IV

The No. 1 secret to working with others is getting into the personal power mind-set, because other people are but our mirror reflections. If you are not in this mind-set, all of the tricks, tips, and advice in the world are useless. At the same time, you must have your heart in the right place. People can spot phonies instantly and see right through them. Trust is lost.

If you get into the personal power mind-set and have your heart in the right place, Part IV will help you polish your communication skills and make working with others easier and more enjoyable.

This part examines what drives the human heart and how to deal with angry people. You'll learn about righting important relationships, bringing out the best in others, leading others using personal power, and establishing and using a network. This part also presents simple ways to develop yourself.

# Tuning In to People's Hearts

## In This Chapter:

* Discover and use the power of "heart"
* Increase the quality of your relationships with others
* Learn ways to take exceptional care of people
* Discover one of the greatest secrets to getting along with others

This chapter is about people's hearts, the place where the most powerful and intense of all emotions lie. The best husbands, wives, doctors, nurses, police officers, salespeople, parents, and friends aren't necessarily the best because of what they know, but because of their extraordinary ability to touch the hearts of others. If you tune in to and touch people's hearts, you, too, will be one of the most loved, respected, and important individuals in their life.

Six-figure communicators' understanding of people's hearts is partly what helps them do extraordinary things. Their understanding helps them better identify with, talk to, and work with others. It helps them become more effective communicators by making them better judges of character, better speakers, and better leaders. It makes them better able to deal with difficult people, improve their conversational outcomes, and establish trust, which makes building rapport faster and easier.

Tuning in to people's hearts gives you the energy to accomplish more and helps others feel more appreciated, important, and loved. And when all of this happens, you are able to work with people more easily and effectively.

# The Three Cravings of the Heart

Every heart craves three things: appreciation, a feeling of importance (significance), and love. These are our core human emotions and at the source of all of our pleasure or lack thereof. People who know how to touch the human heart become powerful forces in social and business circles, for they have more friends and contacts and become better at understanding and working with others. This makes life better not only for them but for everyone they come in contact with.

> *"If I had enough colored ribbon, I could rule the world."*
> — **Napoleon Bonaparte**

Napoleon understood how people work and went on to conquer much of the world. He knew that his soldiers would do almost anything for a little bit of sincere, honest appreciation. Indeed, it seems that men will risk life and limb for a 50-cent ribbon. But Napoleon understood that the ribbons and medals carried little meaning; it was that he gave his soldiers a sense of appreciation and significance that made them do almost anything for him.

As a pharmaceutical salesman I was dependent on getting in and out of many offices quickly to sell my wares. But I used to find it exceedingly difficult to get into the busiest offices. Then one day I tried something new. I made the doctors feel important and the receptionists feel appreciated. This worked wonders and made access to the customer (the doctors) significantly easier, thereby increasing my sales. I soon quit wearing a name tag because they would see me walk in and say: "Pete, come on back." No doubt they were having a hard day and craved a little appreciation and importance and knew I could give it to them, satisfying their cravings. Remember, no one cares what *you* want, only what *they* want.

Still, the greatest power in the universe is love. Love will make us do things we wouldn't do for anyone else. People will run into burning buildings for their loved ones. This emotion wins over logic. Everyone needs and craves it.

> *"God put a little piece of love in our hearts for something greater than ourselves. It is up to us to figure out what to do with that love."*
> — **Mom**

# Treating the Cravings

So how do you treat the heart's cravings? The only way to satisfy a heart's cravings is by helping others feel appreciated, important, and loved. This satisfies your cravings and the cravings of others. The more you give, the more you get in return. You get by giving. Put another way, what you sow is what you reap. You can only temporarily satisfy your heart's cravings by, for example, buying something lavish or getting promoted. To satisfy your cravings long term, you must take the time to make others feel appreciated, important, and loved. It is really as simple as think, show, and do. Let's look at each of these in more detail.

## *Think* of Others First

People with big hearts genuinely care for others and think of them first. They give others 110 percent, care for them 110 percent, and expect nothing in return. A family-practice doctor once told me, "If you look out for people and take care of them, good fortune will come your way in ways you never expected. For this you need to have faith, my friend."

The doctor said that the danger is when you start to become too concerned with yourself. When we become self-focused and not others-focused, we are not satisfying our heart's real cravings. We are chasing decoys to temporarily satisfy an internal gnawing. The only way to feel appreciation, a sense of importance, and love is by giving all three away. And for this we need others!

## *Show* Your Interest in Others

How do you show people you care for them? Or do you? Do you just assume people think that you care for them? Six-figure communicators make sure they consciously show an interest in others. They make people feel respected, appreciated, important, cared for, and loved. They talk to people with a sense of curiosity and warmth.

This caring comes across easily to others on your face as well, consciously or unconsciously through nonlinguistic movements (Chapter 11). But it is not your NLMs that make people like you. It's that you look genuinely interested in them. Six-figure communicators show this interest and concern using NLMs.

# Demonstrate You Care by *Doing*

Action is a powerful way to demonstrate how much you appreciate, admire, or love others or what they have done.

> *"I care about you. Is there anything I can do to make your day brighter?"*
> **—President George W. Bush, in a speech in**
> **January 2002**

One of the fastest, easiest, and most effective ways to feed the heart cravings of others is by using the two- or three-sentence technique (Chapter 14). Simply say or write two or three sentences to someone, including one of the three cravings of the heart.

Six-figure communicators keep their notes short and heartfelt, which enables them to send out many more cards than others. They know that two high-quality sentences today are far more powerful than a lengthy card next week, after the fact. Imagine this cumulative effect!

Too often we get tricked into thinking that we need to fill a page in a book to tell someone how much we care. Don't be bashful about the TST. It's a wonderful and easy way to strengthen relationships.

Even better is to use the TST in person. Pull someone aside and say your two sentences using one of the three cravings of the heart. To make it even more powerful, use the body language of NLMs. Of course there are an infinite number of things you can say, but a few are listed below:

- Joe, I just wanted to tell you how proud I am of you. You sure turned out to be a terrific kid.
- Diedra, I just wanted to thank you for a wonderful weekend. I enjoyed it immensely.
- Honey, I just wanted to tell you how much I love you. Sometimes I get caught up in my own little world and forget to tell you, but I do.

**Any of the following NLMs will make your TST more powerful:**
- A light touch on the arm
- Eye darting
- The smile
- Hand over heart
- Hands on both shoulders (when talking to a loved one)
- A hug
- Holding someone's hand

# Take Exceptional Care of People

When our heart is in the right place and people know that we really care for them, they are magically more forgiving, open, honest, and tolerant. They will cut us some slack, even if we are wrong. Don't be afraid to let people know (how much) you care for them.

I had the unique pleasure to meet a woman named Wanda Johnson at a high school graduation ceremony. A high school truancy officer, Wanda is one of the most pleasant, down-to-earth people I have ever met. Her job is to track down students that have not been coming to school and find out why. Although problem high school students can be notoriously difficult, Wanda is exceptional at learning why these students skip school. She told me that she finds out things that the parents don't even know about their own kids, such as drug use, sexual activity, violence, and other problems teenagers struggle through.

With a little prodding, I got her to share with me her steadfast secret to dealing with people, especially teenagers. Wanda said this one secret has worked more wonders than she cared to remember. Her secret was this: really care about people from the bottom of your heart.

She told me that kids are not stupid. They know whether you really care about them. She said if kids think you are there just to send them back to school, not only will they never work on the problem, but they will never open up to you and trust you. Kids, just like adults, can tell where your heart is and if you really, really care. Don't underestimate the power of the heart.

Wanda understood that when you really care for people, many smaller problems are prevented or magically disappear. She knew that when she really, really cared for the truant kids, they recognized that and were more honest with her. She was getting to the heart of their problems, not fighting decoy problems, such as missing school. Often, the decoy problems are just ways that kids (people in general) try to get our attention, in an attempt to get us to say that we love and care for them.

# Leading from the Heart

Great leaders lead from the heart. They show their subordinates that they genuinely care for them. In return, their subordinates go out of their way to make their leader happy.

Great military leaders always let their troops eat first. No one tells them to do this; it is an instinctive quality of theirs to take care of their soldiers first. I learned this lesson one day in the field, sharing a lettuce sandwich with an Army colonel—it was all that was left to eat.

When subordinates (and people in general) know that you are genuinely looking out for them, they tend to go out of their way to help you. They are more forgiving, open, honest, tolerant, and even harder-working. Leadership is miraculously easier. Subordinates want their leader to succeed, and they take it personally if they disappoint their leader. This is a key distinction between poor leaders and exceptional leaders.

## Caring for Your Customers

While interviewing top salespeople in various industries, I repeatedly noticed a common theme. Almost everyone interviewed made it a point to tell me that they treat people the way they want to be treated. They put themselves in the customer's shoes. And they take exceptional care of people always.

One top auto salesman said, "If you are good with people, have goals, and really, really care for people from the bottom of your heart, you should be able to make six-figures—easy." He said you must give first. He said he treats customers as if they are a guest in his own home. It is about serving people and letting them know that you care about them personally. It doesn't matter if they want to buy a high-end car; he takes exceptional care of everyone, no matter what. Many times people come back to the dealership a year later and buy a car from him then, when they are ready.

Many top salespeople interviewed told me that they spent almost half their time following up with customers. That is two to three days weekly taking care of current customers, and not selling or prospecting. They spend half as much time selling as poor salespeople and significantly more time following up.

> Most top salespeople have their cell phone number printed on their business cards or hand-write it there for customers. This is indicative of their genuine desire to serve and their level of commitment.

One top yacht salesperson said his secret was just keeping in touch with customers and letting them know that he still cared for them after the sale. Then he pointed to a luxury yacht and said, "Do you see that one on the end? That is the fourth one that I have sold to the same family in seven years." Lesson: take exceptional care of people!

Most people think that as long as they offer customers a seat and don't offend anyone, they are taking care. But there is a huge difference between doing the minimum and taking extraordinary care.

# Care for People When They Need It Most

Invariably, all of us have times when we feel that life is either the greatest blessing or the worst of all curses—it is just part of being human. My strongest relationships have come from either helping people (including customers) when they needed it most or when I needed it the most in my life. How about yours? If you take care of people, especially when they need it most, they will never forget you for it.

On July 8, 2001, the town of Mullens, West Virginia, was severely flooded after a storm when a nearby river overflowed its banks. Water rushed into offices, homes, and other buildings within inches of many ceilings. Many homes were washed away, and the ones that weren't were filled with several feet of mud. A postal truck, car, refrigerator, and even a casket (empty) were seen floating down Main Street. The town of about 1,800 was crippled.

A few days later, after realizing how bad the town got hit, I went down to help where I could. I picked a flower shop and started dragging debris into the street and doing whatever else I could.

Consequently, I started about 50 quality relationships with complete strangers that have lasted now for years. Few ever thanked me for my work in that town, but they knew what I had done and treated me warmly. What a feeling it was to walk down Main Street and know the majority of people in town. To have 50 people waving or talking to you is an unbelievable feeling.

You don't need tens of thousands of gallons of water, mud, and debris rushing through the streets of town to help people. Maybe one person's "flood" is a tough relationship he is going through. Maybe someone else's flood is a problem at home and she just needs someone to talk to. People don't forget when you genuinely and sincerely help them, especially when they need it most!

Look for ways to help people when they are at their wit's end, stressed, scared, and going through tough times and a lot of uncertainty. This will build incredible, insurmountable bonds between the two of you. Whether they say thank you doesn't matter. What does matter is that helping them is the right thing to do. It not only makes life a little better for them, but also satisfies your heart's craving to feel appreciated, important, and loved.

One of my heroes is Juan Rodriguez, a former Army sergeant. He once told me about a soldier he knew who had a mental breakdown at work. Unfortunately, he got a pistol and threatened his own life. Everyone, even the battalion commander, tried to talk to this soldier and get him to hand over the pistol, but to no avail—until Juan showed up. Juan was the only person in the crowd the soldier would listen to.

I asked Juan how he got the soldier to turn over the weapon when everyone else had failed. I asked him what negotiating tactic or technique he had used. I asked him what clever words and phrases he had used to end this life-threatening standoff. He smiled at me and simply said, "I gave the soldier my piece of cake once, when no one else would! He trusted me from then on."

Then Juan recounted the story: There had been a birthday cake in the office one day and everyone had gotten a piece except that soldier. The soldier was going through some tough times, and not getting a piece of cake had made him feel even more left out. So Juan offered his. At that point Juan cared more for that soldier than for himself. His heart was in the right place.

*"Do you know how to live forever, Pete? Help someone out big time!*
*They will never forget you for it — even after you're gone!"*
— **Juan Rodriguez**

It sometimes doesn't take much to help people with their "flood." Show kindness to everyone you meet, for you have no idea how badly they may need a kind word or a little kindness.

# Help as Many People as Possible

Six-figure communicators are always listening for ways to help people, and they have an extraordinary ability to match people and resources. They make phone calls, write letters, or get out and help someone hands-on.

Helping as many people as possible differentiates you from others in several important ways:
- People who genuinely want to help others are rare. Other people know this and quickly realize how important you are. They want to hang on to people like you. Helping people shows where your heart is. It shows that you care about others. It shows that you are looking out for people.

- You have more confidence talking to people when you are always thinking of ways to help. Your focus is not on yourself but on helping others. You are outwardly focused, not self-focused. Because of this, you are rarely nervous or self-conscious around others. If you do need help from others, you are not afraid to ask, because you are just as willing to help others if and when they need help.

- You are more positive than other people because your mind is on the solution to problems, not complaining about problems. Why? Because you are carefully listening for ways to help people. Because of the law of attraction, your conversations are positive, happy, pleasant, optimistic, and receptive. And people are drawn to you. Positive conversations give people energy. Negative conversations take energy from people. People like to be around people who are pleasant and want to help and do business with them.

- Helping as many people as possible enables you to develop a huge network of contacts. You help these people genuinely and sincerely because they need help, but by helping others you also meet other people who like to help others. And this a great way to build a network. By helping others, you grow your network exponentially because everyone knows at least 100 people (family, friends, classmates, colleagues, club members, etc.). You meet people you might not ordinarily meet— people in different circles.

- Almost all of the people you help are more than willing to return the favor one day if they can. Through the law of reciprocity, people feel an unspoken obligation to help those who have helped them.

- People who help others have lots of friends, contacts, and solid relationships. People who have no one to help them either have not helped enough other people yet or haven't helped others in a significant way.

## Make People Feel Comfortable

Before top communicators talk with anyone, they usually try to make the other person feel as comfortable as possible. It feels good to take exceptional care of people and treat them better than anyone else, the way we all wish we were treated. Top communicators do this genuinely and sincerely.

This helps put people into a positive, receptive state. In this state, people are more relaxed, open-minded, forgiving, giving, fair, and rational. In a sense, you are giving the other person a sort of sanctuary from the outside world. Any action you do to make someone feel more comfortable will always be appreciated and will set a positive conversational tone.

An example of this was Captain Gumph, a company commander of mine in the Army. One time in the dead of winter, right around midnight, Captain Gumph had six soldiers return to the perimeter after a long mission. Instead of "pouncing" on them as soon as they got back, he had them all go into the tent and get themselves a cup of coffee to warm up before they said a word. Only after his soldiers warmed up and had a chance to take a seat did he ask how it went.

Captain Gumph always took care of his soldiers first. He would do anything for them, and every one of them knew it. It was not surprising that his soldiers also would do anything for him and performed exceptionally during the exercise.

Making people feel more comfortable or giving them "sanctuary" means taking care of their mind and body. You may want to give them a glass of water or wine, have them sit down, offer them something to eat, give them a cushion or footstool to make them more comfortable, or put on some relaxing music to help them relax and put their mind at ease. Even if it is simply a warm comment or gesture with a smile, it counts.

My brother Steve takes exceptional care of guests in his home. He makes sure his refrigerator is always stocked with plenty of drinks for company. His soda, lemonade, beer, and water are all in individual bottles. He usually has fruit juices and a bottle of wine on hand as well. When people come over, he invites them to sit down and then offers them choices of something to drink (he doesn't ask if they want a drink). Then he puts on some fun music. Next he walks into the kitchen and fills a bowl with pretzels or chips and then fills a second bowl with salsa to bring out (he always has an unopened bag of chips set aside for company). Later in the afternoon or evening he might make his guests a pitcher of margaritas or a pot of coffee.

What do most people offer you to drink when you go to their home? Usually it's whatever is in their refrigerator. It may be what's left of a two-liter bottle of cola (flat) or orange juice with a funny smell. But whatever it is, a lack of effort to make guests feel special becomes known, for presentation counts.

Take exceptional care of all guests to your home. Moving? Provide pizza and drinks for the movers. They will return the favor and take special care of your belongings. If a plumber, gardener, or electrician comes to your home, always offer them a drink or just give them one without their even asking. Not only is this the right thing to do, but through the law of reciprocity, they will do a much better job and make sure that they repay you in some way.

> *"Look out for people and take care of them,*
> *and good fortune will come your way in ways you never expected."*
> — **Eric Lavalee, M.D.**

# Bandage First, Talk Later

If someone comes to you broken and bent, "bandage" the person immediately and talk later. Just keep quiet and comfort the other person. Take care of the other person emotionally if need be—no "I told you so."

My editor told me a harrowing story about having been carjacked. When she finally escaped unharmed 12 hours later, she called her parents, among others. The first thing her mother asked was, "Were you carrying your keys in your hand?" This was not the kind of "comfort" my editor had hoped to get from her mother. Instead, it came across as lecturing, or "blaming the victim" (even though she had indeed been carrying her keys in her hand). Much later, my editor was receptive to advice about what she could have done to prevent the attack, but immediately after the ordeal, all she needed was a "bandage."

As difficult as it may be, avoid lengthy discussions, preaching, or yelling. The last thing someone needs under the circumstances is to get lectured. The person will not be in "receive" mode. Wait to calm down and collect your thoughts. This will ensure that you don't do irreparable damage while you are upset.

# Reading Others by Where Their Heart Is

From time to time, everyone accidentally or mistakenly says or does something to upset someone—it happens. Everyone gets tired, stressed, and emotional sometimes. People usually mean to do the right thing, try really hard to do it, but things don't quite turn out the way they meant them to. From time to time people "goof up" or make a mistake—it is just part of being human. How do you react when this happens?

One of the greatest secrets of understanding people better, thereby improving your relationships, is to judge people less by what they say or do—and more by where their heart is. If people's hearts are in the right place, you have something to work with. Looking at "where they're coming from" will make you a better judge of character and help you read others significantly better. This simple secret can and will work wonders for you.

Here is an example. When my brother Steve—who is 11 years younger than I—was 3 years old, he loved to draw pictures with crayons. My parents would always "fuss" over his artwork and tell him how beautiful his drawings were. One day he overheard my parents talking about how important it was that we start decorating for a social function at our house.

Before we knew it, Steve drew all over the white walls from the upstairs to the downstairs, "decorating" for the party. He thought that since my parents liked his artwork so much, he would share it with everyone and try to help out! His heart was clearly in the right place, and he wanted to help. But I'm sure you can imagine our reaction.

Be careful of scolding people when their heart was in the right place and things didn't quite turn out as you or they would have liked. Understand first where their heart is, and then judge.

A common mistake we make when working with people is to take literally what they say. When someone you're working with does or says something that you find a little offensive, ask yourself if the other person meant to do or say that. Was the person's comment intentionally designed to be cruel, or did it just come out wrong? Look beyond these comments if the person has a good heart, for we all have stuck our foot in our mouth at one time or another.

Then again, some people intentionally want to do harm. These people are cruel and malicious. Judge these people differently and don't confuse the two. Understand where their heart is and stay away from them. It is difficult to change a person's heart. If someone's heart is in the wrong place, any nice thing you say is usually suspect. Keep your guard up around such people.

# Chapter Summary

• If you understand and touch people's hearts, you will be one of the most loved, respected, and important people in their life.

• The three cravings of the heart are appreciation, feeling of importance (significance), and love.

• The only way to satisfy the heart's cravings is by helping others feel appreciated, important, and loved. You get all three by giving away all three. And the more you give, the more you get. Remember to think of others first, show them you genuinely care, and do something nice for them. Using NLMs with the TST can be extremely powerful.

• Take exceptional care of people. As truancy officer Wanda Johnson said, kids (and people in general) recognize whether you really care about them. When people know that you care for them, they are magically more forgiving, open, honest, and tolerant.

• When you take care of people, especially when they need it most, they will not forget you for it. Help as many people as possible. Make people feel comfortable. Bandage people first and talk later.

• A potent secret to understanding others is to judge people not so much by what they say or do, but by where their heart is. If their heart is in the right place, you have something to work with.

## Daily Challenge

Use the two-sentence technique today by writing three cards to people. Write from the heart! Use each TST to satisfy one of the three cravings of the heart: appreciation, feelings of importance (significance), and love. Mail each of these cards or leave them for others to find. If you do not have blank cards on hand, buy some to use now and in the future.

## Executive Challenge

Use the TST in person today on three people. Speak from the heart. Try different nonlinguistic movements while using the TST. Experiment with each and notice how each NLM changes the effectiveness of your message.

# Avoiding Conflict with Others

## In This Chapter:

- Use overwhelming energy to your advantage
- Recognize decoy issues that draw attention away from what's really upsetting someone
- Understand how to avoid upsetting others or getting upset yourself
- Learn 13 tactics the pros use to deal with difficult people

On a Likert scale from 1 to 10, with 10 being full of positive energy and "in the zone" and 1 being very tired or angry, at what level do you have to be when dealing with difficult people? Let's say you were at a level of 4. What kind of results do you think you would get? Most people would say they need to be at a level 9 or 10—and for really difficult people a level 12! Here is the first secret to dealing with difficult people: the more positive energy you have, the easier it is to handle difficult people.

## Resisting the Forces of Negativity

Infantry officers will not attack an enemy unless they outnumber the enemy by at least a 4-to-1 ratio. The rule is to use overwhelming force if you are going to stand a chance. It is the same when dealing with difficult people—you need to use overwhelming positive energy!

If your positive emotional energy is low and you talk with someone with a high level of negative emotional energy, you will lose. You will not be strong enough to resist. These people will move in and zap your energy and leave you worse off than before you started.

When this happens, the first thing that goes away is your charm, style, and charisma. You lose your high ground, as they say in the military.

If this should happen, withdraw and save yourself. Fight your battle or talk to the other person another day. You will never get anything accomplished with anyone who overwhelms you with negative emotion. You will also never win your case if someone overruns your positive emotion.

To put it another way, think of dealing with difficult people as playing a video game. Both you and your opponent, a monster in this case, have an energy bar over your head while you are playing the game. The stronger/longer your energy bar, the more you are protected from the evil creature. It shields you and you will not be affected by its attacks. But as your energy bar shrinks, the more vulnerable you become and the easier it is for the monster to destroy you. You must keep your positive energy high not only for your own protection, but to allow you the positive energy to deal with monsters. People are no different.

# Why People Get Upset

When you can identify why someone is upset, you are better able to understand the situation and reassure that person. Listed below are the universal reasons that people get angry or upset:

- Hurt feelings and need for empathy
- Predetermined beliefs
- Add-on information
- Fear of the unknown
- Feeling threatened
- Because they care
- Lacking a feeling of importance
- Lacking respect
- Lacking appreciation
- Tired or irritable
- Under stress
- Under time constraints
- Lacking information or openness
- Comments made around others
- Talking behind someone's back
- Unprofessional or poor behavior
- Sharp tongue
- Need for help

By understanding why people get angry or upset, you will be better able to see the big picture and avoid future confrontations and conflicts. This section looks at the most common reasons.

## Hurt Feelings and Need for Empathy

Perhaps the most common of all reasons that people get angry or upset is hurt feelings and a need for empathy. People need to feel listened to and understood. But this need is often disguised among other objections and issues, most of which are decoys. They just draw your attention away from the real issues, which are hurt feelings and a need for empathy.

For example, a salesman I knew went to a lot of trouble to put together a special dinner for two key groups of customers in the same business. The dinner was to introduce the two groups to each other. But on the day of the event, one group cancelled because of an emergency. The group casually mentioned that they were not going to be at dinner that night because of the emergency.

The salesman was outraged and thought to himself: "After all the trouble I went through to introduce you two together, I can't believe how ungrateful you are. I will never do anything out of my way for you again."

Deep down the salesman knew that this was an emergency and nothing could have been done to prevent it. But what bothered him was that his feelings were not addressed. It was as if the group didn't care for all of the effort he had gone through making reservations, sending out invitations, making phone calls, and so on.

Always remember that even if you have an unassailable reason to cancel out of an engagement, you have to show the other person that you really care about him, about the engagement, or about how much effort he went through. When human beings really care about something, their limbic system, which is their emotional side, takes over; and logic and reality go out the window. A comment or two (TST)—"I really appreciate all the work you went through to set up this dinner. It really means a lot to us that you did this for us, but due to certain circumstances, …"—will help the person know that you care.

If you do not address this real concern, the conversation will shift to a decoy—an issue other than the hurt person's real concern. Most people understand that situations arise and plans must be cancelled, but if you don't address the real concern, which is the person's feelings, then you will find yourself arguing over the reasons that you can't make the engagement. You can never win arguing over a decoy topic!

Get the idea? How many times have you heard shouting and yelling from someone and didn't realize that it had nothing to do with what you did or didn't do—that it had only to do with the other person's feelings? Maybe someone made you dinner and you didn't show up for it, or you showed up late, regardless of how good the reason was. Did you end up arguing about your reasons for being late, rather than acknowledge that you let the other person down?

Realize that the other person's upset has more to do with hurt feelings and wanting empathy than whether the dinner went to waste for a good reason or not. Arguing over decoys is why people get to thinking they shouldn't have to apologize after an argument. Both people are "right" from their perspective. One person argues over hurt feelings not being addressed and the other argues because missing the engagement was unavoidable.

## Predetermined Beliefs

In some situations, we have already consciously or unconsciously predetermined our responses even before an actual event or happening. We operate on autopilot. When the event happens, then "bam," we react. It's like solving for X in an algebraic equation. Events plugged into our equations determine whether we will get angry and in what way.

You cannot control the way other people perceive an event or comment, but you can control the way you perceive it by consciously predetermining how you will interpret it before it happens. Then when it does happen, you can react with a "battle drill," discussed in Chapter 1 and later in this chapter.

## Add-On Information

In his book *Psycho Pictography*, Vernon Howard writes that people do not necessarily get upset by what actually happened, but they scare themselves with the information that they themselves add to an event. And often this information is completely false.

For example, if you called your girlfriend Jennifer and she did not answer the phone, then, in fact, she simply did not answer the phone. That's all the information you have. But your imagination can get the best of you. What if Jennifer didn't make it back home? What if she is out with someone else? What if she is off gallivanting around town?

It is the information that we unnecessarily add to an event that gets us upset. Perhaps Jennifer was simply upstairs taking a shower and did not hear the phone ring.

## Other Decoys

People get upset or angry for many reasons that they will never admit. People are reluctant to admit that they lack feelings of importance, respect, or appreciation, or that they fear the unknown or are feeling threatened. Few people will admit these issues so they throw out decoys to cloud their true feelings. This is a kind of protective mechanism. These superficial smoke screens merely mask the true trouble. But with a little practice you will learn to see through the pond of decoys and identify the genuine issue.

A classic example of using decoy issues to mask true feelings of upset is something parents do often as they raise their children. Parents often express anger when a child comes home later than expected. But really, are the parents angry because the son or daughter came home 15 minutes or even two hours late? Probably not.

Anger over the child's lateness is often a decoy issue masking the parents' fear of the unknown and add-on information that might never have happened. The ultimate reason for the parents' upset is that they care and they don't want anything to happen to their child!

Don't waste your time addressing decoy issues. Learn to identify the real issue and address that.

## Avoid Getting Upset or Upsetting Others

The old saying that an ounce of prevention is worth a pound of cure is never truer than in dealing with people. Indeed, it is easier to talk and work with people before they get upset than after they get upset. The following are three basic truths about people that can keep us from getting upset:

- People are just being themselves, not intentionally trying to be rude or brash
- People are doing the best they can most of the time (honestly!)
- Most problems are misunderstandings

# The Downside of Arguing

When you finish arguing with someone, do you think you are usually liked, respected, or loved more than you were before you ever began the argument? Do people actually say, "Wow, that guy is so smart"? Will people feel better or worse about you? Will arguing make the other person treat you better?

No, people always have worse feelings about you at the end of an argument. They will never treat you better and may even do something to get back at you if you humiliated or embarrassed them. Remember that you have nothing to gain and a lot to lose if you argue or yell at someone.

Of course our goal really isn't to yell at people, but to get others to alter their behavior or rectify a situation. Most people yell first and ask for behavior change later. But this takes away people's motivation and their wanting to help you out of the goodness of their heart.

> *"A gentleman has definite beliefs, but he thinks before voicing his opinions. He recognizes that other people's beliefs are valid. He argues only over an issue that could save a life."*
> — **John Bridges and Bryan Curtis**
> *As a Gentleman Would Say*

Here is an example. One night after picking up my dry cleaning, I noticed that the pants were missing from one of my suits. I decided to go to the cleaners first thing the next morning to rectify the situation.

If I yelled at the clerks behind the counter about losing my pants, would they be more willing to go to any extra effort to find my pants? Would they make my life easier in the future? Would they like me more? The answer to all of these questions is no. Instead, I complimented them on their excellent service and then told them about the one exception, my pants. Now they had a reputation to live up to! Now they wanted to genuinely and sincerely help me. They ended up finding my pants and cleaning my next suit for free.

Yelling might have cost me the suit and a lot of time and energy to find a similar one. But more important, it would have taken me out of the personal power mind-set and destroyed much of the day's productivity. Most minimum-wage workers care more about how they are treated than about someone's pants. Because minimum-wage jobs are plentiful, they generally have nothing to lose by "sticking it to you" or making your life more difficult.

*"There are more pleasant things to do than beat up people."*
— **Muhammad Ali on the occasion of
one of his retirements**

## 14 Ways to Keep Situations Positive

1. Allow people to feel important, especially around others.
2. Ask yourself if someone really meant to do or say that.
3. Don't take what people say so literally (does she always hate me?).
4. Don't take things personally; it seldom has anything to do with you.
5. Don't add information to an event.
6. Never embarrass or talk down to anyone, especially in front of others.
7. Never put anyone on the defensive.
8. If you are unsure why someone got upset, show the other person a lot of empathy.
9. Mitigate someone's mistake or bad feeling; don't feed it. When people "mess up," they usually know it all by themselves.
10. Always treat people with respect.
11. Use extraordinary manners.
12. Take extraordinary care of people.
13. Smile when you talk. It's not what you say but how you say it.
14. Focus on the solution, not the problem.

*"If you take care of your customers, there is nothing to get upset about."*
— **Jeff Wing, Saturn Salesman**

# Battle Drills for Dealing with Difficult People

Be your own general and come up with your own battle drills for handling difficult people. This section looks at specific tactics to help you formulate your personal plan to handle difficult situations and people. By knowing how you will deal with people and situations before you are faced with them, you will "keep your cool" and handle them with finesse and grace. Keep in mind to always build rapport with people first and treat people well. Ultimately, this will win you more friends and help you influence more people.

## Create Allies

Six-figure communicators create allies before they need them. They are pleasant to everyone right from the start. They make friends with everyone they meet and get their name, so they start off on good terms in case they ever need help or encounter a problem later. Then they will "have a friend on the inside," whether they will ever need help or not. People will go out of their way for nice people and do far more for them, especially if they know them.

When my brother got married, we had all family staying in the same hotel for two or three nights. Right from the start, we hit it off and made friends with the hotel receptionist. Whenever we needed something special, she went out of her way to help, including giving us special access to the employee refrigerator, helping us collect cans to tie behind the newlyweds' car, and bending a rule or two to help us out.

The opposite could have happened. If we'd come across pushy and curt, for example, the receptionist would have remembered that. Then when we'd needed her help later, she might have told us there was "nothing I can do about it" or "that is just the way it is." Sometimes people who have been treated poorly will then purposely go out of their way just to "show you," for they have nothing to lose.

I wish I had done a better job with one of my first platoons in the military. I came across too strong and one-sided, primarily because I was taught to be that way from my company commander. I should have done a better job creating allies with my noncommissioned officers (sergeants) right from the start. I should have taken them all out initially and talked over a beer to build rapport. Then, if I had made a mistake later, they would have been more likely to "bail me out."

I survived my time as a platoon leader without first building this rapport, but it was tough! Make it easier on yourself and create allies from the start wherever you go and with whomever you talk. You never know when you may need help.

## "Nice'm to Death"

Bob Walker, a professional salesman for more than 24 years, is one of those guys that everyone likes. But being a salesman, he has had to put up with many hostile people as well.

One day I asked him what his secret was for talking to irate people. Bob replied with his countrified accent, "Nice'm to death." He said that eventually most people will come around, but there will always be a few who won't.

*"Try not getting upset, even if the other person deserves it."*
— **Bob Walker**

Most people are far more forgiving, tolerant, and reasonable if you are pleasant and if they like you. "Nicing people to death" with exceptional customer service should make you feel good too. Top salespeople are always asking customers, "What else can I do for you?" This subtly shifts the focus from problem griping to problem solutions.

Bob's technique will work for you too! Give it a shot. We all know that we will "catch more flies with honey than with vinegar."

## Show Empathy

Most people, particularly frustrated people, just want to feel understood and get a little empathy. They know that the situation that frustrated them probably couldn't have been prevented or that there was little that could have been done. Arguing about the details or decoy issues will just cause bad feelings.

Instead, pour on the empathy, not to be fake, but because that is usually what the other person needs. Address people's feelings! Show them you care. Here are a couple examples:
* "I feel horrible about not making your birthday party."
* "It is days like this when I hate my job. I know how special this day was to you. Let me make it up to you by …"

## Use the "Feel, Felt, Found" Technique

My friend George, a salesman with a leading pharmaceutical company in Texas, once told me of a technique for dealing with difficult people that he learned from a top Xerox salesperson—the "feel, felt, found" technique. George said that it has helped him through countless selling situations and dealing with difficult customers. Here's how it works:

Let's say George's customer is a physician who is angry that she is not able to prescribe a preferable medicine for a patient because it is not on an insurance company's formulary. George might reply, "I can imagine how you must feel about this situation (acknowledge her feelings). I would have felt the same way if I were you (empathize). What I have found is that this is happening to other physicians as well. And they are handling it by, or getting better results by ... (solution)."

# Preface with "I Appreciate"

While going through the police academy of a major U.S. city, my brother Joe learned verbal judo. This is defined as "the gentle art of persuasion that redirects others' behavior with words and generates voluntary compliance."[1] Also called tactical communications, verbal judo has been taught to police officers because many of the people they deal with are among the roughest, toughest, and most challenging people around.

Joe told me that one simple technique has helped him in more situations as a police officer than any other. He said this technique makes people feel that they are listened to and that what they said is at least considered. The technique is quite simply to start a sentence with "I appreciate."

- I appreciate your bringing this to my attention; I will look into it.
- I appreciate what you are trying to do here, but …
- I appreciate your honesty, but I am still going to have to …
- I appreciate all of the trouble you went through, but …

This preface not only softens what you are saying to someone, but, more important, it acknowledges the other person's efforts.

# Let People Know You Are Listening

Often people just want to be heard. They want to feel listened to and understood. Sometimes we spend too much time talking and arguing and not enough time listening. People feel better when they are listened to, even if no solution is found.

How do people know if we are listening to them? How do they know that what they are trying to say is being heard or even making sense? One way six-figure communicators naturally show others that they are listening is through parroting (Chapter 10).

Parroting is simply repeating a word, phrase, or sentence back to the other person to show that you are actively listening. Simply grunting "Hmmm," "oh," and "well" don't do a very good job of showing others that you are listening. Instead, try parroting. Below are a few examples of parroting:

**Angry Person:** And then my boss stormed into my office!
**Parroter:** He came into your office?

**Angry Person:** He started yelling and screaming about the Johnson account!
**Parroter:** The Johnson account?

**Angry Person:** He said that each day we delay on that account, the company loses $3,000.
**Parroter:** Wow, $3,000!

Obviously you don't want to parrot every single sentence an angry person says, for that would only inflame their anger. Change it a little, summarize or paraphrase what the other person says, and ask a few questions like *Why?* and *When?* All of these small acknowledgements show others that you are actively listening. People feel better simply knowing you listened and acknowledged their feelings. There is no need to get into the minutiae.

## Shift the Focus

Rather than dwelling on the problem, shift the focus to the solution. Acknowledge that it may be a tough, tragic, or trying situation, but then brainstorm together what can be done to rectify or remedy the situation. Taking your eyes off the problem and redirecting them onto the solution will create goodwill and energy.

Anthony Robbins, the renowned motivational speaker and success coach, counsels that sometimes people are so irate that it is hard to talk to them and redirect their focus. So he uses the NLP technique of a "pattern interrupt." Here's how he describes this technique:

As someone is getting upset, you might ask her what is hanging out of her nose. She almost always will stop instantly, often mid-sentence, wipe her nose, and ask if she got it. You might then point to the other nostril or say that it was a little more to the right. Then you would quickly jump in and do what you need to do to refocus the conversation.[2]

The genius of this is simply interrupting someone's negative thought patterns, allowing the two of you to shift from the problem to a solution.

It's amazing how easily distracted people can get. When I'm working as a salesman and someone asks me for a free lunch, I suddenly shift the focus. I might reply, "Let me ask you a question. Do you play tennis? We will have to play sometime." The phrase *let me ask you a question* is but one focus shifter and a preparatory question. Come up with your own.

*When angry, count to ten before you speak; if very angry, one hundred.*

— **Thomas Jefferson, third President of the United States**

## Let the Other Person Run Out of Steam

Let difficult people talk until they run out of steam. The more they talk, the better they'll feel. Let them talk 95 percent of the time and encourage them to keep talking. Let them know you're listening by making small acknowledgments along the way, parroting, or asking a question or two to clarify. After they have said everything they can think of and have nothing more to say, then smile and politely end the conversation. This way, you never had to challenge or fight them.

If they are venting, don't take offense while they are doing it. Just let them talk. Take what they are saying with a grain of salt. The less you say, the better.

## If You Are Wrong, Say You Are Wrong

We all make mistakes; we are human. It is okay to admit them. Once you do, it takes away others' "ammo" and there is little more they can say. It takes the wind out of their sails so that both of you can move on.

A lot of people will argue until you admit defeat. But they don't know what to do if you simply agree with them that you might have made a mistake. This leaves them speechless! Don't be stingy with an apology.

## Blame Yourself

If you put other people on the defensive, they will fight you. If you get upset, they will begin to justify their actions. So instead, try this interesting approach—blame yourself! The harder you are on yourself, the more likely the other person will jump in and save you from yourself and either accept some of the responsibility or begin to mitigate the issue. He might even tell you that it is really not that bad. This can be a fun tactic to use.

Let's say you made an awful comment to someone by mistake, or it came out wrong. Pull that person aside later and apologize for the comment or what you did. Say something like what a horrible person you are for making that comment. Say you can't believe you said that and how totally unacceptable it was. Talk about how being under stress or pressure can make you extremely insensitive and judgmental. Say that these are deplorable qualities in your personality and that you are really working on them to become a better person.

About halfway through beating yourself up, the other person will start to smile, laugh, or let you off the hook. It is almost a comical way to address other people's feelings and let them know you may have been a tad out of line.

If you blame yourself without going to the comical extreme and seriously take responsibility for your actions, it still works. Talk about how you lose your head sometimes, how every now and then things come out wrong, or that you don't think before you speak on occasion. Even with these meek apologies, people will feel that you addressed their feelings and usually will let you off the hook.

One time I saw a doctor use a version of this tactic on a golf course. Two doctors started out nice, but after the younger doc made several bad shots, he started yelling and getting angry. The older doctor, in his late sixties, used the "blame yourself" tactic to tactfully get his younger colleague to calm down and to tell him how to shoot better. This is what the older doc said on the tee box before teeing off (when everyone is supposed to remain quiet and he had everyone's attention): "I always have to remember that I play better when I relax. Otherwise, I get too tense and forget to keep my head down and my eye on the ball."

It worked! The angry doctor carefully listened between the lines and kept his head down and relaxed. I will concede that this newfound attitude lasted only about three more holes, but golf really pushes the limits of this tactic. So if it can work on a golf course, it can work anywhere!

## Make the Other Person Feel like Royalty

When someone is upset, make that person feel like a king or queen and watch the tension go away. In other words, make the other person feel important, respected, or appreciated. You might tell someone that she is one of your best (top) customers, so you will work extra hard to rectify the situation. You might tell the person how much you appreciate or respect her and will take the problem directly to the top: "I respect the fact that you ... We need good customers like you to bring this to our attention. Let me make it up to you." Make others feel significant and treat them exceptionally.

# Be Firm

Valerie Quick, an experienced nurse, once told me her secret to dealing with difficult patients: be firm, but polite and respectful. She said that this one technique made a dramatic impact on how she came across and helped her stay professional and polite. She said this technique has helped her talk to some of the most difficult patients and "calm them down." She told me that she had even had patients later come back to her and apologize for getting upset.

To employ this technique, you don't have to get upset or yell at people—just look them in the eye and talk directly to them. Talk sternly and firmly without getting angry. People will be able to tell by the tone of your voice that you are serious and you mean business, so they will not only tread lightly, but many will quickly change their attitude.

# Pinpoint and Fix the Problem

Pinpoint exactly why people are upset, and do whatever you can to help. Too many people assume too much and never take the time to clearly identify a problem or even ask how someone wants to resolve it.

One top auto salesperson told me that a customer of his who'd recently bought a new vehicle came in angry and screaming. No one knew what to do to pacify him. The receptionist sent him from department to department because the customer service people were at lunch. The customer felt overwhelmed and neglected, making him all the more upset. Finally, this salesman simply asked the customer exactly what the problem was. Turned out it was merely a clutch that needed a slight adjustment. A mechanic fixed it and the customer left the dealership happy.

When you pinpoint exactly what the problem is, ask the other person what a reasonable solution would be, if it is unclear. By asking people what they think is reasonable, they are usually more reasonable, realistic, and understanding.

# Four Tips to Getting Along with Others

1.  Ask yourself: Is what you are doing or saying going to make the other person want to help you, work with you, or like you more? Or will it make it exponentially more difficult to work with the other person? The last thing you want is to make things more difficult for yourself. Once you get off on the wrong foot, it is extremely difficult to work with people.

2.  Avoid talking about the problem if you can help it. Talk about everything else. Bonding is more important than fixing the problem. Why? Because a large majority of problems are simply misunderstandings or disagreements over trivial issues, especially when it's family. Don't waste time bickering. People become far more reasonable when rapport is established. Women notoriously tell men that they weren't looking for a solution to their problem; they just wanted the man to listen. Bonding is often more important than fixing the problem, for not all problems can or should be fixed.

> *The three people in the Army you don't want to upset are the cook, the supply sergeant, and the finance officer!*
> — **Old Army Expression**

3.  Take the person out for coffee or lunch to talk to them about the problem. Build rapport! Touch on an apology if you must by using the "blame yourself" tactic. This will almost always trigger the law of reciprocity. When you start blaming yourself, the other person generally will jump in to accept partial blame. Then if you pick up the check, the law of reciprocity will kick in—others will naturally feel obligated to you. They will feel a need to make it up to you somehow. Often they do this by accepting more blame or going out of their way to do you a favor.

4.  Remember not to embarrass people in front of others. Most people think and act differently when others are around. If you have a concern, it is better to pull someone aside or into a private area. People usually respond better in private than in public.

# Chapter Summary

- Resisting the Forces of Negativity: On a Likert scale from 1 to 10, with 10 being full of positive energy and "in the zone" and 1 being very tired or angry, you should be at a level 9 or 10 when dealing with difficult people. Limit or avoid exposure to angry people when your positive energy is low.

- Universal Reasons That People Get Upset or Angry:
  - Hurt feelings and need for empathy
  - Predetermined beliefs
  - Add-on information
  - Fear of the unknown
  - Feeling threatened
  - Because they care
  - Lacking a feeling of importance
  - Lacking respect
  - Lacking appreciation
  - Tired or irritable
  - Under stress
  - Under time constraints
  - Lacking information or openness
  - Comments made around others
  - Talking behind someone's back
  - Unprofessional or poor behavior
  - Sharp tongue
  - Need for help

- Avoid getting upset or getting someone else upset. At the end of an argument, people will feel worse about you than before the argument began. Your goal isn't to yell at people, but to alter the behavior or rectify the situation. It is always easier to talk and work with people before they get upset. Practice the 14 ways to keep situations positive.

- Battle Drills for Dealing with Difficult People:
  - Create Allies
  - "Nice'm to Death"
  - Show Empathy

- Use the Feel, Felt, Found Technique
- Preface with "I Appreciate"
- Let People Know You Are Listening
- Shift the Focus
- Let the Other Person Run out of Steam
- If You Are Wrong, Say You Are Wrong
- Blame Yourself
- Make the Other Person Feel Like Royalty
- Be Firm
- Pinpoint and Fix the Problem

- Four Tips to Getting Along with Others
  - Ask yourself: Is what you are doing or saying going to make the other person want to help you, work with you, or like you more?
  - Avoid talking about the problem if you can help it. Bonding is more important than fixing the problem, for not all problems can or should be fixed.
  - Take people out for coffee or lunch to talk to them about the problem. Build rapport! Touch on an apology if you must by using the "blame yourself" tactic. This will almost always trigger the law of reciprocity.
  - Remember not to embarrass people in front of others. It is better to pull someone aside or into a private area if you have a concern—people will respond better.

# Fixing Important Relationships

## In This Chapter

- Understand the difference between blaming people and merely blaming actions
- Discover the five truths to healing broken relationships
- Use the "clean the slate" formula to fix broken ties
- Reestablish lost relationships while saving face
- Learn the secret to strengthening relationships

**S**ix-figure communicators know how important it is to get along with others both personally and professionally. They keep their relationships with customers, clients, co-workers, business associates, friends, family, and neighbors not only intact, but strong. These powerful relationships enable six-figure communicators to do extraordinary things in life and are responsible in a large part for their success.

They know that everyone has a need to feel important. They know that if they are successful in making others feel important, the vast majority of people problems will fade away—if they even get started to begin with. There is little need for negotiations or apologies. More important, people will like them, appreciate them, and even go out of their way to help them simply because they made others feel important. We all want to surround ourselves with people who make us feel good. It is human nature.

Problems arise when people no longer feel important or respected, when they feel like second-class citizens. Whenever this happens, people feel as if a piece of their soul is taken away. After a while, feelings run so deep that they turn to feelings of hatred. The longer this goes on, the harder it is for people to change.

How bad do these feelings of hatred get? Well, people shoot, stab, beat up, alienate, curse, or otherwise try to destroy people who gave them those feelings! We see this nightly on the news.

Let's hope you don't have any relationships this extreme. But do you have some relationships worth fixing, or at least strengthening? If you do, you are not alone. Most of us have at least one family member or friend from whom we have drifted apart. This chapter looks at the pain of damaged relationships and how they can be healed and strengthened.

## The Pain of Broken Relationships

I know of two brothers who did not see each other in more than 50 years! One of them recently died without seeing his brother again. As sad as this is, many people don't forgive others, even after the others die; they are still holding a grudge! I have a friend in his thirties who hasn't talked to his father since they got into a big fight 15 years ago. And I know of parents who haven't taken their children to see their grandparents in years because of a fight between the younger and the older couple years before. Unfortunately these stories are all too common.

*"The weak can never forgive. Forgiveness is the attribute of the strong."*
— **Mahatma Gandhi**

What a regrettable thing not to see, talk to, or communicate with friends or family members for any reason. Family ties should be stronger than any other ties you have. Even not talking to a friend because of something she said years ago is unfortunate.

If you're in this situation, ill feelings may have been eating at you for years. You may be plagued with these feelings every time you see something that reminds you of that person or every time you think about her. Sometimes with the passing of time, the painful gnawing subsides, but it is always there. It is a dull, nagging, often lifelong pain.

You may talk to the person occasionally, but the conversation feels awkward and artificial. The conversation is probably shallow. More is going on with her than she will tell you. You sense this and don't say much in return.

Or maybe the two of you simply went your own separate ways, never to see each other again. Such broken relationships often come about because one person blames the other for something that went wrong, or each of you blames the other.

# Blame Actions, Not People

Blaming people cripples relationships. It slowly dissolves a relationship's backbone, undoing years of enjoyment and togetherness. Why? Because blame attacks a person's soul. When you blame someone, you attack the person he has been striving to become. Blaming can undo all of the good he has done for others. One sentence labels him personally and even publicly for a single negative action, incident, day, or behavior.

When we blame people, we are essentially saying that they are bad— thoughtless, inconsiderate, uncaring. Blame curses others with a stigma or title. Blame makes it almost impossible for them to recover. We assign and label them and can never go back and take the label off.

Blaming people makes it exceptionally difficult to get past the problem. When we blame people, there is little that they can do to get back in our good graces. It does not grant them a way to fix the situation or improve next time. The options they have to remedy the situation are quickly taken away. Blaming takes away a person's will to change, and it destroys not only relationships, but also hope.

Focusing on behavior and actions, by contrast, saves relationships because it changes the focus. If you blame a person's actions, not the person, then the person has something to work with. Telling someone that a particular behavior or action was inappropriate or could have been handled better enables the person to change and save face. It assumes that the other person is essentially a good person, but has a quality that could be improved. It changes the focus from "bad person" to "undesirable action." This is what enables the person to change.

Actions don't have feelings. Actions don't take things personally. Actions don't get offended, for actions are not people. Actions are inanimate. Actions are temporary behavior that can simply be corrected next time.

Healing a broken relationship relies on people making changes. And what enables people to make changes is a focus on behavior and actions, rather than the person. The next section provides a formula for reestablishing your connection with the person.

# Healing Broken Relationships

The first step toward healing any relationship is realizing a few truths, listed below:

- Being human means that we all make mistakes.

- People do and say things sometimes that they don't necessarily mean. Sometimes things come out wrong but, once said, can't be taken back even if the person wanted to. (The action was bad, not the person.)

- Whatever happened between the two of you probably happened a long time ago. You are different people now, even at different stages in your lives. Most of us develop a greater perspective of life over time, putting one fight or one year into better context.

- Most of us become wiser, more easygoing, and tolerant as we get older because we see more and gain more perspective. What seemed like a big deal then probably isn't as important now.

- Forgiving someone is even better for you than for the other person.

*"Hate doesn't change people (for the better); love changes people."*
— **Charles BouAbboud, M.D.**

## "Clean the Slate" Formula

Many of us tend to bottle up feelings and harbor ill will against others. But it helps to realize that both parties are probably right from their own prospective. Both could have handled the situation better. And both need to put this incident behind them or risk losing or weakening the relationship.

If you want to mend a relationship or reduce ill will, but you are not sure where to start, then try this clean-the-slate formula. This can be tough sometimes and even a little scary. But it is a way to put a negative situation behind you quickly and allow a relationship with another to move forward again. The formula is:

**Apologize + Heartfelt Comment + Smile and Trial Closure**

This formula works like pulling off a bandage—do it quick and it'll be painless. It is not intended to embarrass anyone or dredge up bad feelings. It helps both of you get over the incident and move on with your relationship quickly.

If you have a lot of pride, and if apologizing is tough for you, try this formula. I tend to have a hard time apologizing and swallowing my pride when I am wrong. Instead, I sit around and try to figure out how the other person was wrong so I won't have to apologize. But this formula has worked magically for me and has helped me take my foot out of my mouth on many occasions. Let's look at each of the steps in more detail.

## Step 1: Apologize

As soon as I say the word *apologize*, many people cringe. The first thing they think of is that it is not their fault, or that it should be the other person who apologizes first. But the only thing that really matters is fixing the relationship. So this is how you fix it.

Apologizing is key. Apologize quickly; don't think too much about it. What is important is that you do it, and you do it quickly. A fair or mediocre apology is a thousand times better than none at all. The saying "better is the enemy of good enough" certainly applies here.

Never talk specifics of an incident or problem. The No. 1 mistake people make when they apologize is that they go into the incident and drag it up again. This often starts off innocently enough, but it turns ugly fast, which certainly makes the apologizing more difficult. Don't do it.

The apology should be short and just a few words, such as:
- "I apologize"
- "I'm sorry."
- "I want to apologize for [fill in the blank]."

This is all you need to do for step one. Simple, right?

## Step 2: Heartfelt Comment

The heartfelt comment is the smoother. All you need is one or two comments, as long as they come from the heart. Keep them general with no details or excuses. Sometimes gently blaming yourself is okay. I can't tell you what to say because it must come from your heart, but here are a few examples:

- Sometimes I tend to go overboard, but that is only because I really care.
- Sometimes I get so caught up in what I am doing that I lose track of what's important in my life. And you are important to me.
- You are really, really important to me. I truly care about you!
- I love you so much.
- I can be a real jerk sometimes.

Use nonlinguistic movements (Chapter 11) when you deliver your heartfelt comments. Using them will help your message touch the other person's soul, show that you are sincere, and play a critical role in cleaning the slate.

A few NLMs that could be used are the eye dart, holding your hand over you heart, eye squint, a gentle touch on the arm or shoulder, or simply a hug. Use NLMs to help convey your message only when you are sincere. If you are not going to be sincere, don't waste your time or the time and emotions of others.

## Step 3: Smile and Trial Closure

Give the person the warmest smile you can muster as you go for a trial close. Your smile shows that you are sincere, and the trial close checks with the person to make sure all is well again. If it is, you have successfully cleaned your slate. A few examples of trial closes are the following:

- Would you give me another shot?
- Could you find it somewhere in that big heart of yours to forgive me?
- Is there a tiny little place in that big heart of yours to forgive me?
- Would you forgive me?

Notice that with the clean-the-slate formula, you never talk about the specifics of what happened between the two of you. You both save face. You never have to go into accepting blame or who is right and who is wrong. (Remember, if there is any blame to go around, it is the actions, not the individuals, that are to blame.)

# Moving On

Take advantage of your newly created goodwill and move on with your lives. Just make a mental note to yourself of what you learned from this; and be careful next time, for you now know that this is "hot" territory.

Enjoy the great feeling of being close to someone again. You'll benefit not just from being close but also from feeling free, as if a huge rock has finally been lifted off your shoulders. You'll feel as if your conscience is once again clear. You are no longer archenemies. The relationship is new and exciting again, and somewhere the chemistry that the two of you had will again manifest.

Take pleasure in catching up or getting to know someone again. Learn what you have been missing and what had happened to the other person during the months or years that you were out of touch. You may be surprised. Don't run out of time!

> *"Remorse: regret that one waited so long to do it."*
> — **H.L. Mencken**

# Strengthening Existing Relationships

A young woman in rural West Virginia made me realize one of the keys to fixing or improving important relationships. The year was 2001, and I was sitting in a waiting room at a local hospital, talking to a young woman in her late teens or early twenties. We were talking about families, and I asked her if she had any brothers or sisters. She replied that she had a half brother living in Richmond, Virginia. I then asked her if she was close to him. She replied that she was close to him when he called.

That's it—that is the secret! You can be close to people only when you communicate with them. It doesn't have to be on the phone; it can be through letters, notes, e-mail, or personal visits. But you have to communicate some-how, and frequently! The frequency of communication, even if it is only a voicemail message or a two-line e-mail or note, is far more important than the length of the message or its content.

How many of us live with others but rarely talk to them? I have a brother stationed in Sarajevo that I feel closer to now than when he was stateside. The reason is that we either call or e-mail each other weekly. Before, we would talk only once in a blue moon. Increasing the frequency of communication with someone takes any relationship from the superficial to the next level.

---

Parents spend an average of six minutes daily in meaningful conversation with their children. How many quality minutes a day do you spend with your spouse, child, or other family member?

---

# Chapter Summary

- If you are successful in making people feel important, the vast majority of people problems will fade away—if they even get started to begin with. Problems arise when people no longer feel important or respected. Whenever this happens, people feel as if a piece of their soul is taken away.

- Not seeing, talking to, or communicating with friends or family members for any reason is painful. Such broken relationships often come about because one person blames the other for something that went wrong, or each of you blames the other.

- The first step toward healing any relationship is realizing the following truths:
  - Being human means that we all make mistakes.
  - People do and say things sometimes that they don't necessarily mean. (The action was bad, not the person.)
  - Whatever happened between the two of you probably happened a long time ago. Most of us develop a greater perspective of life over time, putting one fight or one year into better context.
  - Most of us become wiser, more easygoing, and tolerant as we get older so that what seemed like a big deal then probably isn't as important now.
  - Forgiving someone is even better for you than for the other person.

- The clean-the-slate formula helps both of you get over the incident and move on with your relationship quickly:

  **Apologize + Heartfelt Comment + Smile and Trial Closure**

- When you renew a broken relationship, you can enjoy not only the benefits of being close again but also a new freedom, as if your conscience is once again clear. You get to learn what you have been missing and what happened to the other person during the months or years that you were out of touch.

- The key to strengthening relationships is realizing that you can be close to people only when you communicate with them. The frequency of communication is far more important than the length of the message or its content.

## Daily Challenge

Strengthen a relationship today by calling someone you care about whom you haven't talked to in a long time. Say that it's been a long time and you just wanted to call to see how they're doing. Then let them do most of the talking.

## Executive Challenge

Make the first call to reestablish a past relationship. You get credit just for calling. If you can end the conversation on a positive note, do it. If you need to use the clean-the-slate formula, use it. Just make the call.

# Bringing Out the Best in Others

## In This Chapter:

- Understand that people change through persuasion, not force
- Learn to bring out the best in people in three easy steps
- Discover the secret of the four magic keys
- Learn how 16 grilled cheese sandwiches bought 1,000 gallons of water!

There is so much good in people! The problem is that most of us aren't very good at bringing it out in others. It's far easier to bring out the bad. We usually don't mean to; it just happens. And when it happens, it makes us feel bad. All of us naturally want to prosper and be successful, have fun, laugh, and enjoy life. In fact, if we don't have these good feelings, we feel that something is wrong with our lives. We don't feel satisfied. We befriend, admire, trust, love, and respect the people who make us feel good. These are the people who know how to bring out the best in us.

## Swaying People with Your Personal Power

Understand that you can't force people into a positive state of mind to bring out the best in them. But often you can sway their thinking, thus their state. You don't do it by force or by using your power of position; you do it by using your personal power. This is illustrated charmingly in the story about the wind and the sun making a bet.

One day the wind said he was more powerful than the sun, and he bet the sun that he could strip the coat off the traveler walking down the road. The sun took the bet and let the wind go first.

The wind blew and blew at the traveler, trying to strip the clothes off the man. But the harder the wind blew, the tighter the traveler clenched his coat. After some time and a valiant effort, the wind finally gave up.

Next it was the sun's turn. Little by little, the sun shone down on the man and heated the air. Soon sweat beaded on the traveler's forehead. After 20 minutes the traveler couldn't take it any more and took off his coat.

The sun won the bet. Not because he tried to force the man to take off his coat like the wind, but through gentle persuasion. It was the traveler's decision. People are the same way.

Remember that people have to change their own minds; you can't do it for them. But also realize that they can do it in less than a second when they decide to. If you go the rehash route, people may never change their minds or want to better themselves.

Talk about what you want, not what you don't want. Talk about what you want to happen, not what you don't want to happen. For some reason we think we need to prove to others that they were wrong, or that they messed up, to be able to move on. We think that people cannot change their behavior unless they clearly know how wrong they were.

But people can change their behavior—even if they don't see the darker side of their mistakes, or future events—as long as they see a better method of doing something or a more fruitful life. Our job is not to correct others' mistakes but to paint a better picture for them. Mitigate mistakes and paint the good.

If you can paint a picture of a grander life or appeal to people's greed, they will change to the positive much more quickly and easily. Show people a better way by painting a better picture. If you do this, their brain will automatically discard the old method or ways and change to the grander method.

This chapter looks at how to bring out the best in people gently, genuinely, and politely in three straightforward steps.

# Step 1: Get Yourself into State

You cannot bring out the best in others if you cannot bring out the best in yourself. If you want to bring out the best in people, get into the personal power mind-set first (Chapter 1). If you are not in a powerful state, people will know it. If you are not in a powerful state, you will accidentally say the wrong things. If you are not in a powerful state, you won't be able to help, inspire, or bring out the best in anyone. Remember, whoever has the strongest state wins!

Keep in mind, as you learned in Chapter 1, that you can transmit and receive certain traits only when you yourself are in certain states. Certain qualities or traits are unattainable in certain states. You cannot transmit love, caring, patience, understanding, empathy, charisma, charm, class, or confidence when you are outraged. It is impossible. People will see right through you if you try to fake it. You will come off as insincere and fake. By getting yourself into more powerful states, you will be better able to transmit and receive emotions critical to bringing out the best in others.

*"You get the best out of others when you give the best of yourself."*
— **Harvey Firestone**

# Step 2: Decide What You Are Going to Give

In his book *Closing the Sale*, Zig Ziglar says, "You can get everything in life you want if you just help enough other people get what they want."

Bringing out the best in people is exactly the same. You must give to get! Don't think that you can bring out the best in someone without giving something first. Too many people think that they can reap without sowing. They walk around and take, take, take, draining others of everything they have. Freeloaders never inspire, influence, or invigorate others.

So what are you going to give? Better yet, what have you already been giving to others during your contacts with them? How solid and how real are your relationships? The Bible says, "It is more blessed to give than to receive" (Acts 20:35). There is only one "problem" with giving—you get back 10 times more in the long run! Even in the short term, you usually come out ahead. Here is an example:

Once during the holidays, in my job as a salesman, I gave a receptionist a few plastic pens with the name of my product on them. She thanked me for the pens and gave me two oranges from a case that she had bought to support a local high school fund-raiser.

I didn't want the oranges so I gave them separately to two people in the next office. One invited me to sit down and gave me a piece of birthday cake, and the other person thanked me for the orange and invited me out for a cup of coffee the next day. When I went out with him the next day, he introduced me to several new business clients.

One broke off a colorful branch of a poinsettia and gave it to me to spread some Christmas cheer. That was a nice gesture, but I really didn't want the branch, so I gave it to my elderly neighbor when I got home. I told her that I just wanted to say hi and brighten her day. I told her the branch would probably die in a few days, but she could enjoy it now. The neighbor thanked me for it and gave me a piece of pie to take home.

Everything people gave me I gave right back to others. I couldn't get rid of this stuff; people kept giving me more. This was the law of reciprocity in action: When you give something to someone, people respond in kind.

This is the key principle in this chapter. You give genuinely and sincerely to help others or to brighten their day, not just to get things in return. But people usually do respond in kind!

## Four Magic Keys of Giving

The four keys listed below will open doors to bring out the good in others. Your goal is to become proficient at using all four keys. The keys used in combination will yield even greater results.

- Positive Words (must be in a positive state first)
- Positive Deeds (must be in a positive state first)
- Material Objects
- Positive Energy (must be in a positive state first)

Give to get; get by giving. Either way, you must give first. You don't have to buy expensive items to give away; you can give positive words, deeds, energy, and inexpensive items to people. Give people everything you can. Send flowers, give gifts, write notes, and make phone calls to give words of encouragement. The more keys you give away, the greater the probability you will bring out the best in people.

When people help you, reward them. When they go out of their way or do something for you that they didn't have to do, reward them. Whether it is their job or not, they made a special effort for you, so make a special effort to show your appreciation. Give them a pat on the back for their trouble.

This pat on the back can be physical, but most of the time it is verbal. The goal is to give them something as a reward for helping you. Give them a joke, verbal appreciation, words of support, encouragement, or special contact information from your network. Brighten their day or make their life a little better for helping you. You owe them.

# Step 3: Now Bring Out the Good

Everyone has different sides, so look for the side you want to see in others and bring it out. In essence, you create the person you want to see. Look for the good in people, and find it! You may have to look a little, but find it. Skip over people's weaknesses. We all have them. Too many people see weaknesses and have a nasty habit of digging into them—or they simply run off.

Use simplified buttonomics (Chapter 4) to find people's positive hot buttons quickly. Look for positive hot buttons around something near and dear to their heart. This might be something they are proud of, something they enjoy, or something important to them. People will love you for genuinely asking about something they are passionate about.

Once you find a button, dig in and ask the other person specific questions to expand the button. If someone just bought a new car, for example, that may be their positive hot button. You found it; now ask questions about the color, style, and features. The more the person talks about it, the more good will flow.

Nonlinguistic movements (Chapter 11) are another way to show interest in people. Lean forward while the other person is speaking. Smile or use eye movements or hand gestures while using simplified buttonomics. Such NLMs subconsciously show people that you are actively listening to what they are saying. People need to feel listened to.

Unlock the good in people by using the four magic keys to giving—positive words, positive deeds, objects, and positive energy. Share your sense of humor, do something nice for them, look good for them, smile, or reassure them. Make people feel important, special, respected, admired, inspired, loved, proud, attractive, happy, or just plain warm all over. Your goal is to leave people on a high note. You want people to feel better off than they did before they met you.

> *"My best friend is the one who brings out the best in me."*
> — **Henry Ford, U.S. industrialist and automobile manufacturer**

Continually build conversational momentum. Build positive energy and emotions. Because you are in the personal power mind-set, start where the other person is and then slowly build him up to where you are. Keep conversations light and pleasant. Don't bring up negative subjects or things that might be construed as negative. The law of attraction will doom you. You could end up getting mired in that negativity, unable to extract yourself.

Remembering something about others is a shortcut to building conversational momentum. This shows interest and instantly makes people feel good. Remember their name, birthday, how they like their coffee, where they are from, or something else significant.

Again, the two-sentence technique (TST, Chapter 14) is a powerful way to bring out people's positive emotions. Say just two positive sentences, such as "Congratulations. I am proud of you!" Use the TST in person, over the telephone, or on a note card.

I have seen six-figure communicators start conversations by giving people a reputation to live up to. Tell someone right off the bat the behavior you want from them. You might say, "You seem like such a nice person, let me ask you [a question, for a favor]." Without thinking, people respond as if indeed they were a nice person. "You seem like you are in a great mood ... how do you ...?" Subtly tell people how you want them to respond. This plants a little seed and gives them something to live up to.

Taking exceptional care of people also brings out the best in them. Do everything possible to make others feel comfortable and content. This continually builds positive feelings. It is easier to bring the good out of people when they are in a more positive state.

Charm, flattery, and compliments pick people up. It's okay to use them gently. Here are a few examples:
- I love being around [inspiring, interesting, enthusiastic] people!
- Talking with you has been the highlight of my day.
- Do you know what I love about my job? It's working with and helping nice customers like you.

> *"Charm is the power to make someone else feel*
> *that both of you are wonderful."*
> — **Anonymous**

Six-figure communicators are good "closers." They end conversations on a high note and send people off feeling good. They may end by saying something like:
- What a pleasure it was to see you again. Good luck with your finals!
- It sure sounds like life is going great for you. Have fun on your new boat this weekend!

- I had a wonderful time tonight and just wanted to tell you how much I enjoyed our conversation.

## Choose Your Golden Minute

To bring out the best in others, you need to be mindful of what they are doing at the time. Using the two- and three-track minds, consider the environment, who else is around, how much time people have to talk, their mental state, and so on. Maximize your impact by choosing your golden minute.

Remember, too, that different things motivate different people at different times. I will never forget the power of a grilled cheese sandwich in the right circumstance, as the following story illustrates.

I was on an Army training mission at Camp Lejeune, North Carolina. I had a supply platoon that had water purification units that could turn swamp water into drinking water and even desalinate and purify ocean water. My unit had been in the field for an extended period.

One day a storm blew in and two marine landing crafts came ashore needing an urgent resupply of fresh water. The chief of the boat invited me and a couple of my soldiers on board to "talk business" in their galley— over grilled cheese sandwiches.

The chief of the boat used his golden minute and the law of reciprocity wisely. He knew his marines were not in our chain of command; we owed them nothing. It was extra work for us to help them with their water needs.

Still, as tired as we all had become of Army food (imagine that), the grilled cheese sandwiches were the "magic key." The chief got all the fresh water he wanted, not by using his power of position, but his personal power to choose a location conducive to negotiations—the galley.

The grilled cheese sandwiches wouldn't have worked back at the base, but they worked perfectly on this deployment.

# Chapter Summary

- The best way to bring out the good in people is by using your personal power. Paint a better picture for people rather than trying to correct their mistakes.

- Step 1: Get yourself into state. You cannot bring out the best in others if you cannot bring out the best in yourself, for you can transmit and receive certain traits only in certain states. Whoever has the strongest state wins!

- Step 2: Decide what you are going to give. You must give to get! Don't think that you can bring out the best in anyone without giving something first. Freeloaders never inspire, influence, or invigorate others.

  Four Magic Keys of Giving:
  - Positive Words (must be in positive state first)
  - Positive Deeds (must be in positive state first)
  - Material Objects
  - Positive Energy (must be in positive state first)

- Step 3: Now bring out the good. Look for the side you want to see in others and bring it out. Bring out the best in people by making them feel important, special, respected, admired, inspired, loved, proud, attractive, happy, or just plain warm all over. Bring out the good using simplified buttonomics, asking good questions, using NLMs, remembering something about them, giving them a reputation to live up to, using the TST, complimenting them, taking exceptional care, and ending conversations on a high note.

- Choose your Golden Minute wisely. Use the two- and three-track minds to consider the environment, who else is around, how much time the person has to talk, and the person's mental state. Different things motivate different people at different times.

## Daily Challenge

Use each of the four magic keys of giving today to bring out the good in different people. Before you talk with someone, decide which of the four keys you will use and then use it by giving something to someone else. Open the "door" by using simplified buttonomics, asking good questions, using NLMs, and giving compliments.

When you are using the "deeds" key, try an anonymous act of thoughtfulness or kindness. You could send someone flowers with a warm and inspiring anonymous card or leave a nice anonymous note on someone's windshield. All day, both you and the other person will be uplifted. You will be curious about the other person's reaction and how it made him feel, and he will be glowing inside with his wonderful secret and great curiosity. All day good things will come to and out of both of you.

## Executive Challenge

The first three keys are the easiest to get the hang of. Today, practice giving someone energy when you talk to people. Circumstances tend to beat us up all day, draining our energy and making us more prone to getting angry and short-tempered. Build up your energy and give some of it away to help someone through the rest of their day. Children do this when they smile and giggle when they see us. They instantly hug us and ask us off-the-wall questions to take our minds off whatever we are thinking. Others can get people laughing. No matter how you do it, give people some of your energy and then bring out the best in them.

# CHAPTER 21

# Personal Power Leadership

## In This Chapter:

- Avoid the perils of being a "three-day leader"
- Learn the value of mentoring, teaching, and developing employees
- Apply the Pygmalion effect to bring out employees' best qualities
- Discover how parental qualities can make you a better leader

Using the power of position, you can order people subordinate to you to do the things you want them to do—or risk the consequences. Subordinates don't have to like what you tell them; they just have to do what you say. You can tell soldiers, for example, to eat with their helmets on, but if you are crude about it, they will take them off as soon as you leave.

It's not what you say that counts, but how you say it. If you are in a situation in which you have power of position over others—a leader, manager, teacher, parent, police officer—this chapter will help you see the ways that you can be more effective if you use your personal power instead of your position power.

## Leading Effectively When It Matters Most

I've mentioned Juan Rodriguez elsewhere in this book. It was he who told me about the "three-day leader." He said that in wartime, when soldiers are under enormous stress and pressure, it can take as few as three days to burn them out. At this point poor leaders rapidly become ineffective. Their "leadership" deteriorates and things begin to snowball. Soldiers become frustrated and fed up. They begin arguing among themselves and morale quickly disintegrates. Unit effectiveness is reduced.

Back on post, almost anyone can lead soldiers. "Leaders" look good sitting behind a desk with a freshly starched uniform, and they bark orders and go to meetings. Soldiers may not like the way they are being treated, but they tolerate it because they are well-fed, they work fairly set hours, and have most weekends off to rest and recuperate.

But in the field, when soldiers are sleep-deprived, tired, hungry, cold, wet, miserable, and under enormous pressure, you see leaders at their best and at their worst. Stress accelerates the process and quickly brings out their true colors. True leaders emerge and the "three-day leader" crumbles. What differentiates them?

Stressed three-day leaders tend to use more and more of their position power as circumstances become more difficult. In the military, expressions like "Move out, Sergeant" and "Listen, Private" start to become common-place. These leaders constantly seem to be quoting the higher-ups as a justification for their actions. In a business setting, they might say, "the president wants us to …" or "the boss told me that we need to …"

In contrast, strong leaders under stress are successful by using a high degree of personal power, not their power of position. Although they have the power to simply order their people to do what they want (which is far easier to do when you're stressed), they instead choose to use their personal power to talk and work with others.

At this point, it's not their knowledge that makes them strong leaders; it is their strong people skills. Not only are they themselves stressed; but they know that their subordinates are, too, and they treat them differently. They know that the better they are at understanding, talking to, and working with others, the more successful they will be when the going gets tough.

> *"Leadership: the art of getting someone else to do something you want done because he wants to do it."*
> **—Dwight D. Eisenhower, five-star general and 34th U.S. President**

# Leading by Mentoring

How many times have you heard a leader, upon being given an award at a ceremony, say something along the lines of "I just have good people working for me"? Such leaders are humble and act as if they had little to do with the award or organizational success. They make it seem as if they were dealt a winning hand and just played it.

Others may be thinking to themselves, "Oh, if I had the people you had, I could get great results too." For years I have heard military leaders complaining about receiving substandard soldiers whose specialty wasn't a perfect fit for a particular position. They'd want to be given better or more experienced soldiers to do their work.

## "Growing" Your Employees

One of my mentors at work pulled me aside one day and told me that too many leaders just didn't get it. He said that you must "grow" good people! Rarely do they just show up at your door.

The best leaders are good teachers and are extremely knowledgeable about their own expertise, the company's, and the industry's. Employees respect, admire, and truly appreciate leaders who care about them and take the time to explain and teach higher-level information. This is a huge part of mentoring—being a good teacher and being knowledgeable.

Another mentor of mine was so knowledgeable and passionate about his subject matter that people often gathered around his desk during their lunch hour or stayed after work just to learn from him. People understood the importance and value of what he taught. He showed people specific books, manuals, and paperwork to use. He explained the reasons that systems and other matters were the way they were.

By the time you left a meeting with him, you always felt inspired, more knowledgeable, and better off. But just as important, you respected and admired him for being one of the few leaders to really take time with you and help you grow. At the same time, by thoroughly explaining concepts, often on butcher-block paper or a note pad, he made the organization more efficient and productive, all the while reducing future problems. This also made his job easier and more enjoyable.

The lesson is to develop your employees. Learn their strengths, weaknesses, and goals—write down three of each. This will give you a starting point so you, too, can take employees to the next level. Although it is important to work on employees' weaknesses, it is more important to spend time developing their strengths, for it is their unique strengths that you hired them for and that will make you and your organization successful.

*"Take out a sheet of paper and I will tell you the great secret for learning what motivates employees best. Write at the top: 'Ask them!' Put your pencils down."*
**—Dr. Lewis Bender, professor, Central Michigan University**

I knew one leader who would keep a personal notebook on each of his soldiers. It wasn't to write down how his soldiers "messed up," but everything he knew about his soldiers and what he could do to help develop them. He kept their home-of-record address and information. He said he could refer to this book years later to follow up with former soldiers to see how they were doing. "You don't want to lose people's potential," he often said.

He would write down everything he knew about his soldiers, including their strengths, weaknesses, goals, family information, and so on. He then devised a customized plan for developing each soldier or simply listed what he wanted to do to develop each one. "Leaders must teach and mentor; you can tell the ones that don't," he would stress.

He cared about everyone who worked for him. He showed a genuine interest in all of his soldiers and was serious about developing them. And anyone who ever worked for him genuinely knew it.

One of his soldiers, for example, was very smart but didn't feel confident speaking in front of others. His experienced leader/mentor said this about his plan for him: "I listed things I could do to help him develop confidence speaking in front of others, like giving a review and analysis brief every once in a while and teaching the CLOAC (Combined Logistics Officer Advanced Course) when the officers came down [to take the course]." Slowly the soldier became a better speaker and a stronger leader.

## Empowering Employees for More Responsibility

Employees need to be told the direction and the goals of the organization. Tell them what will happen six months out and beyond. Tell them why they are doing the task or job and the importance of it. Take employees up a level or two, behind the scenes to show them how their job fits into the larger picture. This is an important part of mentoring and growing quality people within an organization.

Another way to help employees grow and get more involved in their organization is to turn group or organizational problems into employee problems. Assign employee ownership to problems, and challenge employees to solve them. Giving employees ownership of organizational problems helps prevent a "we/they thing." They will usually step up and take on additional jobs and responsibilities to meet or exceed the challenge.

Three-day leaders don't teach, mentor, motivate, develop, encourage, or challenge. They have a "take it or leave it" attitude. I once knew of a new manager who got rid of everyone he had a concern with in the first 90 days.

Unfortunately, he lost most of the experience on his team, just starting out. The mistake new managers often make is firing people to fix or eliminate problems. But after about a year, they realize, to their dismay, that the new people they hired to take their place have weaknesses too. They are right back where they started and behind in experience.

# Using the Pygmalion Effect

Several years ago I read about a fascinating scientific experiment involving elementary school children. The class was divided by eye color. Children with brown eyes were instructed to sit on one side of the classroom and children with blue eyes on the other side.

The teacher told the children that she had just learned about a study that found that children with blue eyes were smarter than children with brown eyes. She went on to say that the blue-eyed children developed faster, learned information more quickly, and always scored better on tests. These children were more intelligent than the brown-eyed children.

The teacher continued to teach, and after a given amount of time, administered the same tests to the class as a whole. Indeed, the children with the blue eyes scored higher on their tests than did the brown-eyed children.

Then the teacher told the class that she had had it all wrong. It was actually the brown-eyed children who were superior. All children were born with blue eyes, she said, but it was the stronger and wiser children that went on to develop the brown eyes. These children were truly the intelligent ones, she said.

The teacher once again continued to teach, and after a given amount of time, similarly administered tests to the class as a whole. Interestingly, the test scores reversed, and the children with the brown eyes outperformed the children with the blue eyes!

This is an example of the Pygmalion effect, or self-fulfilling prophecy—planting the seed of belief in individuals or groups ahead of time to increase future performance. When people really believe that they can do something, and as a leader you treat them as if they can, they will step up and figure out how to do it. Increasing your expectations of an employee's performance will actually improve that performance. Tell people they are smarter than others or are above average and they will begin to think so and do better.

*"Make people seem slightly nobler than they are, and they will want to live up to the reputation that you have given them."*
— **Dale Carnegie**

I experienced this myself. When Microsoft Office was new (and I had not yet worked with it), my boss gave me an important document to prepare for a meeting the next day. He wanted me to use Microsoft Excel to run various sort options and print out various top 10 lists for the division. Then I was to take that information and make slides for the briefing the next day with Microsoft's PowerPoint. In hindsight, I think my boss knew I was unfamiliar with the software.

Using a high degree of personal power, he applied the Pygmalion effect on me! He explained what he wanted done and gave me a general idea of how to do it with Microsoft Office. He told me how lucky he was to have a young employee who understood computers and could learn new programs quickly.

After leaving his office I felt that I could tackle any computer project he could give me. I thought to myself that he was right—I did learn things quickly and I did take a computer class in college. This would be easy.

I stayed at the office working on that stupid project till late into the night. I hated computers, but I had one heck of a reputation to live up to. The new boss thought I was smart! I couldn't let him down, I thought to myself. I completed the project and presented it with flying colors at the briefing the following morning.

Much later, when it came time for me to leave my job in that division, I asked my boss about the computer project he'd given me on my first day. He said he knew the project would take me out of my comfort zone but that I would do what it took to accomplish the task at hand. In fact, he said he checked in on me several times before leaving for the night and saw that I was asking others questions and learning how to do the various sort options.

*"I'll tell you what makes a great manager: A great manager has a knack for making ballplayers think they are better than they are. He forces you to have a good opinion of yourself. He lets you know he believes in you. He makes you get more out of yourself. And once you learn how good you really are, you never settle for playing anything less than your best."*[1]
—**Reggie Jackson, baseball star**

Giving someone a positive reputation in front of others can intensify the Pygmalion effect. To say, in front of others, that this guy is a mover and a shaker, is going places, is a hard worker, and is going to do great things for the company gently puts pressure on him to live up to those expectations and to make himself look good. Now he has a reputation to uphold and will usually respond in kind.

Another way to use the Pygmalion effect is to tip people off to your expectations right from the start. "You seem like such a nice person, let me ask you for a favor." People will think of themselves as a nice person and will usually respond in kind. Talk-show hosts use this tactic by starting their shows with "what a great audience we have here today!" The audience responds by hooting, hollering, and clapping. People usually respond in kind; this is the law of reciprocity.

## Selfless, Caring Leadership

Some of the best leaders use their personal power in a very caring, almost parental, way. They simply take extraordinary care of the people who work for them, as they might a family member. They seem to give people special time and attention to help them succeed.

The best military leaders in the field were the selfless ones, the ones who would not eat till their soldiers had eaten or would not sleep till everyone had a place to sleep. If an employee forgot her lunch money, the selfless leader would tactfully stick a few dollars in her pocket to buy something to eat. If the employee's car broke down at work, the selfless leader would make sure she got home safely.

Here are some ways you might demonstrate such caring leadership:
- Take the time to explain to subordinates why they are doing something and the importance of it.
- Tell them how much you appreciate their hard work.
- Tell them if you are proud of them or how impressed you were at the way they handled a particular situation.
- Call them into your office and simply ask how they are doing on a personal level, such as in their new marriage, with their new child, how their spouse is doing after the surgery, and so on.
- Buy your employee a cup of coffee or lunch, and get to know the person who is working for you.

Most employees really care for and want to work for leaders of this type. They revere such bosses and will do almost anything for them. In fact, if employees ever let down such a boss, they feel so bad that they will go out of their way not only to rectify the situation, but to get back into the boss's good graces.

Think of a time that you disappointed one of your parents or someone else you really respected. No doubt you felt awful about it. Your parent didn't even have to yell and scream at you; you just knew that you could have done better.

Selfless, caring leadership has this parental quality to it. When you employ this form of leadership, it usually is unnecessary to "chew out" employees. Instead, you can talk to them as if you are disappointed in them and then encourage them to do better by showing confidence in them, like a caring parent. You will be amazed at how well this approach works.

> *"True leadership comes from the heart, not the collar."*
> *(referring to rank).*
> —**Peter Stankovich**

## Chapter Summary

- Leading Effectively When It Matters Most. Under extreme circumstances, people can burn out in as few as three days. This is the point at which true leaders emerge and the "three-day leader" crumbles. Three-day leaders rely primarily on their position power when the going gets tough. In contrast, strong leaders under stress are successful using a high degree of personal power.

- Leading by Mentoring. Successful leaders don't just happen to have good people working for them—they create them. The best leaders groom employees for advancement. They are good teachers and mentors. They access their employees' strengths and weaknesses and learn about their goals. This serves as a starting point for their development.

- The Pygmalion Effect. This is planting the seed of belief in individuals or a group to increase future performance. When people really believe that they can do something, and as a leader you treat them as if they can do it, they will step up and figure out how to do it. Increasing your expectations of an employee's performance will actually improve that performance.

- Selfless, Caring Leadership. Some of the best leaders use their personal power in a caring, almost parental, way. They simply take extraordinary care of the people who work for them, as they might a family member. They seem to give people special time and attention to help them succeed. Most employees revere such bosses and will do almost anything for them. In fact, if employees ever let down such a boss, they will go out of their way not only to rectify the situation, but to get back into the boss's good graces.

## Daily Challenge

Teach someone who works for you something he didn't know about your company or what you do. If you are a manager, introduce a few low-level employees or subordinate managers to some of what happens at the head office. Show them some of the decisions you make daily, introduce them to people in the office, or let them sit in on a meeting or teleconference. When they leave, they will better understand the company they work for and will better appreciate and respect you for showing an interest in them. This will help establish a greater trust and working relationship.

## Executive Challenge

Mentor someone today. Invite the person to sit down with you and assess where she is, where she wants to go, and how you might help her get there. Write down three of her strengths, three weaknesses, and a few of her goals. Create a plan for her and provide direction and leadership.

# CHAPTER 22

# Building and Using Your Network

## In This Chapter:

- Realize you have 10,000 contacts in your network
- Discover the greatest secret to making your network work for you
- Learn how to organize your network
- Explore how to tap into your network—and build a new one
- Understand the importance of maintaining your network

**N**etworking is perhaps the greatest of all communication skills. It takes skill to be able to develop a network and to maintain a network. Magically, mysteriously, miraculously, the better your network, the easier and more enjoyable life will be for not only you, but everyone you help along the way. Good networkers have an extraordinary ability to help others. In fact, the first rule of networking is to apply it to help make the lives of others better. When you help others, it comes back tenfold. This in turn strengthens your network and improves your life.

There are many great books on networking. The purpose of this chapter is not to tell you everything about networking, but to give a quick networking overview and some key thoughts on the subject. After learning the art of networking and creating your own, you will wonder how you ever survived without it.

## Your Network of 10,000 Contacts

Ten thousand contacts! Where can I find 10,000 people, you ask? Well, have you heard of "six degrees of separation"? This theory states that you are connected to everyone, somehow, somewhere by way of six people. Everyone in the world is six phone calls away! The President of the United States is six people away. Perhaps you know someone who knows someone who has a friend who went to school with John Doe, who went to Yale, and is now an advisor to the President. You don't always know the chain that connects you to someone else, for there are so many people in it.

If we whittle down this same theory, we can come to the conclusion that 10,000 people are only two phone calls away! Let's look at the math. Almost everyone knows at least 100 people—family, friends, former classmates, people you grew up with, neighbors, teammates, fellow church members, club members, present and former co-workers, random folks you've met through the years, and many more. In fact, 100 is probably conservative for most people.

So if you know 100 people, and each of them knows or has access to 100 people, that makes at least 10,000 people (100 x 100) that either you or your friends know or have access to. Wow! Have you ever heard of a couple getting together through a friend of a friend whose neighbor made the introduction? Mathematically, the neighbor was tapping into an extended network of 100,000 people (3 people away).

## Applying the Network "Litmus Test"

It's easy to think you have a great network if you look in your address book and see 50 to 100 names. But how many of those would go out of their way to help you? How many of them would go above and beyond to help when you needed real help?

Whether you are moving, looking for a job, or needing advice or a loan or a bail out of jail, you have to wonder how many people in your network would go out of their way to help you. How many people from your network could you call at 1 A.M. and get real help? This is the network "litmus test."

Most people think that the more people they "know," the better their network. And certainly "knowing" people helps. But again, how many of the 10,000 people you have access to would go above and beyond to help you? There is a huge difference between "knowing" people, "knowing of people," and simply having people's phone numbers or addresses.

Why would anyone want to help you? Why would anyone go out of his way to help you find that one-in-ten-thousand person? It takes energy and is time-consuming—and people have their own lives to worry about! What makes people want to genuinely and sincerely help you?

# What You Sow Is What You Reap

The greatest secret to networking is helping as many people as you can. Help people in a big way, especially when they need it most. Help people when they are at wit's end, in trouble, jobless, going through tough times, moving—and they will never forget you for it. The quality of your relationships with people is far more important than the quantity of people you "know."

It is so true that what you sow is what you reap! What you give is what you get. People who need help, and don't get it, have not sown enough. Put another way, if you ever have trouble getting help with something, you have not helped enough people, or haven't helped them in a big way.

Networking is about the sowing. Sow everything you can now so that one day you, too, may reap. You have no idea at this time how you may need future help or how you may reap any of the benefits. But because you sowed, often years earlier, you will reap—someday. It is amazing where help comes from when you need it.

Many people think that if they help someone, and that person never helps them back, that they will have wasted their time and they'll regret helping. But you never waste your time helping others. It always comes back, often in ways you did not expect. The person whom you helped may not be the person who directly helps you later. You may be helped by a third party that you met while helping someone else.

The point is, the more people you help, the more people may help you if you ever need it. When you help people genuinely and sincerely out of the goodness of your heart, you enact the law of reciprocity. Again, this law states that people feel a natural obligation to pay you back for doing something for them. They respond in kind. It is sort of a mental IOU. And the bigger favor you do, the greater this sense of reciprocity. Even if those you help aren't in a direct position to help you later, they most likely will know of someone who can help you, and they'll call in a favor.

# Expanding Your Network

A result of helping people is all of the new circles of contacts you get into. This diversifies your network. Plus all of your new contacts have their own networks. If you are joining a program to mentor teenagers, giving a speech at a high school's career day, or helping people at a church, you will expand your personal network and meet people whom you would not ordinarily have met. You will meet others who like to help people. These are great people to have in your network.

Too many people think only big shots in the business world can help them. This is a mistake. Help everyone you can. I know a woman who started a business cleaning the homes of some of the most successful people in the metropolitan area. She has not only known her clients for years, but has become personal friends with many of them. I met another woman who was a secretary for one of the most successful businessmen in the area. Although she is no longer working for this man, she still maintains a relationship with him.

Don't judge people to see if they are "important" enough. Everyone has a friend, cousin, spouse, neighbor, hairdresser, or other acquaintance who might be able to help you. They will call in favors from people they know. Help people genuinely and sincerely and it will come back tenfold. The better care you take of others, the better care they will take of you. As I quoted from Zig Ziglar earlier in this book, "You can get everything in life you want, if you just help enough other people get what they want."

### Cup-of-Coffee Approach

Want to learn about a new subject or a different organization? Want to get someone's thoughts on a subject or just get to know someone better? Then offer to buy him a cup of coffee and chat. Does he have children or family in the area? What does he do for fun when he is not working? Starting a new relationship or improving an existing one is as simple as buying someone a cup of coffee and chatting over it. Great networkers have bought hundreds of cups of coffee for others.

## Using Your Network to Help Others

When you establish a strong network, you begin to realize that you can help even more people with it. When anyone in your network needs help, you can use your network to help your network.

Let's say that someone in your network is having trouble with his 1969 MG Midget car. He has tried everything he can think of to get it to start, but nothing works. After learning of this frustrating problem, you think of a friend of yours who has been restoring British cars professionally for the last 23 years and might be able to help. You make a phone call, and your friend takes his car to see your car expert. Your expert looks at it and realizes that it is not starting because it is not grounded to the engine block and needs only an inexpensive grounding strap. The MG owner is now delighted that his car starts and the British car expert now has a new customer. Both are happy and grateful for your help, naturally feeling the law of reciprocity.

Now let's say that one of your clients is a travel agent who specializes in Balkan travel. You have a friend who has never been to Serbia, and because of complicated travel restrictions is having trouble with her trip. You use your network to help both of them. You're helping them because they need help, and then both of them will be grateful to you. The travel agent gets a referral and the friend gets real help—and you are in the middle. Now two people owe you one. And three people benefit!

The greatest networkers help the most people! They are always listening for ways to help people, and they mentally search their networks to see how they can help. They ask people what they can do to help or suggest people who may be able to help them. For example:

- Oh, you are moving this weekend—do you need help?
- Oh, you are traveling to Boston this summer; let me give you a couple names and phone numbers of relatives there if you get into an emergency.
- Oh, you are starting a new Toastmasters group; what can I do to help?
- Oh, you need help on a Scouting event, what can I do to help?

## Organizing Your Network

The No. 1 problem most people have with their networks is that they have slips of paper, old phone lists, sticky notes, and business cards all over the house with names, addresses, and other miscellaneous information. These networks at best are sorted alphabetically with scratched-out names and hard-to-read writing. Querying these address books for needed information is difficult, time consuming, and inefficient.

The best networks have names and phone numbers and as much additional information about others as possible (birthday, spouse's name, etc.). It is this information that makes a database so valuable and useful. It is preferable to organize this information electronically as in a spreadsheet or database. This makes it easier to read information, organize it, search it, print it (like address labels), synch it to a personal digital assistant (PDA), or even have it online to access anywhere, anytime. Traditional card files are better than nothing, but they lack many electronic benefits.

Everyone you know is a contact. Build a contact database (spreadsheet or card file) by recording people's names and other information. Record everyone you meet too. Once your names and other information are entered electronically (preferable), the network becomes powerful; it is activated!

Going to Atlanta on business? Query your network to see whom you know in Atlanta. Perhaps you can have dinner or a cup of coffee with an old friend. Let's say your car broke down in Atlanta, you got fogged in at the airport with all hotel rooms taken, your wallet was stolen, and you have no money to get home. Whom can you call? Have no fear—just query your network by searching on "Atlanta."

Remember that by just knowing one person in Atlanta, for example, you will have access to 100 other people in Atlanta. Your one contact can connect you to lots of people. You really aren't as alone or helpless as you might think. One person can introduce you to countless others and take great care of you.

## Tapping In to Your Network

All right, now you have at least 100 people organized in your network. How do you tap the network? How do you use it to get help?

The first thing you must realize is that at any given time, the vast majority of your network is "invisible." You can't see most of the connections or links to others. You only know a little about people. You probably don't know their connections, the groups they belong to, whom they grew up with, whom they went to high school with, who played sports with them, whom they went to college with, whom they are related to, and so on. These connections are always there; you just can't see them.

General conversations may or may not yield the help you are looking for. Someone might know someone who can help you but it might not come up in casual conversation. Someone might stumble upon a helpful connection to others or he might not. Someone might mention her cousin who has exactly what you are looking for, or she might not.

*"It takes about 80 pairs of eyes, and ears, to help find the career, the workplace, the job that you are looking for. Your contacts are those eyes and ears."*
**—Richard Nelson Bolles, *What Color Is Your Parachute***

To make your network more "transparent" in the face of a particular need—to tap into your network to find the help you need—follow these steps:

1.  Decide what you want.

2.  Tell every contact that you need help and ask everyone if they or anyone they know can help you: "Who do you know that …?" Always ask contacts to make an introduction for you (phone or e-mail) and give you the contact information. All you need is one person to help you get your foot in the door and get you started. One person in an organization usually knows how to reach other people in the organization. That person also knows the competition.

3.  If your contacts can't help you, ask them whom they know that could help. Ask them to tap into their networks. Your goal is to get one step closer after talking with someone. Always ask people what they can do to get you "one step closer" (use these words).

4.  If they can't think of anyone, ask them whom they know that might be able to get you "one step closer."

5.  Ask your network contacts if they know of anyone in a particular industry, company, city, or other group. People there know other people there.

6.  Use the two-or-three-sentence technique (TST) to send thank-you cards along the way. Send them to anyone who helps you get in to see someone and to the person you actually got in to see.

## Targeting Specific Individuals or Groups

Often it is easier to use your existing networks and relationships for help, for many of our strongest connections with others are one or two people away. Other times it is better to directly target the people and organizations we need help from. What Richard Bolles said earlier is true, that we need about 80 pairs of eyes and ears to help us find what we want, but they also must be the right eyes and ears.

For example, if you want to change professions and sell high-end medical equipment, like X-ray machines, you might have to ask 200 people in your existing network to be able to find someone in the medical equipment business. (Other times you might get lucky and find the right person by asking only three or four people.) And after spending a lot of time and energy finding that person in your network, or that person referred to you by someone in your network, it may be a wheelchair salesman who may or may not get you "one step closer."

Instead, focus your efforts and specifically target the people you need to get you "one step closer." That is, expand your network and bring targeted people into it. In essence, you are starting a new circle of contacts in precisely what you are looking for. This is a faster and more efficient way to meet the right people. Take the following steps:

1. Decide what you want
2. Target new contacts and organizations
3. Talk to new contacts
4. Ask them for help or to get you "one step closer"
5. Send thank-you
6. Follow-up as needed

Now let's see how this works in the example of the medical equipment sales job search. After you have (1) decided what you want, your job is to get into the right circles by (2) targeting new contacts. You come up with four groups to target: medical equipment reps, customers of medical equipment (hospitals), medical equipment manufacturers, and recruiters. Gather information on companies, addresses, phone numbers, names, and other contact information. Look at company calendars online to see where various people from different organizations will be and when. The Internet is best used for information gathering, rather than contacting people. Most people delete unsolicited e-mail.

Now go out and (3) meet your targets wherever they may be. Use the information in previous chapters to talk to them. Introduce yourself, explain what you are looking for, and (4) ask questions to gather information. Ask them how they would proceed if they were you. Remember to ask people for help and to get you "one step closer."

*"You have to show people that you are serious about something and mean business. People have to differentiate between casually asking and being serious."*
— **Staff Sergeant Walker, Supply Sergeant, U.S. Army**

Remember that you are targeting (in this case) a circle of people. Everyone is connected to the product, person or organization in some way. The manufacturers make the equipment and look for reps to sell it. The reps go out and meet the customers in hospitals and clinics—receptionists, physicians, nurses, purchasing agents, maintenance personnel, clinical engineering departments, and others. Each department works with other departments. Recruiters who hire for these manufacturers do their research by contacting local hospitals and asking for names of top salespeople or people whom they would recommend for selling equipment. Companies also research prospective candidates and call hospitals for references. Then the company hires the candidate who will go back into the field and work with the customers.

It is an endless circle of contacts. Each person is connected to the next. Each person knows the person one step above them and one step below them. Each person can lead you to the next person in the circle, then the next, and then the next until the chain eventually circles back.

When you come full circle, you will understand the business, the industry, and key players, and you will have many, many specific contacts added to your network. Make sure you (5) send thank-you cards to all. And remember to (6) follow up regularly to maintain your valuable contacts.

# Maintaining Your Network

One of the most difficult challenges of networking is maintaining your network. Keeping addresses, phone numbers, and titles current is certainly important. But the greater challenge is maintaining contact with your network. If you haven't talked with people in your network in years, it is hard to call them out of the blue and chat. And it's even more difficult to ask them for help.

So here is the golden rule of network maintenance: the frequency with which you talk to people is far more important than the length of time you talk. A two-minute conversation every other month is far superior to an hour-long conversation once every year and a half.

During a recent interview, I asked a top business executive what quality differentiated her from the pack and most contributed to her success. She replied that it was her desire to take time out of the hectic pace just to connect with people and to stay in touch with associates in different work units (locally and nationally). She went on to say that she not only does this over the phone but also sometimes over lunch. She understands the importance of having a good working relationship with everyone in her piece of the banking organization, not just one or two people. This ultimately makes it easier for her to understand the organization and its people and use it more effectively.

## Staying in Touch

At the very least, keep your contacts current through monthly phone calls just to touch base. One way to keep conversations short is to do very little of talking. Let the other person bring you up to date. Being a great listener keeps conversations short and ensures that you don't miss anything. If you do a lot of the talking, then conversations drag on and you limit the number of people you can talk to that day. Instead, keep conversations energetic, short, and genuine.

Some people might take every Sunday night and call 10 people in their network. My former boss would try to see how many phone calls he could make while driving around on business or waiting at the airport (although I don't recommend using a cell phone while driving), so by the time he got to where he was going, he had touched base with 10 people. Sometimes he would call people on the road just to keep himself company. This not only made him feel better (law of attraction), but enabled him to maintain his network constantly.

If you get people's answering machines or voice mail, good. Leave a pleasant message. At least you tried to call and you get "credit" for calling and thinking about them. Then if they need help or have a crisis, they will call you if necessary.

Another technique for maintaining your network is correspondence. Use the two-sentence technique, as discussed in previous chapters, to keep communication brief and frequent. Write two or three sentences on a card and drop it in the mail. Many people do this annually with Christmas cards. E-mailing people or groups from your database certainly makes touching base fast and easy.

Your card might read: "Just wanted to take a moment and drop you a line. I know we haven't spoken in a long time, but I certainly care about you and wonder how you are doing. If I can ever do anything for you, please don't hesitate to call." Another card might read: "Congratulations on your promotion! I always knew you could do it." It takes only two sentences to keep in touch with people.

# Reactivating a Lost Connection

Not maintaining your network has its consequences. What if you need help from someone to whom you haven't talked in a long time? It might feel awkward and a little daunting to call this person to ask for a favor. What do you do? How should you handle it?

Many people would invite this person to lunch with an ulterior motive. At first, the person might be impressed that you would think of her again and want to know how she was doing. But then when you revealed the favor you were seeking, you would instantly go from seeming like a nice person to being a phony. Your contact would feel used!

So what should you do instead? Do the best job you can in maintaining your network so these things don't happen! But in a predicament like the one mentioned, follow these guidelines:

1.  Apologize for not staying in better contact. Say something along the lines of: "I apologize for not staying in contact as well as I should have. Sometimes I just get all caught up in my own little world."

2.  Tell the person that you need her help with something.

3.  Thank her for anything she can do to help you.

4.  Follow up with a card, short phone call, or voice mail message to thank her again after the favor. Don't offer to take her to lunch or dinner right afterward; people don't want to feel bought. A thank-you is enough.

5.  Follow up in two to four weeks with a coffee, lunch, or dinner invitation. Don't tell her that you are buying, but when the bill comes, pick it up.

6.  Maintain your renewed contact.

You don't have to make a career out of talking with people in your network. You just have to think about each person occasionally and make contact in some small way. By doing this, you keep your network current and you know if someone is about to move or has changed phone numbers. The more frequent your interactions with others, the shorter your conversations, for there is not as much information to convey.

# Chapter Twenty-two

# Chapter Summary

- **Your Network of 10,000 Contacts.** The "six degrees of separation" theory states that you are connected to everyone, somehow, somewhere through six people. This means that 10,000 people are only two phone calls away from you! If you know 100 people and each of them knows 100 people, then that is 10,000 people within your grasp. All you have to do is ask the people you already know for an introduction or help.

- **What You Sow Is What You Reap.** People want to help you when you have helped them; this is the law of reciprocity. You help people genuinely and sincerely because they need it, but you also get back in kind from those you've helped.

- **Expanding Your Network.** A result of helping people is all of the new circles of contacts you get into, which diversifies your network. Plus all of your new contacts have their own networks. Don't judge others by whether they are "important" enough to be in your network.

- **Using Your Network to Help Others.** When you establish a strong network, you begin to realize that you can help even more people with it. Great networkers are always listening for ways to help people.

- **Organizing Your Network.** Organize your information electronically, in either a spreadsheet or database, to make querying easier and more efficient.

- **Tapping In to Your Network.** Realize that the vast majority of your network is invisible; you must ask people you know for help. Decide what you want, tell contacts that you need their help, and thank them for their help. Sometimes it is easier to target specific people for help and expand your network. To do this, decide what you want, target new contacts and organizations, talk to new contacts, and ask them for their help or to get you "one step closer." Always thank people for their help. Follow up as needed. Continue this process until you find the help you need and come back full circle to the original contact.

- **Maintaining Your Network.** Keeping addresses, phone numbers, and titles current is important, but the bigger challenge is maintaining contact with your network. The rule of network maintenance is that the frequency with which you talk to someone is far more important than the length of time you talk. Keep networks current by calling contacts, e-mailing them, or sending them cards.

## Daily Challenge

Today, make an electronic file of contact information for everyone you want to have in your network. Use a database program like Microsoft Access, Excel, or one of many others. Make sure you can query by various fields, such as city or state.

I synchronize my laptop computer with my personal digital assistant daily so if one of them fails, I have a backup. I also synchronize my laptop computer with Yahoo, so my entire database can easily be accessed online, anytime, from any computer. So if anything ever happened to my PDA or my laptop, I would still have access to my database.

## Executive Challenge

If you already have an electronic network, set up a system for keeping in touch with people. Categorize people you want to stay in touch with monthly, quarterly, semiannually, and annually. Maybe check off their names so you know with whom you have touched base, or contact 10 people a week, or call all contacts weekly that start with a particular letter, or use some other method to keep up to date. However you do it, come up with a system for keeping your network current.

# CHAPTER 23

# Advance in Your Communication Skills

## In This Chapter:

- Sharpen your ax
- Be the best you can be

braham Lincoln once told a story about walking through the woods and seeing a man frantically trying to chop down a tree. The man was covered in sweat and making little progress. Lincoln was so interested in the woodchopper that he decided to sit down for a while and watch him. After a while Lincoln finally said something: "Don't you think you would have an easier time at it if you stopped and sharpened your ax?" The woodchopper quickly replied that although that might be a good idea, he didn't have time to stop and sharpen his ax—he had too many trees to chop down.

Like the woodchopper, all of us get into the hurry, hurry, rush, rush mentality. We get into the habit of just surviving the day. We get trapped in our own microcosms. Our axes are all too often dull, and we don't take the time to sharpen them. Someone once said if we are satisfied with the results we are getting, we should keep doing the same things we have been doing. But if we want to change the results we are getting, we must change the things we are doing.

This chapter is about taking the time to stop and sharpen your ax. But you don't stop and sharpen your ax once and for all—it's an ongoing process. It's about learning new people skills, refining old ones, and taking what you have learned to advance in your communication skills. It's about winning the game of life, not just surviving it.

# Chapter Twenty-three

# Observe and Take Notes

All serious students take notes on subjects they are learning and so should you. Are you a people watcher? Good—write down what you have learned. Do you like the way someone handled a particular situation or behaved in that position? If so, write down some notes on it. Did someone handle a situation poorly? What would you have done differently? You can learn just as much from someone else's mistakes as your own. In fact, learning from your own is better. Do you know someone who has a lot of charisma and charm? What do they do differently than you? How do they get things accomplished differently?

Catherine Cox, a researcher in the 1920s, studied more than 300 geniuses throughout history. She noted that one sign of genius—which was displayed not only by aspiring writers but also by generals, statesman, and scientists—was a predilection for eloquently recording thoughts and feelings in diaries, poems, and letters to friends and family.[1] Thomas Edison, for example, produced more than 3 million pages of notes and letters during his lifetime. Great people don't become great accidentally; they become great purposefully.

Buy a journal or notebook and jot down thoughts and notes throughout the day, week, or month about people and your communications with them. You don't necessarily have to write something every day. But as you get ideas, learn new things, and hear or read interesting information, write these down in your notebook. Keep track of what works and what doesn't work, qualities you admire about others, and qualities and skills you want to work on or develop. This notebook will become one of your most treasured possessions.

> *"I never travel without my diary. One should*
> *always have something sensational to read."*
> — **Oscar Wilde (1854–1900)**

# Practice Your Communication Skills

Not very good at starting conversations with others? Then practice. Not very good at meeting strangers? Then practice. The more you practice and the more types of people you talk and work with, the more you learn, the greater your perspective, the greater your network, the more friends you will have, and the higher quality of your relationships.

Consider this: Do you even know the name of the mail carrier who has been delivering your mail for the last 11 years? Is he or she married? Does he have children? Ever have a real conversation with him? I talked with my mail carrier and was amazed to learn that he walks 9.6 miles a day six days a week, carrying a 35-pound mailbag, making more than 700 stops in the rain, ice, snow, or sun. I didn't even know he had a bad back because he is always so cheerful. It was fascinating to hear what he has delivered throughout the years—packages as diverse as cremated dog remains, bees, and more exotic items. He not only knows the profession of most people on his route but also who they write to and who writes to them. He is not nosy; it's just that he has been hand-carrying everyone's mail for 11 years. If your mail carrier knows so much about you, shouldn't you at least take a minute or two to get to know him?

Enjoy talking to people. A little genuine concern for their well-being will go a long way. Have fun trying out and experimenting with the skills and techniques in this book. Use them to improve your own unique style of communication. Soon great communication will become second nature to you, and your relationships with others will just get better and better.

# Read

One of the greatest ways to learn is through the written word. Almost everything you ever wanted to know about has been written about. You can learn from a single book what took someone else a lifetime to learn through trial and error and the school of hard knocks. Imagine gaining a lifetime of experience in the time it takes to read a single book. Imagine the mistakes you could avoid and how much easier and more enjoyable life could be.

> *"Some people read so little they have rickets of the mind."*
> — **Jim Rohn, business philosopher**

The selected bibliography section of this book includes a great reading list of books about dealing with and communicating with people. Remember that you don't have to read a book cover-to-cover to benefit from it. Simply reading the table of contents and choosing the topics or areas you would like to learn more about can still be valuable. If you learn one good idea from a book, the entire book may be worth it! And if you learn a couple new ideas from the book, better yet.

Nowadays, of course, another way to access information on practically any topic is to go online—for newspapers, magazines, journals, dictionaries, maps, encyclopedias, directories, e-books, local art, local history, local events, and various databases. You would think all of this information would cost you a fortune. But it's all free and can be accessed from your local library or from the comfort of your own home.

## Attend Seminars

The great thing about attending seminars is that you are surrounded by people who are interested in the same subject as you. Thus, attending seminars is an ideal way to network and meet people who share at least one interest with you. Additionally, seminars let you interact with others and trade ideas and thoughts about your subject. Seminars are a safe environment where you can learn and practice new information. You will discover new things about yourself doing practical exercises and learning from talented people. The great majority of people leave seminars better off than before they started.

## Listen to Educational Tapes

You can listen to audiotapes while traveling and learn about relationships, networking, finances, discipline, motivation, negotiation, psychology, the Bible, real estate investing, leadership, and management, just for starters. You can listen to biographies and feats of the world's greatest explorers, writers, philosophers, inventors, scientists, and more. Or you could learn a foreign language.

Listening to a tape or two might not seem to make much of a difference in your life, but listening to many tapes for many years will have a cumulative effect that will most certainly give you an edge. It has been estimated that we can get the equivalent of two years of college simply by listening to various topics daily. Never stop learning!

# Chapter Summary

- It is normal to get into the hurry, hurry, rush, rush mentality. But take time to sharpen your ax. Advancing in your communication skills is a constant process.

- Observe and Take Notes. As you get ideas, learn new things, hear or read interesting information, write it down in your notebook. Keep track of what works and what doesn't work, qualities you admire about people, what you want to work on, and skills you want to develop.

- Practice Your Communication Skills. The more types of people you talk to and work with, the more you learn, the greater your perspective, the greater your network, the more friends you will have, and the higher quality of your relationships.

- Read. Remember you don't have to read a book cover-to-cover to benefit from it. Just select interesting or beneficial chapters. Learning one new idea can make the entire book worth it.

- Attend Seminars. Seminars are a great place to learn, network, and share ideas. Most people leave seminars better off than when they started.

- Listen to Educational Tapes. Listening to many tapes for many years will have a cumulative effect. Never stop learning!

## Daily/Executive Challenge

Take time to sharpen your ax today. Start a journal, buy an educational tape or book, or sign up for a seminar. Take action.

# The Personal Power Mind-Set

## Achievable Traits per Dominant Emotion

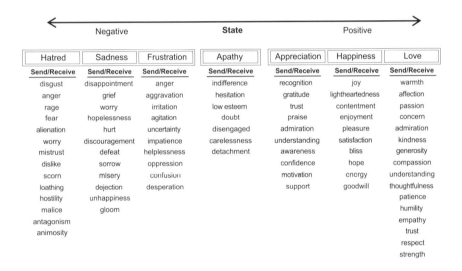

| | Negative | | State | | Positive | |
|---|---|---|---|---|---|---|

| Hatred | Sadness | Frustration | Apathy | Appreciation | Happiness | Love |
|---|---|---|---|---|---|---|
| Send/Receive | Send/Receive | Send/Receive | Send/Receive | Send/Receive | Send/Receive | Send/Receive |
| disgust | disappointment | anger | indifference | recognition | joy | warmth |
| anger | grief | aggravation | hesitation | gratitude | lightheartedness | affection |
| rage | worry | irritation | low esteem | trust | contentment | passion |
| fear | hopelessness | agitation | doubt | praise | enjoyment | concern |
| alienation | hurt | uncertainty | disengaged | admiration | pleasure | admiration |
| worry | discouragement | impatience | carelessness | understanding | satisfaction | kindness |
| mistrust | defeat | helplessness | detachment | awareness | bliss | generosity |
| dislike | sorrow | oppression | | confidence | hope | compassion |
| scorn | misery | confusion | | motivation | energy | understanding |
| loathing | dejection | desperation | | support | goodwill | thoughtfulness |
| hostility | unhappiness | | | | | patience |
| malice | gloom | | | | | humility |
| antagonism | | | | | | empathy |
| animosity | | | | | | trust |
| | | | | | | respect |
| | | | | | | strength |

## Three Steps to the Personal Power Mind-Set

1. Thoughts set the law of attraction in motion. One thought attracts another thought that attracts still another thought until they snowball into a state. Six-figure communicators are others-focused. They look for and find the positive.

2.  Action physically changes our state and stimulates the release of neu-rotransmitters, such as dopamine, serotonin, norepinephrine and endor-phins, thus altering our body chemistry. This gives us a sense of well-being, pleasure, and excitement.

3.  Savor the now. Enjoy the present. Make it a point to consciously savor your friends and family, your work, the weather, and having fun.

Remember that thoughts change actions and actions change thoughts! If you are at wit's end and cannot think positively, change your actions. This will naturally and effortlessly change your thoughts. See the list that follows.

### Fifteen Actions to Transform a Mental State

*   Change your physical surroundings (buildings, view, desk, room, inside/outside, etc.)
*   Change your physical activity level (walk, run, lift weights, etc.)
*   Change your environment (go to the park, restaurant, shopping mall)
*   Change your city, state, or country
*   Change your activity (take a shower, do something fun, go on vacation)
*   Change the variety of people you are around
*   Take a nap or rest
*   Call a happy or pleasant person
*   Change your focus (others-focused vs. self-focused)
*   Change clothes (dress up or down)
*   Listen to different types of music
*   Laugh
*   Help people
*   Do something nice for someone (send flowers, write a note, etc.)
*   Go shopping (you don't necessarily have to buy something)

## Resolving Conflict

### Universal Reasons That People Get Angry/Upset

*   Hurt feelings and need for empathy
*   Predetermined beliefs
*   Add-on information

- Fear of the unknown
- Feeling threatened
- Because they care
- Lacking a feeling of importance
- Lacking respect
- Lacking appreciation
- Tired or irritable
- Under stress
- Under time restraints
- Lacking information or openness
- Comments made around others
- Talking behind someone's back
- Unprofessional or poor behavior
- Sharp tongue
- Need for help

## Three Basic People Truths

- People are just being themselves, not intentionally trying to be rude or brash
- People are doing the best they can most of the time (honestly!)
- Most problems are misunderstandings

## Two Questions to Ask Yourself in a Conflict

1. What was your positive energy level on a scale of 1 to 10 when the conflict happened? Almost all major conflicts happen when your positive energy level is low. The higher your positive energy level, the greater the likelihood that you can avoid conflict.

2. Think about your predetermined beliefs in this situation. Are they accurate?

## Battle Drills

- Create Allies
- "Nice'm to Death"
- Show Empathy
- Use the Feel, Felt, Found Technique
- Preface with "I Appreciate"
- Let People Know You Are Listening

- Shift the Focus
- Let the Other Person Run Out of Steam
- If You are Wrong, Say You are Wrong
- Blame Yourself
- Make the Other Person Feel Like Royalty
- Be Firm
- Pinpoint and Fix the Problem

## The Healing

The first step toward healing any relationship is the realization of five truths:

- Being human means that we all make mistakes.

- People do and say things sometimes that they don't necessarily mean. Sometimes things come out wrong but, once said, can't be taken back even if the person wanted to. (The action was bad, not the person.)

- Whatever happened between the two of you probably happened a long time ago. You are different people now, even at different stages in your lives. Most of us develop a greater perspective of life over time, putting one fight or one year into better context.

- Most of us become wiser, more easygoing, and tolerant as we get older because we see more and gain more perspective. What seemed like a big deal then probably isn't as important now.

- Forgiving someone is even better for you than for the other person.

## Clean-the-Slate Formula

Apologize + Heartfelt Comment + Smile and Trial Closure

# GLOSSARY

**Alternate Routes of Communication**: Communicating with others in a form other than face-to-face, including by letter, card, note (handwritten or e-mail), telegram, picture, and film.

**Attraction, Law of**: One thought attracts another thought that attracts another thought until they build momentum, either positively or negatively, attracting like things into your life, with things getting better and better, or worse and worse.

**Auditory Charisma**: The ability to draw people using the sound of your voice, including modulating tone, pitch, tempo, and pauses.

**Battle Drills**: Responding to situations without hesitation in a predetermined fashion to come across as calm, cool, and collected, thereby reducing stress, anxiety, and second-guessing.

**Buttonomics, Simplified**: Connecting with people on a mental level. It is the art of finding and pushing people's positive hot buttons and staying away from their negative buttons. These hot buttons are topics that emotionally charge people. By finding these positive buttons, you make conversations more genuine and inspiring, drawing the good out of people.

**Caring Leadership**: A leadership style of taking extraordinary care of the people who work for you, almost as if they were your own family. You give subordinates special attention to help them succeed by taking the time to talk to them, mentor them, thank them for their hard work, or even tell them how proud you are of them.

**Charisma**: The ability to draw people to you using only your personal power, relentless belief, and uplifting rapport. See also auditory charisma, kinesthetic charisma, visual charisma, and uplifting rapport.

**Cheese-and-Cracker Talk**: Term originally meant literally chatting with someone over cheese and crackers. Now it means simply chatting to establish rapport, and then slowly easing into the business you want to discuss, especially if you are asking for a favor.

**Cognitive Behavioral Strategies**: Using your thoughts to rationally and logically change your behavior, as when preparing to attend an event.

**Clean-the-Slate Formula**: A quick and easy method for mending relationships and reducing ill will between people. It consists of an apology of just a few words, a heartfelt comment, and a smile with trial close.

**Click-Whirr Response**: A term used by Michael Cialdini in his book *Influence* to describe the automatic behavior of people and animals. It is as if people simply pop in a preprogrammed tape of instructions or reactions in various circumstances and then react accordingly.

**Core Buttons**: Central interests that tend to remain constant throughout life, such as sports, classic cars, dogs, or knitting.

**Core Message**: A simple message that top communicators use to focus and simplify their counsel. They boil their message down to its essence, usually no more than a dozen words. It is easy to understand, makes sense, and is something the other person can take with him.

**Congruency**: Transmitting visual, auditory, and kinesthetic information that is all in agreement. For example, if someone smiles while telling you it is good to see you and then hugs you, he is congruent. But if the person says the same thing through clenched teeth, or keeps looking at his watch or over your shoulder, he is incongruent. He is sending mixed signals.

**Delivery Strategy**: The method you choose to increase the effectiveness of your message to others.

**Disarming Statement**: A neutral or general statement used to break the ice and allow others to feel comfortable around you. This statement enables you to learn people's moods and find out if they want to talk.

**Eye Darting**: A phenomenon of truly connected people in which one's eyes naturally dart back and forth, as from one eye to the other, during conversation. Observing this phenomenon means that the other person is truly interested in the conversation and rapport is established.

**Gatekeeper**: Someone who controls access to a person, group or entry into an office.

**Golden Minute**: The first 60 seconds of a conversation or exposure to others, in which people decide whether they want to talk to you, hire you, do business with you, or ignore you.

**Incremental Model**: A graphical illustration of the concept that more people find unity and agreement on a general level rather than at a specific level. The more specific the issue, the fewer people will agree on a particular stance.

**Immediate Statement**: An immediate positive thought or statement you tell yourself to direct your thoughts into a positive direction, before you have time to see the negative. It forces the mind to justify why it is right.

**Inflection Point**: The point during a conversation in which the person speaking suddenly realizes that he has been doing all the talking and feels he should give the other person an opportunity to speak. Usually this happens when he runs out of steam. At this point he may hesitate and then have a goofy look on his face as he realizes he has been monopolizing the conversation. He feels an obligation to at least ask the other person how he is doing.

**Kinesthetic Charisma:** The ability to draw people by making others *feel* good, such as smiling, using humor, and projecting warmth, personality, charm, flattery, emotions, and touch.

**Matching**: Repeating someone's movements to subconsciously create sameness and thus rapport. If someone sitting across from you reaches for a cup of coffee with her right hand, you would wait a few seconds and then match her by reaching for your cup of coffee with your right hand.

**Mind-Set**: The totality of thought, either positive or negative. Mind-set is intimately tied to emotion and mood.

**Mirroring**: Repeating someone's movements, as if you were her mirror image, to subconsciously build sameness or rapport. If someone sitting across from you reaches for a cup of coffee with her right hand, you would wait a few seconds and then mirror her by reaching for your cup of coffee with your left hand.

**Negative Buttons**: Conversational topics that negatively charge people emotionally.

**Neurotransmitter:** A chemical manufactured and stored in a neuron (brain cell) that is responsible for bridging electrical signals between neurons. Different neurotransmitters bridge different signals.

**Nonlinguistic Movements (NLMs)**: Universal distinctions in body language that change the way people see and feel about others, establishing and building rapport and exuding charisma. They are some of the smallest, most reliable building blocks of body language. Some of these distinctions are so small that most people pick up on them only on a subconscious level, while others are larger and are picked up on a conscious level. Common NLMs include pupil and eye movements, subtle movements of fingers and hands, and facial expressions. They are what six-figure communicators do naturally to connect with people on a physical level.

**Notching**: Finding out where someone stands on the incremental model, then trying to move them up or down a notch or two to be more in agreement with your stance.

**One-Track Mind**: Giving other people your total focus, energy, and undivided attention.

**Parroting**: Repeating back to people the last few words they just said, to enhance your bond with them, show them that you are listening, and help the conversation move along smoothly. For example, if someone said he was feeling tired, you would parrot him by saying sympathetically, "You're feeling tired?"

**Personal Power**: The ability to talk to, work with, and influence others using your people skills and not your authority, rank, position, or status.

**Personal Power IQ**: The ability to get into a powerful mental state and stay there all day, regardless of people and circumstances.

**Personal Power Mind-Set**: A powerful mental state that effortlessly draws people and resources to you, enabling you to effectively influence others without using your authority, rank, position, or status.

**Piggybacking**: A conversational technique to get other people talking and expand the conversation. You key off a word or phrase that someone just used and ask him a question about it. For example, if someone said: "Yeah, I learned how to do that in the *Army*," you might piggyback by keying off the word Army, and say, "So, you were in the Army." or "So, what type of work did you do in the Army?" In this context, the term *piggybacking* was coined by Tom Hopkins, real estate guru and author of *Selling for Dummies*.

**Positive Buttons**: Conversational topics that positively charge people emotionally.

**Power of Position**: Using your position, status, or title to get people to do things.

**Predetermined Beliefs:** Set beliefs that influence how you will interpret and respond to future events. It is like solving for X in an algebraic equation. Events plugged into the equation determine your response. Successful communicators have already "rigged" their equations so that, regardless of the event or situation, their value for X will be positive, not negative.

**Perspective**: The ability to separate yourself from a situation and look at it from a different vantage point. The three components of perspective are time, experience, and distance from the situation.

**Pygmalion Effect**: Planting the seed of belief in individuals or groups to increase future performance; self-fulfilling prophecy.

**Rapport**: A mental connection with others, usually created by sameness or similarity.

**Reducers**: A rationale to apply when you hear negative comments or are treated poorly. You can instantly "reduce" the negative emotion and prevent it from quickly building or snowballing.

**Representational System**: Neuro-linguistic programming teaches that although people take in information using all of their senses, they tend to be dominant in one. Thus, people tend to interpret, or code, the world through that one sense, or system—visually, auditorily, or kinesthetically.

**Reciprocity, Law of**: People respond or feel an obligation to respond in kind. Wave to people, and they will wave back. Give something to people, and they will want to give or will feel an obligation to give something back to you. Be nice to people, and they will want to be nice to you in return.

**Six Degrees of Separation, Theory of**: People are connected to each other, somehow, somewhere, through six people. Anyone is just six phone calls away. But you may not always know the chain or connection. You have a friend who went to school with John, whose brother works with Tony, whose father ...

**Snowball Theory**: Another term for the law of attraction. Thoughts begin to attract other thoughts, which attract still other thoughts, until they begin to "snowball," or pick up momentum, either positively or negatively.

**Superficial Button**: A temporary hot button, usually something that happened today or within the last week or so, something that is currently on your mind. Maybe you just got married, had your house broken into, just started a new job, got a new dog, or bought a new house. It might be as transient as having gotten cut off by another car while driving or having developed a blister on the bottom of your foot. Whatever it is, this is a button that is itching to be pushed right now.

**Talk-Show Host Technique**: Talking with others as if they are guests on your talk show—make others the "star" by bringing out in them appealing qualities and stories.

**"Three-Day Leader"**: One whose leadership deteriorates under stress, causing him to use more and more power of position, rather than personal power, when dealing with subordinates.

**Three-Track Mind**: Consists of one track paying attention to the conversation, one track watching the other person, and the third track astutely aware of the surroundings. The third track is taking in as much information as possible before the conversation even begins, such as what is in the room, who is in the room, the mood of the people, what is on the wall or desk, or any unusual behavior. People using the three-track mind are more in tune with what is happening in a particular situation.

**Two-Track Mind**: Consists of one track focusing on the conversational dialogue and the other track watching every movement the other person makes during conversation as a way to determine congruency.

**Uplifting Rapport**: Giving others so many positive feelings that they are attracted to you and want to be around you. People feel good around you. Components of uplifting rapport include positive energy, passive likeability, the ability to help others feel better, class, and humor.

**Verbal Judo**: Term used by George J. Thompson, Ph.D., in his book *Verbal Judo*, defined as "the gentle art of persuasion that redirects others' behavior with words and generates voluntary compliance." As a police officer, Thompson tactfully used his personal power, not his power of position, to generate voluntary compliance from perpetrators.

**Visual Charisma**: The ability to draw people using visual cues, such as gestures, smiles, posture, and movements of the face, hands, and body.

**Zooming**: Moving a discussion from the specific to more and more general statements as necessary until you find common ground with the other party.

## ENDNOTES

### Chapter 1

1. Jerry and Esther Hicks, *A New Beginning II: A Personal Handbook to Enhance Your Life, Liberty and Pursuit of Happiness* (San Antonio: Abraham Hicks Publishing, 1995), 96-99.
2. John H. Richardson, "Dr. Happy: Ed Diener Studies That Elusive State We All Strive For," *Esquire*, June 2002. Reprinted in *Reader's Digest*, November 2002, 94-99.
3. This study was originally reported in *The Veterinary Journal 165*: 296, but the study's abstract used was taken from *New Scientist 178*, no. 2391 (April 19, 2003): 19.
4. This study, "Effect of aerobic exercise at various sub-maximal intensities on circulating beta-endorphin concentrations," conducted by I.M. Dabayebeh et al., was presented at the annual meeting of the American College of Sports Medicine, Seattle, 1999, and reported in *The Black Letter 14*, no. 7 (July 1999): 74.
5. Aileen Milne, *Counseling* (Chicago: Contemporary Books, 1999), 125.

### Chapter 4

1. Leil Lowndes, *Talking the Winner's Way: 92 Little Tricks for Big Success in Business* (Chicago: Contemporary Books, 1999).
2. Bill Gates with Collins Hemingway, *Business @ the Speed of Thought: Using a Digital Nervous System* (New York: Warner Books, 1999), xvi, 446.

## Chapter 5

1. Mark Strassmann, "On the Scene: Holy City Liberated," CBS News, April 3,2003, online ed. A background article to this story, also by Mark Strassmann, is "On the Scene: Winning Over Iraqis," CBS News, April 1, 2003, online ed.

## Chapter 6

1. Tony Alessandra Ph.D., *Charisma: The Seven Keys to Developing the Magnetism that Leads to Success* (New York: Warner Books, 1998), 11.

## Chapter 9

1. Prilosec is a registered trademark of the AstraZeneca Group, AstraZeneca LP, Wilmington, DE 19850. The drug is manufactured by Merck & Co., Inc., Whitehouse Station, NJ 08889, USA.
2. Study was a U.S. multicenter double-blind-placebo controlled study in patients with symptoms of GERD and endoscopically diagnosed erosive esophagitis of grade 2 or above. The percentage healing rates were per protocol. The study was found in the revised April 2000 product package insert.
3. Entocort EC is a registered trademark of the AstraZeneca group, AstraZenca LP, Wilmington, DE 19850. Entocort EC is manufactured by AstraZeneca AB, Sodertalje, Sweden.
4. Data found in the AstraZeneca Entocort EC product package insert under Adverse Reactions, revision 08/01. Data displayed showed the incidence of symptoms of hypercortisolism by active questioning of patients in clinical trials.
5. National Institute of Mental Health. "Depression Research at the National Institute of Mental Health: Fact Sheet 1, 2" (April 2002), NIH Publication No. 00-4501, Bethesda, MD.
6. Zig Ziglar, *The Goals Program* (Dallas: Zig Ziglar Corporation, 1981).
7. Marlo Thomas, *The Right Words at the Right Time* (New York: Atria Books, 2002).
8. Ibid., 62-63.
9. Ibid., 2.
10. Ibid., 115-117.

## Chapter 10

1. Leil Lowndes, *Talking the Winner's Way: 92 Little Tricks for Big Success in Business* (Chicago: Contemporary Books, 1999), 76-79.

## Chapter 16

1. Joseph O'Connor and John Seymour, *Introducing NLP: Psychological Skills for Understanding and Influencing People* (Great Britain: Thorsons, 1995), 17. Original research was conducted by Mehrabian and Ferris, "Inference of Attitudes from Nonverbal Communication in Two Channels," *The Journal of Counseling Psychology 31* (1967): 248-252.

2. Jean Hamilton, "How to Use Your Voice for Charm and Charisma," speech during the Pacific Northwest Chapter of the National Speakers Association's "Super Summit," November 7, 2003. Hamilton's company, Speaking Results, is dedicated to teaching executives speaking and presentation skills.

## Chapter 18

1. George J. Thompson, Ph.D., *Verbal Judo: The Gentle Art of Persuasion* (New York: William Morrow and Company, Inc., 1993). A former police officer, Thompson relates that although he had the power of position in his job, he was more effective using his personal power. He trains law enforcement officers nationwide on how to use their personal power to overcome obstacles when dealing with difficult people.

2. Anthony Robbins, *Unlimited Power: The New Science of Personal Achievement* (New York: Simon & Schuster, 1997).

## Chapter 21

1. Philip R. Theibert, *How to Give a Damn Good Speech: Even When You Have No Time to Prepare* (New York: Galahad Books, 2000), 158.

## Chapter 23

1. Colin P. Rose and Malcolm J. Nicholl, *Accelerated Learning for the 21st Century: The Six-Step Plan to Unlock Your Master-Mind* (New York: Dell Publishing, 1998), 125.

## SELECTED BIBLIOGRAPHY

### Books

Alessandra, Tony, Ph.D. *Charisma: Seven Keys to Developing the Magnetism That Leads to Success.* New York: Warner Books, 1998.

Allen, James. *As a Man Thinketh.* New York: Grosset & Dunlap, 1987.

Amos, Wally, and Gregory Amos. *The Power in You.* New York: Donald I. Fine, Inc., 1988.

Bolles, Richard Nelson. *What Color Is Your Parachute: A Practical Manual for Job-Hunters and Career-Changers.* 31st ed. Berkeley, CA: Ten Speed Press, 2003.

Brooks, Michael. *Instant Rapport.* New York: Warner Books, 1989.

Carnegie, Dale. *How to Win Friends and Influence People.* New York: Simon and Schuster, 1998.

Cialdini, Robert B. *Influence: Science and Practice.* Boston: Allyn and Bacon, 2001.

Covey, Stephen R. *The Seven Habits of Highly Effective People: Powerful Lessons in Personal Change.* New York: Simon & Schuster, 2004.

Curtis, John M., Ph.D. *Operation Charisma.* Los Angeles: Discobolos Press, 1999.

Dawson, Roger. *Secrets of Power Persuasion: Everything You'll Ever Need to Get Anything You'll Ever Want.* Paramus, NJ: Prentice Hall, 1992.

Diagram Visual Information. *Running Press Cyclopedia: The Portable Visual Encyclopedia.* Philadelphia: Running Press Book Publishers, 1993.

Donaldson, Les. *Conversational Magic: Key to Poise, Popularity and Success.* West Nyack, NY: Parker Publishing Company, 1981.

Dubrin, Andrew J. *Personal Magnetism: Discover Your Own Charisma and Learn to Charm, Inspire, and Influence Others.* New York: AMACOM, 1997.

Fast, Julius. *Body Language.* Rev. Ed. New York: M. Evans & Co., Inc., 2002.

Goldberg, Michael J. *Getting Your Boss's Number and Many Other Ways to Use the Enneagram at Work.* San Francisco: HarperSanFrancisco, 1996.

Goodman, Dr. Gary S. *Selling Skills for the Non-Salesperson.* New York: Simon & Schuster, 1992.

Hallowell, Edward M. *Dare to Forgive.* Deerfield Beach, FL: Health Communications, Inc., 2004.

Hicks, Esther, and Jerry Hicks. *A New Beginning I: Handbook for Joyous Survival.* San Antonio, TX: Abraham-Hicks Publications, 1996.

Hill, Napoleon. *Think and Grow Rich.* New York, Ballantine Books, 1983.

Hopkins, Tom. *Selling for Dummies.* Foster City, CA: IDG Books Worldwide, Inc., 1995.

Howard, Vernon. *Psycho-Pictography.* Englewood Cliffs, NJ: Prentice Hall, 1965.

King, Larry. *How to Talk to Anyone, Anytime, Anywhere.* New York: Crown Publishers, Inc., 1994.

Lang, Doe, Ph.D. *The New Secrets of Charisma: How to Discover and Unleash Your Hidden Powers.* Chicago: Contemporary Books, 1999.

Leeds, Dorothy. *The 7 Powers of Questions: Secrets to Successful Communication in Life and at Work.* New York: Berkley Publishing Group, 2000.

Lieberman, David J., Ph.D. *Get Anyone to Do Anything and Never Feel Powerless Again.* New York: St. Martin's Press, 2000.

Lown, Bernard, M.D. *The Lost Art of Healing.* Boston: Houghton Mifflin Company, 1996.

Lowndes, Leil. *How to Make Anyone Fall in Love with You.* Chicago: Contemporary Books, 1996.

Lowndes, Leil. *How to Talk to Anybody About Anything: Breaking the Ice with Everyone from Accountants to Zen Buddhists.* Secaucus, NJ: Carol Publishing Group 1995.

Lowndes, Leil. *Talking the Winner's Way: 92 Little Tricks for Big Success in Business and Personal Releationships.* Chicago: Contemporary Books, 1999.

Molloy, John T. *New Dress for Success.* New York: Warner Books, Inc., 1988.

Mackay, Harvey. *Dig Your Well Before You're Thirsty.* New York: Currency Doubleday, 1997.

Maltz, Maxwell. *Psycho-Cybernetics.* New York: Pocket Books, 1960.

McGinnis, Alan Loy. *Bringing Out the Best in People.* Minneapolis: Augsburg Publishing House, 1985.

Murphy, Joseph, D.R.S., Ph.D., D.D., L.L.D. *The Power of Your Subconscious Mind.* New York: Bantam, 1963.

Niven, David. *The 100 Simple Secrets of Happy People.* San Francisco: Harper San Francisco, 2000.

O'Connor, Joseph, and John Seymour. *Introducing NLP: Psychological Skills for Understanding and Influencing People.* Great Britain: Thorsons, 1995.

Rabin, Susan. *How to Attract Anyone, Anytime, Anyplace.* New York: Penguin Books USA Inc., 1993.

Richardson, Donald Charles. *Men of Style: The Zoli Guide for the Total Man.* New York: Villard Books, 1992.

RoAne, Susan. *How to Work a Room: A Guide to Successfully Managing the Mingling.* New York: Shapolsky Publishers, Inc., 1988.

Robbins, Anthony. *Unlimited Power.* New York: Simon & Schuster, 1997.

Saxon, Bret, and Elliot Goldman. *It's Who You Know: How to Make the Right Business Connections—and Make Them Pay Off.* New York: Berkley Books, 2001.

Schuller, Robert H. *Tough Minded Faith for Tender Hearted People.* New York: Inspirational Press, 1986.

Schuller, Robert H. *Tough Times Never Last, But Tough People Do.* New York: Inspirational Press, 1986.

Theibert, Philip R. *How to Give a Damn Good Speech: Even When You Have No Time to Prepare.* New York: Galahad Books, 2000.

Thomas, Marlo, ed. *The Right Words at the Right Time.* New York: Atria Books, 2002.

Van Fleet, James K. *Lifetime Conversation Guide.* Englewood Cliffs, NJ: Prentice Hall, Inc., 1984.

Ziglar, Zig. *See You at the Top.* Gretna, LA: Pelican Publishing Company, 1982.

## Articles, Multimedia, and Newsletters

Decker, Bert. *High Impact Communication: How to Build Charisma, Credibility and Trust.* Audiotapes (6). Producer: Daniel Strutzel. Niles, IL: Nightingale-Conant Corporation.

Gee, Bobbie. *Image Power.* Audiotapes (6). Laguna Beach, CA: Bobbie Gee Enterprises, 1986.

*Great American Speeches:80 Years of Political Oratory.* VHS. Prod. Parker Payson. Narr. Jody Powell. Pieri and Spring Productions, 1997.

Lowndes, Leil. *Let Your Body Do the Talking.* Audiotape. New York: Applause, Inc.

Mackay, Harvey. *How to Build a Network of Powerful Relationships.* Audiotapes (6). Producer: Karen Stelmach. Niles, IL: Nightingale-Conant Corporation.

Martin, Judith. "Learn the Magic Words." *The Washington Post*, October 5, 2003. D5.

Richardson, John H. "Dr. Happy." *Esquire*, June 2002.

Tracy, Brian. *The Luck Factor: How to Take the Chance out of Becoming a Success.* Audiotapes (6). Producer: JoAnn Nelson. Niles, IL: Nightingale-Conant Corporation.

Zaneski, Cyril T. "Medical Sales Reps Arrive Bearing Gifts." *The Baltimore Sun*, June 17, 2004.

# Send Us Your Success Stories!

This book is dedicated to all who strive to better themselves and the lives of others. It consists of more than a decade of research intended to improve the lives of readers and anyone with whom they comes in contact. Has this book improved or changed your life? Is there one particular technique, piece of advice, or passage in this book that has made an impact on your life, worked particularly well for you, resonated with you, or improved your communication with others? If so, tell us how! We would love to hear your success stories and share them with others!

Send your stories to:   **successstories@six-figureincomes.com.**

Please indicate if your story is to be shared with the author only or if your story and name can be shared with others, such as with live audiences, on our website, or in future publications.

Thank you!